CHINA:

BUSINESS STRATEGIES FOR THE '90s

ABOUT THE AUTHOR

Arne J. de Keijzer was actively involved in the China trade from 1972 to 1989 and president of his own consulting firm, A.J. de Keijzer & Associates, Inc., from 1978 to 1991. During that time he helped numerous American firms with planning, research, project development, and negotiations in the People's Republic. These included work on joint ventures, execution of import/export arrangements and assistance to travel and service companies. He has traveled widely in China and is author of two other books, *The China Guidebook* and *The China Business Handbook.*

A resident of Weston, Connecticut, he currently devotes his time to writing and publishing projects related to international business issues. He also undertakes corporate communication assignments and does specialized project consultancy and support work on China.

ABOUT THE CONTRIBUTORS

Eugene Theroux, who wrote the foreword to this book, is a partner in the Washington, D.C. office of Baker & McKenzie, the largest international law firm in the world. Mr. Theroux made his first visit to China in June 1972. Since then, he has made more than 150 trips to China on behalf of clients of his firm and he has spent, in the aggregate, more than five years in China. He opened the first Baker & McKenzie office in China in late 1980, and inaugurated the firm's Shanghai office in 1985.

Mr. Theroux serves as a director of the U.S.-China Business Council, an Advisory Professor of Law at Fudan University in Shanghai, and a member of the Business Advisory Council of the Fletcher School of Law and Diplomacy. In 1981, Mr. Theroux was a founding Director and Legal Counsel of the American Chamber of Commerce in the People's Republic of China.

Allan Liu, who collaborated closely on the research and development of this book, is a consultant to a number of large multinational corporations on investing and marketing in China. Educated in China and the West, he's had more than ten years' experience starting successful joint ventures and analyzing market opportunities. He lives and works in the U.S.

The U.S.-China Business Council is a private, not-for-profit organization dedicated to providing information and practical assistance to member U.S. firms involved in trade and other forms of business with the People's Republic of China. Through its educational arm, **The China Business Forum,** it organizes policy seminars and publishes studies of various aspects of U.S.-China business relations. The Council also publishes *The China Business Review,* the bimonthly magazine chronicling China's foreign trade and investment practices.

Business International Asia/Pacific Ltd. is the publisher of *Business China*, a twice-monthly newsletter published in Hong Kong. Its parent, Business International, is a member of The Economist Group. BI's purpose is to provide senior managers of multinational companies with highest-quality information, analysis and advice on the critical issues affecting business across borders. Lois Dougan Tretiak is director of BI's China Division and editor-in-chief of *Business China*.

Asia Pacific Resource Group (APRG) is a trade, investment, and consulting company based in Cambridge, Massachusetts. APRG specializes in assisting mid-sized U.S. companies in forming strategic partnerships with companies in the Greater China market: Hong Kong, Taiwan, and the P.R.C. In addition, APRG publishes *China Trade,* a newsletter covering business strategies for the Greater China market. APRG also offers translation services as well as a trade liaison service for the Hong Kong Department of Industry.

The **Japan External Trade Organization** (JETRO), actively promotes Japan's international business relations. Among its many publications is the *JETRO China Newsletter,* a monthly publication that carries detailed analysis of China's economic, foreign trade, investment, and business practices. It regularly carries case studies of the activities of Japanese companies in China.

P. Richard Bohr, Ph.D. has consulted widely on U.S.-China relations, led many trade missions to China and Asia, and is the author of books and numerous articles on doing business with China. He was formerly Executive Director of the Minnesota Trade Office, and President of the Midwest China Center. He is currently working on a book on Sino-Western intercultural relationship as seen through the Taiping Rebellion.

Julie Reinganum is the founder and managing director of Pacific Rim Resources, a San Francisco–based company providing consulting, investing, trading, and market development services to Asian and American clients. Areas of company expertise include pharmaceuticals, telecommunications, and light manufacturing. Ms. Reinganum holds degrees from Vassar, Johns Hopkins School of Advanced International Studies, and the Graduate School of Business at Stanford University.

Roy F. Grow is chair of the Department of Political Science at Carleton College in Northfield, Minnesota and also teaches at the University of International Business and Economics in Beijing. He works with Japanese and American firms active in China and is a frequent traveler to Asia. He has done research on hundreds of technology transfer arrangements to China, has written extensively about them, and also has directly participated in negotiating a number of them.

A. T. Kearney is a leading international management consulting firm with 36 offices located in 15 countries. In Asia, the firm has offices in Tokyo, Hong Kong, and Singapore, and is active in China, Korea, Taiwan, Malaysia, Indonesia, Thailand, and India. Dr. Kim Woodard, an expert on China with many publications to his credit, is the director for China.

CHINA:

BUSINESS STRATEGIES FOR THE '90s

ARNE J. DE KEIJZER

WITH THE COLLABORATION OF
Allan H. Liu

FOREWORD BY
Eugene Theroux

CASE STUDIES CONTRIBUTED BY
The U.S.- China Business Council
Business International Asia/Pacific
Asia Pacific Resource Group, P. Richard Bohr,
Julie Reinganum, Roy F. Grow, JETRO, and A. T. Kearney

Pacific View Press
Berkeley, California

Cover design by Silicon Studios
Text design by Linda Revel

All views expressed in this work are solely those of the author and do
not necessarily reflect those of either the collaborator or the various
contributors.

This publication was previously advertised as ISBN 0-8351-2486-X.
See correct ISBN below.

Library of Congress Catalog Card Number 92-70169
ISBN 1-881896-00-5

Contents

PART I
DEVELOPING THE STRATEGY

PART II
CHINA BUSINESS STRATEGIES —
THE CASE STUDIES

PART III
HOW TO APPROACH THE CHINA MARKET— THE LESSONS LEARNED

PART IV
TOWARD THE 21st CENTURY

APPENDICES

Author's Preface

When asked about the most significant changes in China since this book was written two years ago, my answer is direct: "All trends have intensified." Though optimistic about the pace of reforms, we didn't anticipate the speed with which the internal market has responded and the degree to which international business has picked up the China challenge.

Foreign trade is expected to reach a staggering quarter trillion U.S. dollars in 1995, propelling China to the front rank of world trade. Foreign joint ventures contribute a startling one-third of China's exports. Total foreign investment now surpasses several billion dollars *per year per province*, and in some cases, *per city*. This far eclipses foreign investment in any other Asian nation or, for that matter, most European nations.

As a result, China has been thrust prominently on the agenda of nearly every corporate boardroom in the world. AT&T officials have publicly stated that the company's China business may exceed its U.S. business after the turn of the century. The Union Bank of Switzerland declared that in terms of future competitiveness, the U.S. ranked 19th; the Chinese ranked second, behind only South Korea.

The trend toward an entrepreneurial revival in China was also noted in these pages; what was unexpected was the degree to which the reforms would ignite a grassroots revolution that catapulted new people, new factories, and a host of private and collective enterprises to the forefront of China's economy. This new class of entrepreneurs, not the old state enterprises, are producing the eye-popping statistics displayed on viewgraphs in boardrooms around the world.

The negative side of the new Chinese revolution has also gained a great deal more visibility. Human rights abuses, political uncertainties, a get-rich-quick mentality, social dislocation, corruption, import restrictions, piracy of intellectual property rights, the lack of legal procedures and safeguards—all these and more raise caution flags. China's economy is still prone to sharp ups and downs. Bureaucracies can still be unfathomable. And the Gordian knot awkwardly tying together the "iron rice bowl" with the marketplace has not been cut.

Thus, while realistically optimistic in the long term, the caution expressed in the original preface to this book is worth repeating: companies approaching the market should do so conscious of the risk, aware of the realities, and understanding of the unique (but by no means insurmountable) problems presented. Expect, for example, a major downturn sometime in the latter half of the '90s.

On the whole, the trade and investment trends and priorities illuminated here remain unchanged. Some important shifts of emphasis—all favorable—should be noted, however.

- The invest-for-market-share mentality is officially alive but hard to enforce in practical terms. Companies can enter the market here as elsewhere in Asia: step-by-step introducing product, finding distributors, and selling everywhere. A joint venture can be established as business warrants rather than as entry ticket. Similarly, "compensation trade" has given way to simple sourcing, or process trade.

• There is much less pressure for foreign exchange balance on joint ventures; export requirements have also all but disappeared except with state enterprises in certain sectors.

• Formerly restricted areas of investment have opened up: insurance, energy, transportation and other infrastructure projects, investment banking, and retail, to name a few.

• The thrust of foreign investment has moved away from the glamour projects favored by government planners and away from the loss-making state enterprises. Instead, money is going into projects that utilize the energy and talents of China's extraordinary people. These take various forms: setting up modern sales and distribution networks, opening foreign retail and food chains, and founding independent companies in manufacturing, trading, and services.

• Interest in the special economic zones has diminished. Why? They are no longer unique. There are now vest-pocket zones run by cities and counties all over China. Unlike the old SEZs run by state agencies, the new zones are more like business parks, with partners that act more like developers.

• Early in the '90s, the government, seeking to emulate the success of the Japanese *keiretsu* system, encouraged the formation of large multifunction companies combining production, finance, and trading. Despite some successes in this effort (e.g. Capital Steel, First Auto Works) the countertrend is stronger: independent enterprises, "free" to structure themselves for maximum competitiveness.

In the freewheeling, frontier business climate of China today, companies must stop, look, and listen. The goal of this book is to fulfill the first two of these criteria by presenting in a fresh, reference-style format the hard-won experience of heads long banged against the Great Wall. But the hardest part is the third imperative: listening. China no longer speaks with one voice. Not at the top, amongst the leadership, or in the markets, factories, and streets. Cutting edge information might come at you from the financial towers of Beijing and Shanghai, from behind the walled compounds of the Party, or from your "informal" Chinese employees via fax machines, pagers, and cellular phones. The only genuine China expert is one who says, "I don't know, but I can find out."

Two people who meet and exceed this standard have contributed immensely to the spirit and substance of this book and deserve more than general acknowledgment: Allan Liu, partner, virtual co-author and Chinese entrepreneur extraordinaire, and James Stepanek, a richly experienced China trader whose penetrating insights and apt phrasemaking really deserve a book of their own.

Arne J. de Keijzer
January 1995

FOREWORD

by Eugene Theroux

The passage of time tends to blur one of the most unexpected, even startling, announcements made in this century—the report of the Secretary of State Henry Kissinger's secret journey to Beijing in August 1971 which paved the way for President Richard Nixon's meeting with Chairman Mao Zedong in the People's Republic of China the following February. February 22, 1992 marked the 20th anniversary of the day President Nixon and Premier Zhou Enlai signed the Shanghai Communique. That time now seems far in the past; Beijing was "Peking," Mao was "Mao Tse-tung," and the Prime Minister was "Chou En-lai."

Among other things, the Shanghai Communique was an important foundation for trade between the United States and China. In the 20 years previous to the Communique, there had been a total embargo on U.S. trade with China. In the two decades since that first-ever visit by U.S. officials to the "People's Republic," China's trade with the outside world has grown to such proportions that it represents, in the minds of some countries, the threat of a flood tide of goods.

Confucius said it was "delightful to have friends coming from distant quarters." I have seen that visitors to China over these last 20 years have for the most part come as friends. Lately, though, China has hosted some rather contentious foreign visitors. American trade officials have visited Beijing for the purpose of forcing changes in China's foreign trade policies, in China's domestic laws and regulations, and even in China's domestic policies that are altogether unrelated to trade. Discussions have been difficult, and the U.S. and China each have threatened retaliatory measures over the talks.

These developments darken Sino-American relations. They worry businesses which have trade and investment interests in China. But when these disturbances are considered and balanced in a historical context, I do not think they are as worrisome as some believe. In support of my optimism, I offer a personal perspective.

I was born in Massachusetts and that may explain my early interest in China. My home state's involvement in the China trade began when the first American vessel sailed from Boston to Cathay—the "Empress of China" anchored in Canton in 1784. The American clipper ships which carried out the China trade were built in yards on the Mystic River, in my hometown, Medford, Massachusetts. Later, in 1844, a former member of Congress from Massachusetts,

Caleb Cushing, was sent by President Tyler to negotiate the first treaty between the U.S. and China, the Treaty of Wanghai. By that treaty, the United States gained most favored nation (MFN) status for itself, but not for China.

When I made my first visit to Hong Kong, in 1968, there was a total embargo on U.S. trade with China. No trade, no investment, not even any travel. For Americans, China did not exist. Under the U.S. "Trading with the Enemy Act" President Truman had, in December 1950, prohibited all commercial and financial transactions with China. That embargo remained in effect for two decades.

In June 1972, just four months after the signing of the Shanghai Communique, I was in Beijing. Such a trip for an American was, at that time, nearly as exotic as a journey to the other side of the moon. The two leaders of the U.S.-House of Representatives, Majority Leader Hale Boggs and Minority Leader (and later President) Gerald Ford, had been invited to visit Beijing, and I accompanied them. At that time, on leave from Baker & McKenzie, I served as Special Counsel to the Joint Economic Committee of the Congress.

The lifting of the trade embargo after Secretary Kissinger's secret trip to Beijing in 1971, and the Shanghai Communique made the climate auspicious. In that communique, the U.S. and China "viewed bilateral trade as another area from which mutual benefit can be derived" and they pledged themselves "to facilitate the progressive development of trade between their two countries." The mission of the two leaders of the U.S. House of Representatives helped advance that pledge.

But Sino-U.S. trade was not, at that time, very promising. On China's side, the vice-minister of foreign trade, in a speech to an international conference of the U.N. Commission on Trade and Development, expressed China's apprehensions about foreign trade. He said:

> For over a century, the imperialist powers divided China into spheres of influence, interfered in China's internal affairs, backed the reactionary authorities, subjected the Chinese people to bloody suppression, engineered civil wars among warlords, controlled China's customs, shipping, and insurance, manipulated China's financial and monetary affairs, extorted privileges of running mines and factories, building railways, and engaging in inland navigation. They flagrantly plundered China's resources, fleeced the Chinese people, and seriously disrupted the national economy.

The vice-minister did not exaggerate, and he could also have mentioned the infamous opium trade. Bitter experience produced great caution in China's consideration of economic relations with the outside world. Who, in those days, could have foreseen that China's total foreign trade would rise from $4.3 billion in 1971 to $135.7 billion in 1991?

The U.S., too, had very modest expectations of trade with China in 1972. Total imports from China that year amounted to only $32 million (contrast that with 1991 U.S. imports of Chinese textiles alone—more than $3.2 *billion*), and China seemed uninterested in producing products designed for foreign consumer markets or in importing foreign manufactured goods.

The 1972 report of the congressional mission in which I participated reported to the U.S. House of Representatives that China had little serious interest in building trade relations. I remember our dilemma in preparing the report to Congress, "Impressions of the New China": we did not want to pour cold water on American business interest in China, but neither did we want to mask China's antipathy toward trade with the United States when we wrote: "We did not find among our hosts the same high degrees of enthusiasm for early and measurable increases in trade which has stimulated the interest of American businessmen."

We had found that China had no need for and no interest in American nor any other foreign consumer goods. Not foods, not cosmetics, not soft drinks, not cigarettes, not confectionery products, not home electronics, not films, not music. Chinese officials labeled as "forbidden zones" the prospect of foreign investment or any thought for foreign participation in the exploration or development of China's natural resources. Even tourism, as unbelievable as it may sound today, had a very low priority in Beijing. As a lawyer, I noticed, too, that China had dismantled the legal profession, and dispersed its members, along with other "pests."

In light of all of this, it is no small irony that, as a lawyer, I was later to become involved in projects involving every single one of those "forbidden zones." An inability to see the future prevented me from knowing that our firm, Baker & McKenzie, would one day have offices in three of China's cities, making us among China's major foreign taxpayers, and that the Chinese government would retain our firm to appear on its behalf in important litigation in American courts.

All of this is to say that the predictions and expectations of the pessimists of the time seem laughable today. Even the hopes of imaginative long-term optimists—Arne de Keijzer and I among them—fell far short of today's remarkable reality. These are among the reasons that, however disturbing and important are the sounds of discords in the U.S.-China relationship, I know that things have been far, far worse and that much of the contention in the relationship results from a very healthy and truly mutually beneficial, and still very promising, commercial relationship.

It has always been in fashion, by optimists and pessimists alike, to caution against excessive euphoria. But in the last decade of the 20th century, the evidence is that the "myth of the China market" has itself become a myth.

Washington, D.C.
February 1992

Acknowledgments

This book could not have been written without incorporating the knowledge others have so generously shared with me. Clients on both sides of the Pacific helped test my vague notions against the reality of day-to-day business, and colleagues and friends have contributed their own hard-won insights. I thank you one and all.

When Nancy Ippolito, now of Pacific View Press, asked me to do this book, I found immediate help and support from Henry Ho of Standard Chartered Bank, Rosalind Daly of the National Committee on U.S.-China Relations, Madelyn Ross and Dan Reardon of the U.S.-China Business Council, and James Stepanek, seasoned China trade veteran. Invaluable during the editing process were Helen de Keijzer, the staff of Word'sworth, and Bob Schildgen.

Without my collaborator, Allan Liu, and those who believed in the project and contributed so generously of their time and talent— Eugene Theroux, Julie Reinganum, P. Richard Bohr, Lois Dougan Tretiak, Edward Morrison, Krista Conley, Satoshi Imai, and Kim Woodard—this book would not have been able to answer that most fundamental of all questions: what works when it comes to doing business in China?

On a personal level, Bill Mays, Brian Weiss, and Daniel Burstein are three pillars of wisdom and support. Encouragement and support have also come, as always, from Nel de Keijzer and Dick Reiss. At the core are Helen and Hannah, and it is to you I dedicate this book.

Arne J. de Keijzer

Note on Reference Sources and Currency Values

Footnotes have been kept to a minimum. However, when the work and ideas of others are used, the author is credited and full reference may be found in appendix 1, "Further Reading."

Currency figures used are either in U.S. dollars ($) or Chinese yuan (RMB). As of early 1994, the exchange rate was approximately $1.00 = RMB 8.4.

DEVELOPING
THE
STRATEGY

Seven Reasons Why China Might Be Worth the Risk

Our policy is to talk all the time about socialism, while moving more and more toward the private sector.

—CHINESE GOVERNMENT OFFICIAL (1991)

China is well on its way to lifting one-fifth of humanity out of poverty and backwardness. That this has been accomplished in less than one generation, and that many foreign firms have benefited from helping China achieve such sustained growth, is the complex truth behind the headlines of economic uncertainty, business frustration, and political upheaval.

Yes, turmoil continues. China's search for a modern identity clearly remains incomplete. From the Opium War to the Cultural Revolution, and from the Self-Strengthening Movement of the late 19th century to the Open Door policy of 1980s, China has wrestled with the question of how to modernize while remaining "Chinese," how to achieve fundamental change while remaining stable.

The tragic events of June 3–4, 1989 in Tiananmen Square searingly brought this struggle home to Western eyes. Communist power in China had not become benign after all. Economic reform did not assure a deliberate process of change towards Western political standards. Nor did our extraordinary business behavior—putting up with extra costs, extra delays, extra discounts—eliminate uncertainty.

Dark storm clouds had already gathered over business the year before. Strong austerity measures were imposed in 1988 to regain control over the runaway economy. As a result, the reform program stalled. Imports and needed investment funds were choked off. Foreign business frustration ran high. Tiananmen, many feared, would simply be the *coup de grâce* to economic reform altogether.

The reaction of business to Tiananmen took several forms. Some companies, Johnson & Johnson and Pennzoil among them, closed their doors completely. A few have never returned. Others, while decrying the brutal crackdown, carried on business as usual. Procter & Gamble heeded the advice of trusted Chinese close to their venture and kept factory doors open and foreign managers in place. A few months later the company even announced a major expansion of its business (but well away from Beijing). Minnesota Mining and Manufacturing (3M) reopened its Beijing office within a few days of June 4, and its Shanghai operations were never interrupted.

Most business took a more middle-of-the-road, wait-and-see attitude. Even though their Chinese partners generally expressed— privately as well as publicly—a desire for business as usual, companies ranging in size from MTS Systems to IBM were cautious, scaling back operations and waiting to see what events would bring in China as well as what the reaction would be at home.

By early 1990 it had become evident that the economic reform process was too deeply rooted to be swept away, even by the hard-liners who dominated the power structure in the wake of Tiananmen. As a headline in *The New York Times* would later sum it up: "Hard Line In Beijing Fails to Kill Boom." Indeed, many local and provincial officials clearly began to treat the central government as largely irrelevant, acting as if the old emperors still clinging to power had already lost their "mandate of heaven."

The first highly public signal that China—at least business China—should no longer be treated as a pariah came with the resumption of World Bank funding for selected local projects in late 1990. In the words of Barber Conable, then president of the World Bank, "The Chinese are quite capable of closing the door and turning inward—neither in their interest nor ours—but they don't want to and won't if we encourage their presence in the global economy and the economic reform which can bring that about."

Members of the European Community and the government of Japan soon followed the World Bank's lead. International business, too, got off the fence and began returning to China in significant numbers.

H. J. Heinz, Coca-Cola, and others announced new ventures. Peugeot and Continental Can were once again producing at full capacity. IBM, General Electric, Boeing, and Xerox watched their sales climb. Licensing deals resumed, as did selected export sales. Importers were busier than ever, Avon ladies began knocking on doors all over Guangzhou, and Big Macs were being sold just off Tiananmen Square. By the first quarter of 1992, foreign investors had made commitments worth $6.5 billion in 3,837 enterprises—a rate twice that of 1991, and four times that of previous years.

All this was being done with so little fanfare that in late 1991 a *Wall Street Journal* reporter wondered if this low-profile, hunker-down mentality might not even begin to backfire. As anti-China rhetoric was mounting in the U.S., politicians and the public heard few positive arguments about how trade and investment were benefiting both American companies and hundreds of millions of Chinese living under the reform system.

▼ **SHOULD WE BE DOING BUSINESS WITH CHINA?**

China's economy is outgrowing communism. The leadership, alas, is not. What should business do?
—THE ECONOMIST

Economic freedom without political democracy is a difficult concept for Westerners to grasp. Can market reforms continue to stride ahead while, as *The Wall Street Journal* put it, "China's government has its other foot stuck in the Stone Age?"

The rationale for tight political control given by Deng Xiaoping, and implemented to various extremes by the hardliners now in power, is that only when there is social stability can there be meaningful progress for China. Social stability, in turn, can be bought through prosperity.

One does not have to accept this argument to understand that there are some powerful reasons for not isolating China. Geopolitically, China is the largest military power in Asia, a determinant in the strategic turmoil going on in the region, and an important actor on the world political scene. But perhaps an even more important reason for not ostracizing China is to help its people to a stable, richer, freer future.

American business should not forget Tiananmen, or ignore continued human rights abuses. We can adopt policies that support pressure for change and make clear decisions about who is, and who is not, to benefit from our business. But to withhold ourselves from the direct support of economic pluralism in China until some vision of pure American-style capitalism and perfect democracy takes hold is naive, and holds millions back from enjoying a better future. If we truly believe that complete political and economic freedom are ultimately one and inseparable, then we should continue to take the steps that contribute to the prosperity of the population, thereby hastening the end of the present era and laying a firm economic foundation for a future one.

▲

Just what were American and other foreign companies seeing in China? A decade of reform that has created for China a robust economy well ahead of its counterparts in the socialist world and the Third World. A decentralized decision-making process more participatory and accessible than the nature of the political system might suggest. A growing export sector based not on regimented planning or labor practices so much as on enterprises benefiting from foreign capital and technology. A silent and remarkably orderly upheaval overall that is overthrowing 20 years of political dogma in favor of market freedom.

Here are the reasons underlying this positive assessment:

1. The Economic Fundamentals Remain Strong

The economy shows surprising resilience as it enters the new decade. Economic growth slowed to 4–5% in 1989–90 after expanding at an average of 10% annually for a decade. But by 1991 the annualized real growth of the GNP had gone back up to 7%, well on its way up to the level of the booming 1980s. Industrial output and consumer sales also resumed double digit growth. China's rural industries soared 23% in 1991. Living standards, which had doubled in the 1980s, continued to rise.

China in the 1990s finds itself in the ranks of the world's top 10 exporters. Total trade, having tripled in 10 years, is one-fourth of China's gross national product. Both imports and exports rose at double-digit levels in 1991. There is a substantial trade surplus ($8.1 billion in 1991), solid foreign exchange reserves (about $30 billion), and a modest debt-service ratio (10%).

In short, China has not paid a high economic price for the hard-line political orthodoxy still being preached by its leaders. Indeed, China was enjoying far more vigorous growth in the early 1990s than the economies of the U.S., Japan, or most other countries, rich or poor.

Underlying these statistics is the unshakable feeling that despite all the lurching and uncertainty, and despite a leadership still groping for ways to preserve the socialist legacy of the past in the leadership of tomorrow, the dozen years of reform and change have moved the country into a new era. China is no longer the sick man of Asia or the market of last resort. Every cycle of readjustment has brought China closer to a path for which, as former premier Zhao Ziyang once said, "There is no parallel in history."

Barring some cataclysmic event, the irrepressible pragmatism and determination of the Chinese people ensures that China's position as the next Asian economic superpower is no longer just a vision, but a foreseeable reality.

2. The Reform Process Continues

Much of the rhetoric emanating from Beijing makes it seem as if the government has abandoned liberalization in any form. But the ground is shaking underneath the hard-liners as Deng Xiaoping and other reformers continue to erect the edifice of reform. Blaming China's problems on, among other things, "leftist errors" and its "refusing to make use of capitalism," Deng vigorously propounded a progressive line in early 1992, seemingly intent on carving his reform policies in stone. Equally promising was the call by the National People's Congress in March 1992 to accelerate the trend toward market reform that would be "unwavering for 100 years."

Meanwhile, day-to-day policy changes were being made to ensure the progress of such reforms. Import and export subsidies have been removed, forcing factories and trade organizations to become more efficient. Wholesale markets in commodities (wheat, corn, timber) have opened and will be expanded. Shanghai, Guangzhou, and Shenzhen have modernized stock exchanges; other cities will follow soon.

The pricing of more and more goods and raw materials is being determined by the market. Experimentation goes on with transforming state-owned companies to shareholder ones. An emerging concept of land ownership bears an uncanny resemblance to Hong Kong's colonial system of long-term land-use leases. Even the multi-tiered pricing system governing foreign trade is being eliminated and China's currency will be allowed to float freely.

In sum, market forces are being applied to more and more segments of the economy. The irony is that these reforms and the ensuing rapid growth of the private sector are propping up the sagging state sector and the men who are trying to maintain it. Take the emergence of the capital market, for example. In urgent need of revenues to replace tax shortfalls, the government started selling bonds to try and tap the astounding RMB 1.4 trillion socked away by the populace and out of the State's reach. The effort was so successful that more bonds were offered, then a few stocks. Soon a formal exchange system was being put into place (for a detailed look at China's investment picture, see appendix 4). The result? Pure capitalism in the service of socialist stability. Marx, as *The Economist* noted, always did love contradictions.

Whether by choice or not, reform continues.

3. The Two-China Economy

Given this state of affairs, it is no surprise that today there are really two Chinas. China 1, as business consultant James Stepanek and others point out, is the China inside the state plan. Here we find the lifeless state-run enterprises that drained some $11 billion in subsidies from the treasury in 1991 and remain an enormous drag on the rest of the economy. This is the China that puts up every rhetorical and regulatory fight it can to keep the economy in its orbit. This is the sector, as Stepanek notes, where lavish attention is paid to foreign business, but where business is welcomed only to the degree it can provide the latest technology—even though the sector generally can't afford it, can't absorb it, and doesn't know how to sell it.

China 2, however, is the one outside the state plan—and *it* has all the momentum. Here are the decentralized state enterprises, the medium and small "cooperative" factories, and the private enterprises actively seeking to modernize. China 2 has the special economic zones, the thriving open cities like Dalian and Tianjin, and the prosperous coastal areas of southern China. It's the sector that will by the end of 1992 outstrip the industrial output of the state-owned enterprises.

This is also the sector with which it's become ever easier to do business and which is the greatest source for long-term optimism. Indeed, China 2 is so successful and the government is so intent upon reforming China 1 that there are hints China 2 will be asked to take over the state factories in relatively good shape and let these then gradually absorb the bad ones.

4. Decentralization and the Emergence of Greater China

In addition to a resilient economy, the continuation of reforms, and the blossoming of a private sector, the fourth trend encouraging to foreign business is the emergence of the provinces and large coastal cities as increasingly strong-willed, autonomous entities. The standard image of China as a monolithic entity controlled entirely by the totalitarian whims of an aged group of hard-liners is an increasingly simplistic one. Although the leadership continues to hold immense power and continues to be backed, at least for now, by the Chinese army, it is evident that the center is inexorably being eclipsed.

The process of decentralization shows up in ways large and small. Governors resisted the rollback of reforms in 1989, and are now at the forefront of pushing them ahead. Provincial leaders vetoed the current Five-Year Plan (1991–95) several times in its development stages until it left them sufficient room to maneuver around it. They're also doing their best to contribute as little revenue as possible to Beijing (an average of 53% of tax revenues stay at the provincial level, with Guangzhou withholding 90%).

Major trade and investment decisions have devolved to the cities and provinces. Enterprises large and small are making their own management and marketing decisions. Beyond the confines of the Beijing beltway, people are making their own plans, invoking a classic phrase out of China's past, "The sky is high and the emperor is far away."

Nowhere is there a better example of the impact of decentralization than in Guangdong province. In 1978, according to *The Far Eastern Economic Review*, 90% of Guangdong's total output was derived from farming and 10% from industry. In 1990, the proportions were reversed, with industry accounting for RMB 142.2 billion ($26.3 billion) of the gross provincial output of RMB 164.3 billion. Some 66% of the households in Guangzhou (Canton) enjoy a disposable income of RMB 7,200 per year or more, compared with only 7% of households just four years previously.

When Sir Robert Kadoori, chair of Hong Kong Light & Power, predicted in the late 1970s that Hong Kong and Guangzhou would become one large city by the end of the century, people raised their eyebrows in disbelief. But time has proved him right. Today, Hong Kong industrial companies employ 2–3 million workers at some 16,000 factories in Guangdong. A superhighway linking Guangzhou and Hong Kong is under construction. Kadoori's foresight demonstrates a fundamental lesson: don't sell to the present market, but to the future one. For the Pearl River Delta, that future has already arrived—it is now the most vibrant economic area of China and has moved fully into the dynamic Asian-Pacific economy. It will begin to happen in other areas of China as well.

5. An Expanded Legal Framework

Over the past dozen years vague legal guarantees have evolved into an extensive group of laws and regulations that provide increasing assurance that commercial rights will be protected. Even foreign law firms have now been given the right to practice in China.

Supportive regulations recently introduced facilitate the establishment of wholly foreign-owned enterprises, modify the joint venture laws to allow greater foreign control and longer terms of duration, and establish a unified tax code standardizing foreign income taxes. Investors are also benefiting from such laws as the 1988 "Personnel Opinion on Further Implementation of the Right of Autonomy of Joint Ventures," which allows JVs to conduct their employment affairs independently and in accordance with international practices.

Business is also becoming more optimistic about China's protection of intellectual property rights, which has traditionally been a sore point. In early 1992 China responded to U.S. government pressure and agreed to join the two major international copyright conventions to curb piracy in computer software and sound recordings. Steps were also taken to extend stronger protection to U.S. producers of pharmaceuticals and agricultural chemicals and to promulgate trade secrets legislation. These and other agreements underline China's commitment to foreign participation in its economy as well as its growing willingness to recognize and abide by the rules of international commerce.

6. A More Rational Attitude towards Business

Beyond the improvements in laws, policies, and statistics, the move towards the market economy has brought with it a change of attitudes. The idea of the market and the need for competition have slowly but inexorably followed the structural reforms that worked their way up from the farms and free markets into rural enterprises, then into the cities and the industrial sector, and finally across departmental and provincial barriers.

The best and brightest from China's universities now seek employment at foreign-run enterprises instead of Beijing government ministries. Qualified factory workers are not only freer than ever to move on to better jobs, but less and less subject to the stigma of leaving the womb of stability within the state-factory welfare system for the risk of making more money. Young unmarried women are hoping to marry entrepreneurs or workers who earn extra bonuses through hard work instead of those embarking on a career in the bureaucracy.

The prevalence of this attitude should not be overstated. Yet however limited its spread and whatever its more bizarre side effects (e.g., the corruption associated with the growing attitude of "money talks"), there is emerging a new breed of manager, worker, and farmer in China—people who are willing to take risks, to be measured on the basis of their performance, and to take responsibility rather than hide behind the bureaucracy.

What this means for the foreign trader is that while the heavy hand of government interference remains, the local partner is more often willing to be part of the solution rather than part of the problem and help find a way around nettlesome meddling. In short, it's now possible to work out contracts and manage people in a way that can make the business work for you instead of against you.

7. Companies Can Be More Realistic

If anything good might be said to have come out of the Tiananmen incident, it is that the business community is learning that what we hope to see in China—positively or negatively—should not blind us to what's really there. There is no longer any reason to be in China just for the prestige. We can put aside the rose colored glasses of the early 1980s.

This newfound sense of realism can allow a better look at the comparative advantages (and disadvantages) of China. It also lets us learn from the wide body of experience of thousands of companies who've gone before, particularly those that did not succumb to an un-businesslike "loss-leader" approach and whose priority was to have a deal make business sense rather than political nonsense.

There are plenty of complications and challenges in China, but there are complications and challenges in every new market. What's different in the China of the 1990s is that in most situations, you can now anticipate those problems, and more easily solve them.

Risks

The glass that is half full can also be seen as half empty, of course. Although much progress has been made, there is no doubt that China's 15-year-old economic revolution is full of contradictions and complexities. While that revolution remains vigorous, to a great extent it is also unpredictable. Here is a short list of reasons why some will find it prudent to temper their optimism about the potential for business in China:

• *China's current leadership does not share the West's values, politically or economically.* Despite reforms and the increasingly autonomous nature of provinces, cities, and enterprises, the government remains committed to state socialism as the basis for the economy. Moreover, from the suppression of the slightest semblance of free political expression to the use of prison labor for manufacturing exports, from the sales of advanced weaponry to renegade regimes to the poaching of proprietary technology, China can be the easiest country in the world to love to hate.

• *Politics and economic policy are inescapably intertwined in China and power remains personal rather than institutional.* In other countries governments change, but commercial policies generally do not. That's not necessarily the case in China. There is no framework for succession and, at least theoretically, today's policies could be rendered void by tomorrow's political whims.

• *The long-term outlook may be good, but things are in a colossal mess in the meantime.* The Chinese economy is a nightmare of inefficiency, inconsistency, and irrationality. The price system establishes several different prices for the same product. The central government has lost control of tax collection. Then there are the decrepit infrastructure and the shortages of energy and raw materials. Never mind a few glowing regional success stories. Overall, China faces a predicament straight out of Alice in Wonderland—a burgeoning population and growing expectations means having to run twice as fast just to stay in place. The push-pull, zigzag nature of the reform process makes China susceptible to losing ground overall.

It's also become clear that the attitudes changing things for the better have a dark side. Defiance in the provinces, some say, may lead to economic warlordism. Entrepreneurship can be perverted into a cynical "What's in it for me?"

These and other risks make it clear that China will not soon—or ever—fulfill the myth some have created for it as the El Dorado of the 21st century. There is no market for a billion pairs of shoes, much less an American car in every garage.

At the same time, high dudgeon should not blind us to the fact that unlike the example of the former Soviet states, where perestroika is the policy but the economy is in chaos and the stores are empty, the vast majority of Chinese have benefited substantially from a process of reform that is growing from the ground up, even while the leadership continues to cling to discredited aspects of its ideology.

▼ ISSUES IN U.S.- CHINA TRADE

An undercurrent of mutual mistrust flows through China-U.S. trade relations. On China's part there's been the fear of being economically bullied and culturally undermined. The U.S., on the other hand, has all along been wary of communist motives and aggrieved at unfair trade practices and obvious human rights abuses.

In the wake of Tiananmen, such cross-perceptions have spilled into public anger. Senator George Mitchel argues that China has engaged in "systematic cheating" in its trade relations. Senator Lloyd Bentsen has argued that unless the U.S. takes action, China could become another Japan, exporting cheap goods to the rest of the world while protecting its domestic market behind an impenetrable web of duties, licensing requirements, and trade barriers.

For the record, here are the major issues raised by U.S. business and government officials:

• *Protection of intellectual property rights.* American companies involved in technology deals have complained loudly that intellectual property rights are not respected in China and are costing them $400 million in losses per year. The U.S. and China signed an agreement on January 16, 1992 whereby Beijing promised to join the Berne Copyright Convention in October 1992 and take other steps to protect trade secrets. Both the U.S. Congress and business will display little patience if these promises remain unfulfilled.

• *Chinese import barriers.* There is a broad consensus among federal agencies that China is discriminating against American products and that it shows little willingness to change its policies. These barriers include import quotas and outright bans on some products; complex import licensing requirements; highly specific technical standards that only match domestically produced goods; and a refusal to publish rules so that American business can avoid legal pitfalls. It's for these reasons, officials say, that China will accumulate a $12 billion trade surplus with the U.S. in 1991.

• *Human rights issues.* Congress and human rights groups oppose trade with China on the grounds that it legitimizes the present regime and helps prop it up. Adding fuel to the fire already lit by Tiananmen are reports that forced prison labor is being used in the manufacture of export goods. U.S. Customs agents have raided offices of Chinese trading companies and American importers as part of an ongoing investigation into this issue.

• *Customs fraud.* U.S. Customs believes China has cheated the U.S. Treasury out of several hundred million dollars by not properly reporting the value of goods exported to these shores. Chinese companies also are failing to report revenues they receive by selling each other unused export quotas for the U.S. market, Customs officials say. The offices of U.S. importers have also been raided in search of these violations and indictments began to be handed down in early 1992 as the result of continuing investigations by the U.S. Attorney's office in New York.

• *Irresponsible world power issues.* China sells missile and nuclear weapon technology and parts to "outlaw" nations such as Syria and Pakistan, and arms to countries hostile to Israel.

These are the issues that are putting Congress, parts of the administration, and a segment of the public in a punitive frame of mind. At stake are increased tariff barriers, the continued renewal of Most Favored Nation status, and the continuation of a climate of mutual distrust.

In the absence of a trade policy that can more clearly separate moral, economic, and political issues, the U.S. Congress is likely to continue to debate unilateral trade sanctions in the hope of forcing political developments.

There *is* a gap between rhetoric and reality in China. Unlike the mid-'80s, however, that gap now benefits the man on the street as well as the foreign trader and investor. It's good form to say "socialist China," but most of the economy is now outside the state sector. It's customary to say "monolithic China," but reforms have effectively turned parts of the country into quasi-independent regions. In short, the China of the 1990s is more transparent, and likely to be a far more pragmatic partner.

This is not to excuse human rights violations or the foreign policy of indecency. The challenge for business is to avoid the extremes offered by both idealism and cant. To put aside the tendency to impose our own goals and values and adopt instead an approach that accepts an atmosphere of ambiguity and permits the Chinese to invent their own future. If the government were to fall tomorrow, where is the alternative vision—let alone the Boris Yeltsin—that would take its place? If all controls were lifted from the Chinese economy next week, what would result but huge chaos?

China is not yet on its way to political freedom. Stability and progress are more easily gained and held, China's leaders believe, if the people have full bellies rather than free minds. Economic pluralism, however, which gives people choice, will gradually engender political pluralism, although Western democracies may still not be comfortable with its authoritarian bent.

"China will go its own way," Jonathan Spence, the eminent historian, reminds us. "There is no reason why the People's Republic of China should do what the United States wants it or expects it to do."

The problems and risks involved in starting and maintaining a business in China are great. Nowhere does trade and investment require such a strong vision and sound strategic plan. That these can be achieved and result in benefits to the Chinese people as well as profitable business is the premise of this book.

Doing successful business in China in the 1990s begins—as this book does—with an understanding of the business climate. Then, after looking at the experience of others, we can draw some lessons and begin to sketch scenarios of how business will be transacted with China in the decade ahead.

2

The 15-Minute China Briefing

As a result of the different speeds at which China's economic and political institutions are evolving, the country increasingly resembles a perplexing mixture of Europe at the end of the Middle Ages and a late 20th-century Asian newly industrializing country. Beijing has not yet accepted democracy, nor created a fully consistent legal framework for capitalism, but commerce with the rest of the world is rapidly decentralizing economic and political power within China.

—DAVID HALE, *FINANCIAL TIMES* (1991)

The burden of bringing China into the 21st century cannot be underestimated. It remains fundamentally an agrarian, semi-industrialized country whose greatest assets—a large territory and a great many people—are also its greatest obstacles to progress.

Despite the barriers, China has managed to do what its two largest neighbors have not—create substantial economic progress for its people in the last decade. China shares with the Commonwealth of Independent States (the former Soviet Union) a centralized political structure and state controlled economy. But while industrial output in Russia and the other republics is in free fall, inflation in triple figures, and the economy in chaos, China has a growth rate greater than the U.S. or Japan, a low inflation rate, and an economy driven by private and collective enterprise and aided by vigorous foreign trade and investment.

China shares with India the burdens of a huge population and unforgiving geography. But India's growth rate is a third of China's. Its budget deficit is huge, foreign debt is over $70 billion, reserves are under $1 billion, and its industry is starved for inputs. The growth rate of China's exports is more than twice that of India's, foreign debt is manageable, and foreign exchange reserves are over $30 billion.

There are at least three reasons for China's superior performance. First, reforms began in the rice fields and have worked their way up to where there is now an established market economy that can withstand and/or work around most interference imposed by the state economy.

Second, it's clear to most Chinese that whatever remains within the state economy doesn't work as well as everything outside of state control. In 1991, for example, the output of foreign and private business rose by at least 45%, and that of "collectively owned" business (more or less private) by 25%. State enterprises grew only 11%.

The third advantage China has over its Commonwealth neighbors and India is that it has opened its economy to the outside world. It hasn't just jawboned about the need for trade and investment but has actively pursued a program of concrete reforms to encourage it.

Of course, China remains backward in many ways. Moreover, the lack of a clear economic policy and a murky political situation mean that the chaos and contradictions in the marketplace are likely to continue. In the meantime, however, there is a lot of growth to be had, benefits to be shared, and money to be made. This chapter traces the economic and political foundations that form the basis for China's trade and investment strategy.

Social Statistics
TABLE 2.1

	1991	1990	1989
Labor & Wages			
Rural Net Income (Rmb per capita)	710	630	602
Urban Net Income (Rmb per capita)	1570	1387	1261
Total Savings (Rmb billions)	911	703	515
Average Worker's Wages (Rmb per year)	2365	2150	1950
New Urban Unemployment (millions)	4.0	1.3	NA
Population			
Total Number of People (millions)	1158	1143.3	1127
Increase from previous year	1.1%	1.5%	

Source: China State Statistical Bureau

KEY ECONOMIC INDICATORS
TABLE 2.2

Item	Unit	1987	1988	1989	1990	1991
Real GNP Growth	Percent	11	10.8	3.9	4.4	7.0
Real GVIO Growth	Percent	17.7	20.8	8.3	7	14.2
State-owned industries		11	12.7	3.7	2.9	8.4
Collective Industries		25	28.8	10.7	9	18.0
Private Industries		48	46	24.1	21.1	24.0
GVIO Growth For Heavy Industry	Percent	16.7	19.4	8.2	4.6	14.5
GVIO Growth For Light Industry	Percent	18.6	22.1	8.4	7.4	13.9
Coal Production	Million metric tons	928	980	1040	1080	1090
Oil Production	Million metric tons	134	137	137	138	139
Electricity Production	Billion Kwh	497	545	582	621	675
Steel Production	Million metric tons	56	59	61	66	71
Grain Production	Million metric tons	403	394	407	446	435
Cotton Production	Million metric tons	4.25	4.2	3.8	4.5	5.7
Labor Productivity Growth	Percent	7.1	7.9	1.3	2.6	NA
Total Investment	Billion Yuan	364	450	414	445	528
State Investment	Billion Yuan	230	276	254	292	356
Retail Price Increase	Percent	7.3	18.5	17.8	2.1	2.9
Retail Sales	Billion Yuan	582	744	810	830	940
Average Urban Income (per capita)	Yuan	1012	1192	1260	1387	1570
Average Rural income	Yuan	463	545	602	630	710
Subsidy for Enterprise Losses	Billion Yuan	37.6	44.6	60.0	NA	57.9
Price Subsidies	Billion Yuan	29.5	31.7	37.0	38.0	NA

Source: China State Statistical Bureau

CHINA

THE RURAL ECONOMY TABLE 2.3						
	1986	**1987**	**1988**	**1989**	**1990**	**1991**
Gross Value Output of Rural Production	755423	943161	1253469	1448017	1661921	1893084
Agricultural Output	401301	467570	586527	653473	766209	800839
Rural Industries Output	238079	328426	478116	588602	671973	840865
Rural Construction	59193	72331	89533	91917	97847	110379
Transportation	24540	33447	43444	51510	57962	64390
Rural Collectives	32310	41327	55849	62475	67930	76611
Personal Consumption						
Food	201	220	255	290	295	NA
Clothing	34	34.2	41	44	45	NA
Housing	51	57.8	71	77	69	NA
In millions of yuan, RMB						

The Economic Foundations

Land and People

China's territory is dominated by rugged mountains, great desert plateaus, and vast pasture lands. While the visual grandeur of these features is impressive, their potential for food production is severely constrained: China's arable land is just 12% of its territory.

This relatively small amount of farmland must support 22% of the world's population—1.158 billion people at the end of 1991. Population growth for the 1982–90 period was 1.5% per year, quite low for a developing country (India's is 2.0%), but still enough to have added 126 million people, or about half the population of the United States, in just eight years. China expects a population of 1.3 billion at the end of the century.

Just this month, 1.44 million more people will have been added. In 1992, a record 123 million women were entering prime child-bearing age (23–29) and at least 24 million people are expected to be born—the same as the combined urban populations of New York City, Mexico City, and Tokyo.

This rapid expansion of the population obviously places an immense burden upon China's planners. Twenty-six percent of the population live in urban areas, although in a fast-growing area such as Guangdong Province, it's 37%. Nearly 3% of the populace (29.8 million) is categorized as "migrant," meaning they are restlessly traveling the country, searching for work.

The burden of these statistics falls most heavily on the shoulders of the Chinese peasantry. It is they, constrained by geography and climate, who play the dominant role in determining China's ability to sustain both its population and its aspirations for economic growth.

The Big Farm

Agriculture accounts for more than one-third of the gross national product and employs some 60% of the labor force. Reforms, launched nationally in 1979, allow peasants to use individual plots, contract for labor and commodities, and establish rural enterprises. As long as they sell a set percentage of their produce to the state, they can generally grow what they wish and sell it in a relatively free market.

The results have been impressive. By reducing administrative controls and increasing the role of market forces, the growth in farm output quadrupled from 2% to 8% per year in 1979–84. Over the 10 year period of 1979–89, the gross value of agricultural production nearly doubled. Peasant income doubled in six years. Many peasants built their own houses, and press reports told of farmers worth more than RMB 100,000 who had automobiles and fax machines.

In the last half of the 1980s this growth rate slowed, however. Experts blame the limited scope of the reforms, the pricing system, the decline in investment for large scale development projects, and the diversion of capital from the farming sector to the rural enterprise sector.

Whatever the cause of the slowdown, staple crop yields are now near maximum feasible values for a labor intensive, small-scale agricultural system such as China's. The amount of land cultivated *per capita* declined 50% between the early 1950s and the mid-1980s, a victim of rapid population growth as well as cannibalization for industrial purposes. Add a series of natural disasters in 1987–88 and 1990–91, and by the early 1990s China is again in danger of lagging behind in the race to feed itself.

OUTLOOK FOR AGRICULTURE IN THE 1990S

China's Eighth Five-Year Plan (1991–95) has gone some way toward correcting the absence of a coordinated long-term strategy for the agricultural sector. The plan targets the annual growth of agricultural output at 3.5%. It calls for increases in investment at both the national and local level (large-scale irrigation projects will resume).

The plan also allows greater decentralization and promotes more diversity in the rural economy towards cash crops, small scale industry, and commerce.

Signs of reform continue to appear. In 1990, China opened its first grain commodity exchange. By early 1992, three more had opened for other commodities and raw materials. More are planned. All in all, the farm economy, including rural enterprise, continues its escape from the hands of state planners. Only one-eighth of all farm produce is now sold at government procurement prices.

The trend for the first half of the 1990s, therefore, is for a generally confusing mix of small steps toward market reform with continued government intervention. What this means for the foreign business person is a scenario of relative stability in the farm sector (there is no indication the peasantry is restive) and a continuation of the policy to selectively import grain, agricultural processing machinery, and the necessary technology to bring Chinese farming into the 20th century.

▼ PLANNED OUTPUT OF CHINA'S EIGHTH FIVE-YEAR PLAN

Beijing's objective in the latest Five-Year Plan (1991–95) is to create the conditions for sustained, balanced growth. Broadly speaking, this means GNP growth of 6% per year. Industry has been given the target of 4% growth annually to try and reverse the trend of the 1980s, when industry grew much more rapidly than other sectors.

Priorities for the industrial sector have also changed. The raw and semi-finished materials industries will no longer be emphasized. Steel output is also a slow-growth area, mainly because the Chinese want to concentrate on improving supplies of high-quality finished steel. On the other hand, non-ferrous metals, particularly aluminum, will be emphasized. Only one industrial product—ethylene—is targeted to grow faster than GNP.

The Five-Year Plan (FYP) for agriculture calls for increases in inputs and investment in large-scale irrigation projects. Overall agricultural output should grow about 3.5% annually.

The most significant aspect of the plan is its reaffirmation of the reform process. Although it has been labeled by some as a weak compromise, the significance of the plan is that it clearly moves away from hard-line policies. It proposes to phase out dual-track prices, for example, a move that was subsequently implemented in 1992.

The following are some specific targets called for by the Five Year Plan:

	Five-Year Plan	Increase Over Previous
Grain	447 million tons	8.2 million tons
Cotton	4.64 million tons	120,000 tons
Oil-bearing crops	17.26 million tons	560,000 tons
Sugar-bearing crops	73.72 million tons	2.5 million tons
Meat production	30 million tons	2 million tons over 1990
Fish and shellfish	14.5 million tons	2.32 million tons over 1990
Forestry	afforest 62 million acres	bring national cover to 14% from present 12–13%
Coal	1.32 billion tons	220 million tons
Crude oil	160 million tons	7 million tons
Electricity	810 billion kilowatt-hrs	260 billion kilowatt-hrs
Steel	79 million tons	25 million tons
Chemical fertilizer	110 million tons	NA
Ethylene	2.5 million tons	1 million tons

The Industrial Economy

China's industrial economy has shown itself similarly robust and resilient during a decade of seesaw reforms. Annualized real GNP growth was 10%, living standards and consumption more than doubled, and for most of the period inflation was kept under control.

China is now the world's fourth largest steel producer, third largest energy producer, and the world's leading coal producer. Industrial activity accounts for 46% of GNP—exactly double what it was in 1952. Coincidentally, that's the same growth Japan saw in its first four decades of modernization.

Industrial reform in China began in the early 1980s with the institution of workers' bonuses and a profit retention system for factories. This was known as the "responsibility system," and it meant the more you produced, the more you earned. In a second wave of reforms (1984–85), business was allowed to retain some of its profit and limited ownership privileges were established. By 1988, the number of products allocated through central planning was reduced from 250 in the early 1980s to 20.

Concepts such as competition, supply and demand, productivity, and managerial reform began slowly, even painfully to take hold.

Production went up. Salaries went up. Benefits, subsidies and bonuses—virtually nonexistent prior to the economic reform program—added up to one-third of a worker's income.

Business Week and *The Wall Street Journal* were leaving readers spellbound with stories such as the one of Zhang Guoxi, a Communist Party member who "drinks cognac, hunts pheasant, plays billiards, and is furnishing his mansion with a burgeoning antique collection. He has read *Iacocca* twice. His woodcarving business employs 3,000 people in 32 factories. He runs six commercial factories, seven joint ventures, and has offices in Japan, Germany, and Hong Kong. His net worth is about $540 million."

Such people are the exception. The Chinese economy retains large pockets of poverty. Growth in the 1980s was cyclical rather than steady. Periods of reform, decentralization, and growth alternated with retrenchment, re-centralization, and stagnation as overly rapid expansion led to inflation and shortages of energy, raw materials, and foreign exchange.

Then, too, reforms reached mainly the arms and legs of the economy, not the bloated main corpus. State-owned enterprises, which now account for one-third of China's gross national product and employ 18% of the work force, continued their inefficient ways, providing millions of workers with lifelong employment, guaranteed wages, and an opportunity to underperform for a living. To smash this "iron rice bowl" system while maintaining social stability represents an immense challenge.

OUTLOOK FOR INDUSTRY IN THE 1990S

As China enters the 1990s, industrial output and consumer sales continue double-digit growth. Yet, as China's official *Economic Daily* put it, "If reform doesn't go forward, won't it go backward?" The question encapsulates both the hopes and fears of the Chinese work force. Industrial policy, like the economy as a whole, seems ruled by uncertainty.

Nevertheless, some trends are clear. One is that for all the lingering dominance of Beijing's conservatives and central planners, the reform process moves inexorably forward. Another is that the portion of the industrial economy that is outside state control continues to enjoy robust growth. When Deng Xiaoping launched the reform process, nearly 80% of China's industrial output came from the state-owned sector. In 1991, that figure was 53%. By the end of 1992, it should be below 50%. In every category, state-owned businesses are declining and the non-state ones rising.

But even state-controlled enterprises are being shaken out of their lethargy. A powerful state leader, Zhu Rongji, has been put in charge of reforming the state enterprise system and is again talking about ending subsidies and letting unprofitable factories go bankrupt. In the near future, holding companies for state enterprises will be created. These will begin selling shares, first to employees and then to the public at large.

The most noticeable trend of the 1990s, however, may be the increased regionalization of the Chinese economy. Local officials have substantial autonomy over economic decision-making and show every sign of largely ignoring the government's efforts to rein in their growing power. This is particularly true of coastal and southern China, where the attitude seems to be: "Beijing? Where's that?"

▼ **IS THE GLASS HALF EMPTY . . . OR HALF FULL?**

Trying to evaluate events in China through the daily newspaper can get confusing. For example, both *The Wall Street Journal* and *The New York Times* reported Premier Li Peng's annual report to the National People's Congress of March 25, 1991. The speech was flagged as important because it might signal whether hard-liners or reformers were coming out ahead in the struggle for power.

The Wall Street Journal's headline read: "Premier Describes Economic Woes Afflicting China." Its lead paragraph stated, "China is beset with economic problems; yet the country's leaders have no comprehensive strategy for solving them." It goes on to describe the speech as a "candid litany of woes" (*The Wall Street Journal*, March 26, 1991).

The headline in *The New York Times*, on the other hand, read: "China Sees Greater Role for Free Market in 1990's." Its lead paragraph began, "Prime Minister Li Peng said today that China would move cautiously to expand the role of the market in the 1990's. . . ." While reciting many of the points covered in the *The Wall Street Journal* article, it also said, "In tone, the speech was slightly more enthusiastic about change than previous declarations of policy. Mr. Li said repeatedly, without providing many new specifics, that China would steadily deepen its 12-year-old economic liberalization program" (*The New York Times*, March 26, 1991).

And this brings up the question: is the glass half empty, or half full?

▲

Resources and Infrastructure

The success of the economic reforms ultimately depends not only on a strong agricultural sector and a productive industrial base, but on the ability of China's leaders to adequately exploit latent energy and raw materials resources and develop a transportation and communications infrastructure that ties them all together.

Over the past decade, significant advances have been made. Nevertheless, growth has been unable to keep pace with the demands made by the advancing economy, creating some serious bottlenecks to future growth. Here, too, modernization and greater efficiency will depend upon further reform and the ability of China to attract development loans and foreign investment.

ENERGY RESOURCES

Like the agricultural and industrial sectors, energy experienced economic and structural reform in the early 1980s. After some initial reorganization, output began to rebound, and the first half of the decade saw an average annual growth rate of 6.1% in primary energy production. Such growth was not sustained after 1985, largely because the government kept the industry closely under central control due to its strategic importance. Prices were kept artificially low, for example, thereby discouraging efficiency. Meanwhile, demand continued to increase and soon began to outrace supply. While the economy grew at a rate of 16.7% annually from 1985–1989, the growth in energy output slowed to an average of 4.7%.

Electricity production fell so far behind that many localities suffered regular blackouts and were forced to close plants several days per week. Growing shortages of petroleum products led the government to relax import restrictions on both products and crude oil, which in turn placed greater pressure on dwindling foreign exchange reserves.

By 1990 even usually upbeat planners began to admit that China was facing a prolonged and chronic energy shortage. For China to meet its self-defined goal of being energy self-sufficient, it must make major commitments to sustain foreign and domestic investment flows, increase efficiency, rationalize prices, and step up conservation.

Coal

China relies upon coal for almost three-fourths of its energy needs, mining some 1.02 billion tons in 1990. Less than 2% of that was exported. Only the U.S. and the former Soviet Union have greater coal reserves, but China lacks the modern equipment and technology to exploit such reserves efficiently and properly.

Inefficient production means up to 30% of China's enterprises are operating below capacity. The problem is exacerbated by geography and transportation. The coal is in the north and northwest, but the major consuming centers are in the south and east. Railways are clogged. In late 1988, for example, some 24 million tons of coal had piled up awaiting rail shipment to market.

Petroleum

China is the world's fifth largest producer of oil (ranked just ahead of Mexico) and its potential reserves approach those of Kuwait. Technologies acquired from Western oil companies have allowed greater output from onshore wells, and the exploration and development of offshore wells. Offshore crude production will reach about 100,000 barrels per day in 1992 and is expected to rise to 160,000 barrels per day in 1995.

The demand for petroleum is expected to reach 3.5–4.5 million barrels per day by the end of the decade. To help get there, China will spend some $500 million on importing petroleum equipment and technology over the next five years. China also intends to open up inland and shallow coastal areas for oil prospecting by foreign joint ventures.

ENERGY OUTPUT
TABLE 2.4

| | Power Generation* | | | Coal‡‡ | | Petroleum† | |
	Thermal	Hydro	Total	Output	Consumption	Output	Consumption
1980	242.4	58.2	300.6	626.0	610.1	2,119	1,262
1981	243.8	65.5	309.3	624.3	605.8	2,024	1,188
1982	253.3	74.4	327.7	658.7	641.3	2,042	1,198
1983	265.0	86.4	351.4	697.6	687.1	2,121	1,240
1984	290.2	86.8	377.0	767.7	749.7	2,292	1,309
1985	318.3	92.4	410.7	827.8	816.0	2,498	1,370
1986	355.1	94.4	449.5	873.3	860.2	2,614	1,479
1987	397.3	100.0	497.3	932.6	928.0	2,683	1,595
1988	436.0	109.2	545.2	996.7	993.5	2,741	1,706
1989	462.7	122.1	584.8	1012.6	1034.3	2,752	NA
1990	494.5	126.7	621.2	1022.2	1055.2	NA	NA
1991	551.5	123.5	675.0	NA	NA	NA	NA

* = In thousands of Watt Hours   ‡‡ = In million tons

† = In thousands of barrels per day   NA = Not Available

Source: China Statistical Bureau; courtesy Allan Liu

Natural Gas

Oil provides 20% of the national primary energy supply, but natural gas constitutes less than 3%. Industry dominates consumption (80% of the total, two-thirds of which is used by fertilizer plants, both as feedstock and as fuel). Household use is about 10%. The rest is used in construction and transport.

As the petroleum sector underperforms demand, China's planners are paying more attention to natural gas, especially as a solution to the needs of towns and cities. To that end, Texaco and several other foreign companies have licensed coal gasification technology to China.

Electrical Power

Despite a good record of growth (5.7% annually for the period 1980–85, and 9.4% for 1985–89), electrical power shortages have worsened virtually throughout the land. Power output growth has averaged only half that of GNP growth. In certain provinces, such as Guangdong, estimates of power shortages range from 25% to 30%.

In the early 1980s, the industry concentrated on hydropower, but during the second half of the decade there was a sustained effort to expand thermal generating capacity and to replace oil with coal. By the late 1980s, coal was providing over 90% of the total fuel supply. As indicated earlier, this heavy reliance on coal created immense logistical and transport problems.

To alleviate severe electrical power shortages, China is investing $6 billion in 1992 to expand power output by building 24 hydroelectric stations, 51 thermal plants and 223 substations. On a long-range basis, China has devised a 12-year program of nuclear power development that foresees a dramatic increase in capacity by the year 2000. Moreover, the government has also approved (although far from unanimously) the plan to dam the scenic Yangzi River Gorges and build a $10.5 billion hydroelectric complex to serve power-starved central China.

TRANSPORTATION

Transportation services are still rudimentary. Improving them is another matter of high priority to the Chinese government.

Railways

China's 54,000 kilometers of railroad stagger under the load of huge demand. Passenger volume reached 1.14 billion persons in 1989 and the railways moved 1.51 billion tons of cargo. But the story is the same—never enough.

The government is trying both to deflect demand (by rationing the supply to favored shippers in freight, or a "first-come, first-served" policy for passengers) and add capacity. New routes have been built (primarily to move coal) and by 1989 25% of the rail network had been double tracked and 10% had been electrified.

Some 10,000 kilometers of new rail line are planned for construction in the 1990s, but expansion is hobbled by the need to bring in a new generation of high-tech electronics for signaling and other tasks.

Highways

Two-and-a-half million vehicles are on 1.014 million kilometers of road in China, with roughly 450,000 domestically produced and 100,000 imported vehicles added yearly. Many of the roads are woefully substandard and, in many parts of the country, impassable during parts of the year. Official figures show highway traffic has increased at the rate of about 16% per year recently, but informal observation would seem to suggest this figure is low, particularly around urban areas.

Highway development has focused on the upgrading of existing roads as opposed to building new ones. Resurfacing has been carried out, and since 1988 400 kilometers of expressway have been added to the system (Shenzhen-Guangzhou-Zhuhai, Beijing-Tianjin, and Shenyang-Dalian).

China's Eighth Five-Year Plan seeks foreign investment and loans to build at least 50,000 kilometers of new trunk roads.

Water

Rivers and canals have been a major form of transportation in China since the imperial dynasties. There are 109,800 kilometers of navigable inland waterways (a water depth of one foot or more). Fewer than 5,000 kilometers can accommodate vessels of 1,000 tons plus. Freight volume on the nation's waterways in 1987 totaled 939.7 billion tons/kilometers (a little less than trains, and triple that of roads).

Seaports have received great priority. By 1990, China had a total of 1,200 shipping berths. In the decade to come, coastal ports will establish a system for coal, containers, and mainland-to-island roll-on/roll-off transport. Interport freight services along the affluent coast of eastern and southern China will also be enhanced. The government also has for the first time endorsed development of a foreign-funded port.

Aviation

Freight and passenger traffic on China's airline system has grown about 20% per year, but it still accounts for only about 3% of passenger and less than 1% of the freight hauling.

The major news in this sector is the multiple agreements China has signed with foreign airframe makers. This has not only meant instant modernization for a great part of the fleet, but, through joint manufacturing agreements, a rapid acceleration on the technical side of the learning curve for China's domestic airframe industry.

TELECOMMUNICATIONS

China's antiquated telecommunications infrastructure is a serious impediment to broad scale modernization. While the U.S. has 55 telephones per 100 people, China has but one telephone for every 133 people—the lowest density of telephones in the world.

According to telecommunications expert Ken Zita, the industry is crippled by three strategic weaknesses. First, there is little vertical integration of local and toll services, which skews economies of scale in capital investment and revenue collection, and leads to technical inconsistencies among local and regional networks. Second, R&D and telecommunications manufacturing are split helter skelter between two rival entities, the Ministry of Posts and Telecommunications and the Ministry of Machine Building and Electronics Industry. Third, state funds—especially foreign exchange for imports and joint ventures—are extremely limited.

China hopes to raise the number of telephones to 33.6 million by the year 2000, adding some 10–15 million virtual circuits or line equivalents. Analog service is expected to be extended to the smallest towns and digital switching and transmission corridors are slated to link provincial capitals and big cities. Fiber optic networks and sophisticated switching systems will upgrade urban centers.

THE OUTLOOK FOR INFRASTRUCTURE IN THE 1990S

The Eighth Five Year Plan aims to overcome many of the bottlenecks in the infrastructure.

For example, it calls for an increase in coal production of about 3% annually, to 1.3 billion tons by 1995. To meet these goals China will spend more than $200 million annually to import coal-mining machinery. It will also spend more than $10 billion to build 75 power projects with a combined capacity of 32.8 million kilowatts.

The plan also gives priority to construction of railways, airports, seaports, highways, and communications centers. Major projects on the drawing boards include an airport and high-speed rail link in Shenzhen; water supply projects in Shenyang, Xian, and Chongqing, underground railways in Guangzhou, Nanjing, Qingdao, and Shanghai; and a direct rail link between Hong Kong and Beijing.

In addition to the existing 19 key ports, which are to be further improved, the Five-Year Plan includes the construction of four international transfer ports with deepwater berths: Dayao Bay at Dalian, Beilun port in Ningbo, Meizhou Bay in Fujian, and Dapeng Bay in Shenzhen.

At least these were the plans before the disastrous floods of mid-1991, which created $15 billion worth of damage to farmland, irrigation systems, bridges, roads, railroads, and telecommunication links in 18 provinces. How much of China's limited financial resources will have to be siphoned off from the Five-Year Plan to repair this damage is as yet an open question.

✦ ✦ ✦

People, geography, energy, transportation, communications. These are the raw materials of development, the foundation of economic growth. Yet in the end, progress is largely a function of how the raw materials are drawn together, arranged, and distributed. In China, these are still decisions often made not by the market, but by the political system.

The Political Framework

China stands at the edge of an uncertain political future, waiting. Everyone seems instinctively to realize that the future lies not with the aging leadership in Beijing and their hand-picked heirs. Still, the old revolutionaries cling to power, their legitimacy based not on ideology but rather on their willingness to back the very reforms that are eroding their authority.

This section first considers the formal instruments of control and then evaluates the political climate of the early 1990s.

The Structure of Power

On paper, power is divided between a government and a party structure. In practice they are inexorably intertwined.

GOVERNMENT STRUCTURE

The Chinese constitution establishes a National People's Congress as the supreme legislative body. This 2,859-member assembly, which meets at least once every five years, has three major tasks: amending the constitution and passing all laws, electing or approving appointments to top state positions, and deciding major issues in state affairs like the plan for national economic and social development. Remarkably, it has become less of a rubber stamp body in recent years, forcing Li Peng to include reformist policies in his report to the NPC in March 1992 and failing to give unanimous consent to the controversial plan to dam the Yangzi River gorges.

A permanent Standing Committee of the National People's Congress (NPC) exercises nominal control over the government apparatus by overseeing China's highest administrative body, the State Council. It is the State Council, in turn, which oversees ministries and commissions, and controls the vast bureaucracy. It also appoints the State Council's premier.

THE COMMUNIST PARTY

The top governing body within the Party is the Politburo, an 18-member organization elected by the National Party Congress. The Politburo makes the overall decisions on where China is headed and it, in turn, has an inner circle called the Standing Committee, consisting of a handful of the most senior Politburo members.

Reporting to the Politburo are the Central Committee and the Secretariat. The Secretariat runs the daily affairs of the Party and is the fast track for proteges of the leadership. The Central Committee, made up of 175 members chosen from the National Party Congress, meets periodically to discuss and approve policies sent down from the Politburo. Members have other full-time jobs in the top echelons of government, reinforcing the Party's web of control over bureaucratic power.

More than 2.4 million people have joined the Communist Party since the events of June 1989, according to *People's Daily*, bringing membership to 50.3 million. Even if this figure is wildly inflated, the basic question is, "Why?" At least for now, the Party still offers an umbrella of protection for certain types of jobs, as well as an avenue for promotion in an unstable political climate. If two talented young people are competing for the same job, the senior official may still feel it's "safer" to give it to the one who has joined the Party.

Politics in Practice

The practical effect of this structure is that power in China is not institutional but personal. Institutions owe their power to their leaders. As leaders come and go, so does the power of the bureaucracies they control.

With the leadership divided, the government is unable to lay out a clear vision of the future, or to respond to specific crises such as those besetting the state-owned enterprises. The best it seems able to do is resort to crude nationalism in defending "state socialism with Chinese characteristics." As the center seems to get weaker, the regional and local bureaucracies, controlled by ambitious provincial leaders, get more powerful.

Outlook for the Political Climate of the 1990s

Until the present leadership goes to its reward sometime in mid-decade and a new social compact is reached, China is likely to be in for a murky period of institutionalized instability similar to the one seen in 1990 and 1991. As long as the current leadership can still deliver economic improvement and social stability, it is likely to remain in power.

It will be preoccupied with succession, divided between the need for pragmatic leaders able to manage a growing economy, and the desire to pass the revolutionary legacy on to trusted descendants of the old guard. Because each faction in the leadership will want to install its own loyalists to defend its version of that legacy, no major decisions will be made.

 PEOPLE TO WATCH

Whoever does not support reform will have to leave the stage.

—DENG XIAOPING, JANUARY 1992

Whether hard-liners such as Li Peng and his associates heed that injunction voluntarily or will wait until Marx calls them home, there are plenty of the people waiting in the wings. The candidates most often mentioned in the press are Zhou, and Zhu, but we pick Li Tieying (see chapter 12).

Jiang Zemin. Secretary general of the Communist Party. Former mayor of Shanghai plucked suddenly to replace Zhao Ziyang. Held various technocratic posts. Reportedly has a small power base.

Li Changchun. Governor of Hunan. Former governor of Lianoning, and former mayor of Shenyang, where he championed some of the most important reforms undertaken in any city. Not in central government but a young (b. 1944) dark horse to watch.

Li Ruihuan. A former carpenter who's worked his way up the Beijing and national Party apparatus to become head of propaganda and cultural affairs. Former mayor of Tianjin. Open and active reformer.

Li Tieying. Minister of education. Former leader in Ministry of Machine Building (where he oversaw the building of China's first microcomputer), then head of the Ministry of Electronics Industry. In 1987, appointed Minister of the State Commission of Restructuring the Economic System. Also a State Councillor and member of the Central Committee. Probably a son of Deng

Xiaoping's first wife. Solid reputation as a can-do reformer while also trusted by the present leadership.

Yang Baibing. General secretary of the Central Military Commission. Son of president Yang Shangkun. Solid base within the People's Liberation Army.

Ye Xuanping. Vice-chairman, Chinese People's Consultative Conference. Governor of Guangdong with broad power base in the provinces. Generally regarded as a reformer.

Zou Jiahua. Vice-Premier. Minister of the State Planning Commission. Effectively in charge of day-to-day operations of the State Council. Considered leading candidate for next round of top leadership. Effective technocrat whom analysts consider a mainstream conservative. Believed to have close ties to military.

Zhu Rongji. Vice-premier and director of the State Production Office, whose task is the day-to-day management and reform of the debt-ridden state sector. Also in charge of the new "Economic and Trade Office," a superministry. Former mayor of Shanghai. Alternate member of the Central Committee. Generally identified as a reformer and an "action man." Savvy with foreigners.

▲

Distracted, the leadership is likely to continue to have to trade off local authority for nominal control. The assertion of local interests and autonomy in areas of economic strategy, budgetary control, and foreign investment will continue. As one analyst put it, "There's policy and then there's what really happens."

The question is, will this sea change be sudden and violent? A number of factors suggest not. There are major problems in the economy and the political system, but there are no food shortages and no signs of rampant dissatisfaction (with the notable exception of groups of intellectuals and the rootless unemployed). There is also a general fear of disorder, uncertainty, and a vacuum of authority, particularly among the peasants. Rebellion is not in the air—at least as long as the leadership can maintain some sort of united front, however tenuous. These and other factors make it easy to be persuaded by Sinologist David Lampton's analysis that the greatest difficulty facing China is political gridlock rather than violent revolution.

In the meantime, the major failing of the leadership—an inability to reconcile itself to the reform programs it has launched—will become ever more apparent.

3

Trade and Investment Basics

In 1940, in wartime China, Chou En-lai gave an extraordinary banquet—hors d'oeuvres both hot and cold, bamboo and chicken, then duck livers. And then the main course—unmistakenly pig, a golden-brown, crackle-skinned roast suckling pig.

"Ch'ing, ch'ing," said Chou En-lai, the host, gesturing with his chopsticks at the pig, inviting the guests to break the crackle first. I flinched. I put my chopsticks down and explained as best I could that I was Jewish and that Jews were not allowed to eat any kind of pig meat. The group was downcast, for they felt they had done wrong.

Then Chou himself took over. He lifted his chopsticks once more, again repeating "Ch'ing, ch'ing" [please, please]. This time he was grinning as he said, "Teddy, this is China. Look again. See. Look. It looks to you like a pig. But in China, this is not a pig—this is a duck."

—THEODORE H. WHITE, *IN SEARCH OF HISTORY* (1978)

Foreign trade and investment have been a strikingly successful part of China's reform program, transforming within a dozen years a largely closed economy into one remarkably open to international economic forces. Foreign firms which accept the invitation to look at this banquet of opportunities from China's point of view will benefit from the experience.

In 1978, the first year of reforms, total international trade was $20.6 billion. By the end of 1991 that figure had increased nearly sevenfold to $135.7 billion, equivalent to more than one-fourth of

China's gross national product. Exports averaged 13% annual growth during the same period, a rate matched only by the "little dragons" of Taiwan, Hong Kong, and South Korea.

Foreign investment has also boomed. China has signed more than 42,000 investment contracts worth nearly $50 billion in the period 1979–91. At the same time, China has tapped foreign governments, commercial lenders, and international financial institutions for $44 billion in loans, about 10% of which has come from the World Bank.

The impact of this open door policy on the Chinese economy has been profound. Export incentives, for example, fueled an expansion of industries making labor-intensive light industrial goods. Imports and foreign investment projects have brought technology and have increased quality and productivity, raising the overall standard of living. And trade and investment have helped transform China's coastal areas into mini Hong Kongs.

This chapter looks at the strategy behind trade and investment and the various ways and organizations used to carry it out. Advice on actually dealing with the system is offered in chapter 9.

China's Trade and Investment Strategy

China's trade and investment strategy can be summarized in a phrase used first by 19th century reformers and echoed by Deng Xiaoping: "Let foreign things serve China."

In other words, China accepts foreign trade, investment, and institutional borrowing as an essential part of the development strategy, but only to the extent that they do not create dependence. The phrase heard most often in China to describe this strategy is "self-reliance."

The Chinese view is that a surplus account driven by exports can bring in the foreign exchange necessary to pay for needed imports. Most imports should eventually be replaced by domestic production. Joint ventures and other foreign investments are a useful way of absorbing Western and Japanese technology; they're not, in the main, platforms for foreigners to penetrate the domestic market. Foreign project loans can be an inexpensive way to develop the infrastructure.

Implementing the Strategy

No matter how liberalized foreign trade and investment policy have become and no matter how important foreign participation is to the growth of the economy, foreign trade and investment remain for now creatures of government policy. Quotas, tariffs, licensing, and other administrative measures are used to ensure the fulfillment of a centrally-directed-and-controlled economic plan.

Administrative control of foreign trade begins with an annual state plan setting import and export targets based on need as well as on the balance of payments situation. Responsibility for implementing that plan devolves to the Ministry of Foreign Economic Relations and Trade and the State Planning Commission. They implement the goals through a system of licensing, regulatory taxes, and customs tariffs applied to a three-tiered structure of import and export categories. These allow central control of critical items (certain commodities and raw materials, such as petroleum), mid-level control of others (to let them conform to provincial priorities), and market control of the remainder.

The currency's lack of convertibility acts as another administrative control over foreign trade. By regulating the amount of foreign exchange that can be retained by an enterprise that sells abroad, or by the amount allocated in the case of those seeking to import, the government attempts to guarantee an efficient use of precious hard currency reserves.

The third method of control used by the government has been to subsidize, directly and indirectly, many of the entities involved in foreign trade.

By the early 1990s, these administrative controls were being substantially relaxed and in some cases eliminated. The reasons are varied. To ensure access to global trade and financial assistance programs, top levels of the bureaucracy were increasingly willing to meet the outside world's terms for interdependence. Then, too, the process of decentralization itself served to erode central control.

The result was that by 1992 the government retained tight control only over commodities, raw materials, foreign exchange reserves, and other items deemed essential to the central economy. Looser administrative controls governed the bulk of foreign trade and investment transactions.

The current focus of the strategy is to make the system more self-sufficient and thus better able to respond to market forces. Subsidies are being cut, state trading corporations are being cut loose, and large corporations that integrate trade, investment, and production are being encouraged.

RESULTS

China's "open door" policy officially began in 1978. Institutional and legal changes were made to decentralize the foreign trade bureaucracy, protect the interest of foreign investors, and facilitate borrowing from abroad. Special economic zones (SEZs) were established, joint venture negotiations begun, and trade policies liberalized.

How much China's open door policy has accomplished can be judged by the accompanying charts as well as by the case studies in chapters 4 through 7 in this book. But progress, while truly impressive, has not come without periods of uncertainty and pain. Three times during the 1980s periods of liberalization and rapid change were followed by stiff retrenchment. As analyst Arlene Wilson and others have pointed out, each reform period (1979–80, 1984, and 1987–88) was characterized by expansionary monetary policy, increased investment spending, liberalized measures for exports, imports and foreign investment, decentralization of foreign trade decisions, and the granting of special dispensations to cities and special economic zones to encourage market economics.

Within a short period of time, buying binges created a foreign exchange crisis. Also, easy credit mixed with a shortage of supplies created inflation—which all segments of the population fear almost as much as foreign domination of the country. The government would then retract some or most of the reforms, tighten credit, and recentralize foreign trade and investment policy. The most dramatic shift was as recent as 1988, a year that saw foreign business confidence fall to a new low.

A detailed history of how well foreign companies responded to this process is best left to others (see appendices 1 and 2). Suffice it to say, the record was ambiguous, with a number of well-publicized failures but also hundreds if not thousands of quiet successes. In the arena of foreign trade, suppliers of commodity and capital goods have done well. Selected machinery and technology sales accounted for heavy volume. Importers and those looking for low-cost manu-facturing, or processing and assembly projects, have also fared well.

Investment results have been more mixed. While China is today one of the largest recipients of foreign direct investment among the developing countries, and the total contract commitments have exceeded $45 billion, success has not been unqualified. As World Bank Development Officer Joseph Battat points out, China has not been able to attract the high-technology projects it wants, the actual foreign investment utilized is only half of that contracted, and, except in a few coastal provinces, the impact of foreign direct investment on the domestic economy has been inconsequential.

Nevertheless, interest by foreign companies in investment remains high. Two key developments support their optimism. First, current investors generally view their ventures as successful, both in terms of profitability and strength of market position. Second, the recent willingness of China to acquiesce to U.S. demands to accept world standards for the protection of intellectual property rights (reportedly as the result of direct intervention by Deng Xiaoping) clearly signals a serious commitment to improving the investment climate yet further.

CHINA'S FOREIGN TRADE WITH SELECTED COUNTRIES, 1990–91
TABLE 3.1

	Total 1991	Imported From	Exported To	% of Total Trade	Total 1990	% Change 1990–1991
Hong Kong	$90,906	$37,594	$53,312	66.99%	$40,911	122.2%
Japan	$20,283	$10,032	$10,251	14.95%	$16,587	22.3%
USA	$14,202	$8,078	$6,194	10.47%	$11,768	20.7%
Germany	$5,404	$3,049	$2,355	3.98%	$4,541	19.0%
USSR	$3,904	$2,081	$1,823	2.88%	$4,379	-10.8%
Singapore	$3,077	$1,063	$2,014	2.27%	$2,832	8.7%
Italy	$2,390	$1,458	$932	1.76%	$1,905	25.5%
France	$2,305	$1,572	$733	1.70%	$2,308	-0.1%
Canada	$2,201	$1,646	$555	1.62%	$1,909	15.3%
Australia	$2,110	$1,556	$554	1.55%	$1,809	16.6%
UK	$1,669	$942	$727	1.23%	$2,027	-17.7%
Malaysia	$1,332	$804	$528	0.98%	$1,176	13.3%
Thailand	$1,269	$421	$848	0.94%	$1,194	6.3%
Total World	$135,701	$63,791	$71,910	100%	$115,413	17.6%

In millions of US$

Source: China Customs Bureau Statistics, courtesy Allan Liu

Trade and Investment Priorities for the 1990s

China has established clear trade and investment priorities.

China will try to encourage the development of value-added export products (toys, appliances, electronics) and manufactured goods (machinery) while reducing its reliance on the export of essential commodities such as petroleum, since the latter are now needed for domestic development. Overall, three sectors will have export priority: electronics assembly, pharmaceuticals, and machine tools.

Those selling to China will find priority being given to technology or equipment (rather than finished goods) and to companies willing to sell in the context of some flexible arrangement such as barter, compensation trade, or countertrade (see next section).

Priorities for foreign investment include: (a) projects that make new machinery, materials, and equipment readily marketable domestically and internationally; (b) projects that upgrade existing products, increase their variety, and make them more competitive on the world market; and (c) projects related to building the infrastructure, either by producing materials now in short supply or materials that relate to energy, communications, transportation, and agriculture.

The desire for process technology means that knowledge of the production of key parts and components will have priority over the acquisition of complete assembly plants in areas such as transportation, machinery, and electronics. Given the recurrent shortage of foreign exchange, China will also continue to encourage "patch-up" type joint ventures (renovation of existing plants rather than the building of new ones).

The next phases of investment will also see greater effort being made towards attracting large, well-known global corporations—a Philips for fiber optics, or a General Electric for medical equipment. The ability to attract such large and high-quality companies holds good public relations value, makes China less vulnerable to questionable deals with unqualified partners (it's happened on both sides), and assures them they are dealing with people who have both the technology and the resources to make the ventures succeed.

Ways of Carrying Out Foreign Trade and Investment

China uses various forms of trade and investment to spur economic growth. In addition, its development strategy incorporates foreign borrowing and use of multilateral economic institutions such as the World Bank.

Forms of Trade

BASIC IMPORT/EXPORT

Despite the extra attention given to new methods of doing business with China, most trade is still done the old-fashioned way, by sitting across the table from someone and hammering out a contract for outright purchase or sale.

Basic trade is for the foreign importer who buys machinery, rugs, foodstuffs, rattanware, and the thousands of other items made originally or to order in China. It is for the seller of commodities, textile yarns, medical equipment, telecommunications equipment, and electrical machinery.

CHINA'S KEY IMPORTS AND EXPORTS
TABLE 3.2

	1991	Value Rank	1990	Value Rank	1989	Value Rank	1988	Value Rank
Imports								
Specialized machinery	5500	1	5000	1	5673	2	4599	2
Textile yarn, fabrics, made-ups	3400	2	2748	3	2845	4	2388	4
Fertilizers, manufactured	3100	3	2605	4	2364	7	2336	5
Electrical machinery, Appliances	2400	4	2050	6	2396	5	2304	7
Iron and Steel	2400	5	2852	2	5797	1	4625	1
Artificial resins, plastics	2200	6	1498	12	2206	9	3558	3
Textile fibers	2000	7	1841	8	2286	8	1946	8
Telecommunications & sound	1900	8	1878	7	1793	10	1824	10
General industrial machinery & equip.	1800	9	1732	9	2387	6	2315	6
Power generating machinery & equip.	1600	10	1730	10	1365	15	1049	16
Cereals	1300	11	2353	5	2983	3	1855	9
Total, All Imports			53350		59142		55251	
Exports								
Apparel; clothing accessories	8139	1	6848	2	6130	2	4872	2
Textile yarn fabrics	7106	2	6999	1	6994	1	6458	1
Petroleum; petroleum products	3864	3	4460	3	3581	3	3372	3
Misc. manufactured Items	3175	4	2646	4	2283	4	1645	5
Footwear	2142	5	1607	7	1096	9	727	10
Telecommunications & sound	1907	6	1738	6	1140	8	789	9
Vegetables & fruit	1740	7	1742	5	1623	5	1617	6
Nonmetalic mineral manufactures	1568	8	1316	10	793	14	579	17
Manufactures of Metal	1566	9	1437	8	1210	7	1006	7
Textile fibers	1058	10	1095	13	1546	6	1672	4
Fish-related	980	11	1370	9	1039	10	987	8
Total, All Exports			62063		52486		47540	

In US$ millions   Source: Chinese Customs Bureau Statistics

LICENSING

Although they prefer acquiring it in the context of joint ventures, the Chinese continue to import technology in the form of licensing, technical services, co-production, and technical consulting services.

Chrysler, for example, signed an agreement in 1987 to license the manufacture of engines and supply some production lines. In return, they received an up-front fee as well as a fixed royalty based on the production of a set number of engines each year. (For another type of technology transfer deal, see the Gelman Sciences case study in chapter 4.)

Outright purchases of technology have been sporadic in recent years. Domestic austerity programs and questionable protection of

CHINA'S BALANCE OF PAYMENTS TABLE 3.3						
	1985	**1986**	**1987**	**1988**	**1989**	**1990**
Current account	-11.4	-7	0.3	-3.8	-4.3	8.5
Trade balance	-13.1	-9.1	1.7	-5.3	-5.6	7
Exports	25.1	25.8	34.7	41	43.2	51
Imports	38.2	34.9	36.4	46.4	48.8	44
Nontrade income	1.5	1.7	1.7	1.1	0.9	1.1
Capital account	6.7	5.9	6	7.2	3.7	4
Long-term capital (net)	4.4	8.2	5.8	7.1	5.2	5.5
Short-term capital (net)	2.3	-2.3	0.2	0.1	-1.5	-1.5
Total external debt16	.7	22.8	31	40.9	41.3	45.4
Tourism receipts	1.3	1.5	1.9	2.2	1.8	2
Foreign direct investment inflows	2	2.2	2.3	3.2	3.3	3.4
Foreign direct investment outflows	0.3	0.3	0.6	0.9	1	1.3
Year-end foreign exchange reserves	11.9	10.5	15.2	17.5	17	27

In US$ Billions
Trade data based on customs statistics. Nontrade income includes shipment fees, tourist revenues, investment income, labor contracts, and other nontrade services

proprietary knowledge were two factors, but the lack of foreign exchange was probably the most important. Sales now often come through project funding from multilateral institutions such as the World Bank, the Asian Development Bank, or foreign government loans.

COUNTERTRADE

An increasing number of flexible trade arrangements have been developed by the Chinese during the past dozen years. These practices all have the same goal: to ensure acquisition of the technology and equipment required to help build the domestic economy while at the same time conserving precious foreign exchange.

The terms "flex trade" or "countertrade" are used by the Chinese to cover any type of non-cash transaction. They encompass mainly barter, counterpurchase, and compensation trade (better known abroad as processing and assembly).

Barter

Barter is the one-time exchange of commodities of equal or similar value. Only goods, no funds, change hands. This form of trade is usually restricted to general trade agreements with other nations (e.g., Eastern European or Third World countries). Very few contracts of this nature have been signed between Chinese and individual companies.

Counterpurchase

Also called "countertrade," this is when a foreign firm sells one product and receives payment in another, non-related product. McDonnell Douglas, for example, is selling airframe technology and getting paid partly in fluorspar and industrial hydraulic jacks.

A variation of countertrade, known as "offset," applies to trade in raw materials. Here, one division of a foreign company might sell China plywood, rolled steel, tobacco, or other commodities while at the same time agreeing, through another division, to buy cotton, rice, jute, or chemicals.

Compensation Trade

Compensation trade has enjoyed a good track record in China. Here the foreign partner typically supplies things like equipment, technology, training, and components or raw materials. Once the renovated factory is in operation, the foreigner is paid back by purchasing, at a concessionary rate, part of the products made on the equipment it provided (direct method), and/or perhaps other products made by the Chinese factory (indirect method).

FOREIGN INVESTMENT IN CHINA BY TYPE
TABLE 3.4

	1979/81	1982	1983	1984	1985	1986	1987	1988	1989	1990	1991	1979-1991
Equity Joint Ventures												
# of Contracts	63	20	107	741	1,412	892	1,395	3,900	3,659	4,071	7,859	24,119
$ Committed‡	$102.9	$24.2	$188.4	$1,066.6	$2,029.7	$1,375.2	$1,950.4	$3,133.9	$2,659.0	$2,704.0	$5,670.0	$20,904.3
Contractual Joint Ventures												
# of Contracts	683	110	330	1,089	1,611	582	789	1,621	1,179	1,317	1,731	11,042
$ Committed	$2,427.1	$300.0	$502.7	$1,484.0	$3,496.2	$1,358.0	$1,282.6	$1,624.0	$1,083.2	$1,254.1	$1,873.0	$16,684.9
Wholly Foreign Owned												
# of Contracts	25	8	15	26	46	18	46	410	931	1,860	2,696	6,081
$ Committed	$295.9	$36.0	$39.5	$99.9	$45.7	$20.3	$471.2	$480.6	$1,653.8	$1,443.8	$3,421.0	$8,007.7
Offshore Oil												
# of Contracts	12	1	18	0	4	6	3	5	10	5	10	74
$ Committed	$1,252.0	$170.0	$100.9	$0.0	$359.6	$80.8	$4.7	$58.6	$203.7	$194.3	$92.0	$2,516.6
Other*												
$ Committed	$759.0	$170.0	$185.5	$224.5	$402.1	$496.0	$610.3	$893.7	$694.3	$390.2	$406.0	$5,231.6
Total Foreign Investment												
Number	783	139	470	1,856	3,073	1,498	2,233	5,936	5,779	7,282	12,296	41,345
$ Committed	$4,837.1	$700.2	$1,916.9	$1,874.9	$6,333.2	$330.3	$4,319.1	$6,190.7	$6,294.1	$3,564.0	$11,462.0	$47,822.5
$ Utilized	$1,121.4	$649.3	$916.0	$1,418.9	$1,956.2	$2,244.9	$2,646.6	$3,739.7	$3,773.5	$515.0	NA	NA

‡ = In millions of US$

* = Leasing, compensation trade, processing and assembly

SOURCE: Ministry of Foreign Economic Relations & Trade and US-China Business Council statistics

This form of trade is often used by firms looking for processing and assembling operations and is favored by the Chinese because it gives them hands-on experience in Western technology, management, and processing, as well as the ability to earn foreign exchange.

▼ A COMPENSATION TRADE EXAMPLE

Odyssey International Pte. Ltd. is a Hong Kong-based company with subsidiaries in 15 countries. Comprised of manufacturing and design operations in Asia, the United States, and Europe, the group's subsidiaries include such outdoor and sports companies as The North Face, Sierra Designs, Frank Shorter Sportswear, and Head Sportswear Japan.

Odyssey started buying from China in 1978 and now works with 75 factories in nine provinces to source products. The company has no equity investment in China, but for the period 1989–91 they have been manufacturing a steady 30% of their products there. Instead of a direct investment, Odyssey is involved in two compensation trade agreements, through which it has supplied $3.5 million in machinery and equipment to new factories in Guangdong Province. It supplies these factories with 80% of the raw material—much of it sourced from suppliers in China—that are required to make the complete garments. In this sense, it is both a sourcing as well as processing and assembly operation.

Odyssey prefers China over locations such as Malaysia, Hong Kong, Scotland, and the U.S. to satisfy its need for complex, labor-intensive production. According to William N. Simon, managing director, "We find Chinese factories, when properly informed about our needs, to be responsive, cooperative, and able to produce extremely high-quality products." Moreover, Simon says, the Chinese have met export commitments in an "honorable and timely fashion."

Drawbacks relate to the relatively high degree of supervision required to achieve the necessary quality and production timeliness. Odyssey operates seven official production control offices in China, staffed by Hong Kong and Chinese nationals. In addition, the company maintains a large logistics and service staff in Hong Kong to purchase and transport raw materials, make samples, test materials, prepare the contracts, and schedule the production.

Odyssey plans to continue sourcing about 30% of its overall production needs from China. As it stands, this amounts to about $60 million at FOB value annually. If the U.S. were to rescind most-favored-nation (MFN) treatment for China, Simon says, the company would be forced to move 70–80% of production out of China. At the same time, were MFN not subject to an annual renewal battle, Odyssey would consider establishing four or five new factories in the near-term.

SOURCE: ADAPTED FROM *THE CHINA BUSINESS REVIEW*, SEPTEMBER–OCTOBER, 1991.

UTILIZATION OF FOREIGN CAPITAL
TABLE 3.5

	1990 Contracts Signed			1991 Contracts Signed		
	Number	Funds Involved	Funds Actually Used	Number	Funds Involved	Funds Actually Used
Foreign Loans	98	$5,096.9	$6,534.3	100	$6,371.0	$7,021.0
Foreign Government	82	$719.4	$2,523.6	85	$1,344.0	$1,500.0
Int'l Financial Institution	16	$1,893.0	$1,065.6	15	$2,139.0	$1,495.0
Foreign Banks		$1,650.4	$2,044.0			
Issuing Bonds and Stocks		$3.0	$3.0		$108.0	$108.0
Direct Foreign Investment	7273	$6,596.1	$3,437.1	12296	$11,100.0	$4,000.0
Joint Ventures	4091	$2,704.0	$1,836.1	7859	$5,670.0	$2,045.0
Contractual Enterprises	1317	$1,254.1	$673.6	1731	$1,873.0	$681.0
Wholly Foreign-Owned	1860	$2,443.8	$683.2	2696	$3,421.0	$1,038.0
Other Foreign Investment		$390.2	$267.8		$406.0	$283.0
International Leasing		$51.1	$30.5		$29.0	$15.0
Compensation Trade		$202.7	$158.7		$254.0	$182.0
Processing & Assembly		$136.4	$78.6		$123.0	$86.0
Totals:		$12,083.2	$10,239.2		$17,800.0	$11,300.0

In US$ millions

Source: *China Statistical Yearbook,* MOFERT and State Statistical Bureau Figures, courtesy Allan Liu

Evidence Account

Also known as "clearing account" and "central evidence account," this is a rarely used trade form in which an agreement is made with an umbrella organization (such as a ministry, or a city) to balance import and export sales over a period of time.

Caterpillar, for one, has tried this arrangement. The company reportedly signed a licensing agreement with a division of a Chinese National Machinery Ministry that included supplying them semi-knocked-down kits, components, and some capital equipment. In return, an evidence account was set up through the Bank of China so that hard currency credits from the sale and royalties of the technology and parts could accumulate there. These credits, in turn, could be used by Caterpillar in lieu of cash to buy goods from other divisions of the ministry. Apparently, the inability of the Ministry to generate sufficient sales eventually undermined this evidence account arrangement.

Forms of Investment

There are two basic forms of joint ventures, equity and contractual. Wholly owned foreign enterprises are also encouraged.

EQUITY JOINT VENTURES

An equity joint venture (EJV) is a joint-stock enterprise newly created for the production of a specific product. The Chinese and foreign partner each contribute equity and share in the investment, management, operations, risks, profits, and losses. Earnings are distributed according to their equity shares, which are issued in certificates rather than shares of stock.

The Chinese typically contribute their equity in the form of land, a factory, infrastructure, some machinery and materials, and labor. Occasionally, the Chinese also contribute cash. The foreign partner is expected to provide the technology, capital equipment and machinery, external marketing expertise, management, and possibly additional working capital. A limited liability corporation is then formed to hold the investment and operate the company.

Minimum foreign investment is set at 25%, but may be negotiated as high as 100%. Duration of these ventures has tended to range from 10 to 25 years, but in 1991 the Chinese allowed open-ended terms to counter the impression that they wanted the foreigner around just long enough to establish the business and then reap the residual benefits for themselves. There is a joint board of directors, with a Chinese often retaining the title of chairman (this is no longer a requirement).

Equity joint ventures offer the Chinese factory not only a chance to upgrade their plant, equipment, and product line but also

Utilization of Foreign Capital By Region & Government Department, 1990
TABLE 3.6

	% of Total	Total	Loans	Direct Investment	Other Investment
Total, All Capital	100.00%	$10,289	$6,534	$3,487	$267
Total Regional	53.40%	$5,494	$2,058	$3,168	$267
Guangdong	36.68%	$2,015	$433	$1,460	$122
Liaoning	13.23%	$727	$470	$244	$14
Fujian	7.77%	$427	$107	$290	$30
Beijing	7.14%	$392	$113	$277	$2
Shanghai	5.84%	$321	$147	$174	
Jiangsu	4.51%	$248	$114	$124	$1
Shandong	4.19%	$230	$45	$151	$35
Hunan	2.55%	$140	$126	$11	$3
Zhejiang	2.33%	$128	$79	$48	$1
Hainan	2.13%	$117	$14	$103	
Tianjin	1.80%	$99	$62	$35	$2
Hebei	1.78%	$98	$53	$39	$5
Hubei	1.71%	$94	$62	$29	$3
Shan'xi	1.35%	$74	$26	$42	$5
Guangxi	1.15%	$63	$27	$29	$7
Szechuan	1.15%	$63	$39	$16	$8
Heilongjiang	0.86%	$47	$19	$25	$4
Anhui		$42	$29	$1	$4
Jiangxi		$36	$28	$6	$1
Henan		$34	$23	$11	$1
Jilin		$31	$13	$18	
Xinjiang		$25	$20	$5	
Yunnan		$12	$5	$3	$5
Guizhou		$11	$1	$5	$6
Mongolia		$11		$11	
Shenxi		$8	$4	$3	
Gansu		$1		$1	
Ningxia					
Government Use	46.61%	$4,796	$4,477	$319	
MOFERT	4.42%	$212	$204	$7	
Ministry of Finance	0.10%	$5	$5		
Offshore Oil Corp.	6.78%	$325	$81	$244	
Others	88.70%	$4,254	$4,187	$67	

In US$ millions

Source: Ministry of Foreign Economic Relations & Trade

a chance to qualify for a tax break that reduces their burden to 33% or less from well over 50%. Factories have even been known to establish a joint venture with a "silent" partner just to be able to qualify for the tax break.

Equity joint ventures are the most regulated and defined of all foreign investment vehicles. To make them more attractive, regulations continue to be passed that clarify practices and grant these ventures increased flexibility.

▼ **EXAMPLE OF A JOINT VENTURE ARRANGEMENT**

IBM has had a large presence in China, both to sell computers and to source some component parts. In recent years, however, China has been pressuring IBM and other computer makers to show their commitment to the market by opening a joint venture that would help the Chinese to develop a domestic computer manufacturer that can compete with imports.

In late 1990, after five years of negotiations, IBM announced a joint venture with the state-owned Zhonghuan Electronic Computer Corporation of Tianjin to produce IBM's PS/2 personal computers for sale in China.

According to the *Far Eastern Economic Review,* IBM was granted access to the market because the Chinese believe they have much to learn from the company, particularly in the areas of production-line technology, staff training, and quality control. The price of entry was significant: IBM has agreed to procure from China components such as printed circuit boards, transformers, motors, and semiconductor packaging, not only for the Tianjin venture but for worldwide use. In 1989, such component purchases amounted to about $20 million, according to IBM.

SOURCE: "BIG BLUE GOES RED," IN *FAR EASTERN ECONOMIC REVIEW,*
SEPTEMBER 13, 1990.

CONTRACTUAL JOINT VENTURES

The contractual (also called "cooperative") joint venture (CJV) differs from equity joint ventures in that the funds, equipment, materials, and services provided by the partners are not contributed as equity shares. The foreign company provides its share (in technology, machinery, etc.) at a given value and is repaid at a set rate of return.

Under the terms of a contractual joint venture the profits can be distributed in any proportion agreed upon without regard to the contribution of each side. Each side has separate liability in a CJV, and each party pays taxes separately. Most other terms are similar to those of an equity joint venture.

The approval process follows the same specific set of procedures as those for equity joint ventures: proposal, feasibility study, submission of documents to relevant branch offices of planning authorities and the Ministry of Foreign Economic Relations and Trade (MOFERT), negotiations on the contract and articles of association, and, upon MOFERT approval, submission to the State Administration of Industry and Commerce for the business license.

WHOLLY FOREIGN-OWNED ENTERPRISE

The wholly foreign-owned enterprise (WFOE) is a limited liability entity organized solely for the benefit of the foreign company. It contributes its entire equity, receives all the profits, and has complete and independent control of the running of the enterprise.

Once discouraged by the Chinese (detailed implementing regulations were not promulgated until late 1990) and avoided by Western companies, WFOEs have grown much more popular in recent years. In 1986, there were 18, but four years later there were over 1,800. The reason for their sudden jump in popularity is that they are largely insulated from the ebb and flow of other investment problems (e.g., foreign exchange shortages). Moreover, companies such as 3M, W. R. Grace, DEC, and PepsiCo have shown that these types of ventures can be operated highly successfully.

Foreign Borrowing and Use of Multilateral Economic Institutions

One of the most radical shifts away from the autarchic policies of the Maoist era was the decision, in late 1978, to seek outside development assistance. However ironic, the abrupt shift had quick and salutary results.

China was granted admission into the World Bank Group (which includes the International Monetary Fund, International Bank for Reconstruction and Development, International Development Association, and the International Finance Corporation) in 1980. Membership in the Asian Development Bank came in 1986.

In 1983, China gained observer status in the General Agreement on Tariffs and Trade (GATT). In 1986 it announced its desire to gain full GATT membership, but due to its inability to as yet demonstrate economic and trade policies based upon free market principles as defined by GATT, its application was still pending as of early 1992 (see "Multilateral Institutions," below).

The governments of Japan and most European countries have lined up to grant China highly concessionary development loans. Major international banks also eagerly sought active involvement in joint ventures and infrastructure projects.

By mid-1990, China's total international debt stood at $45 billion. The debt service ratio has remained a modest 10%, and the country's external debt is roughly equivalent to an equally modest 11% of GNP. Peak payment periods will average a manageable $5 billion per year until 1996.

THE WORLD BANK AND RELATED INSTITUTIONS

Before suspending loans because of the violent suppression of student protests at Tiananmen Square, annual World Bank assistance had peaked in 1988 at nearly $1.7 billion.

The bank resumed loans to China in 1990 on the grounds that without the active involvement of world institutions, China would crawl back into an isolationist shell, halting economic growth and hurting the general population. As the bank put it, China "would have little alternative other than to resort to increased planning and policies promoting domestic self-sufficiency."

The emphasis of the Bank's loans has shifted, due both to the events at Tiananmen and the change in World Bank leadership. While still considering a broad range of projects, there is now a focus on humanitarian lending. One of the first loans, for example, was to assist in improving the design of homes that had been destroyed by earthquakes. In addition to humanitarian projects, the bank has made environmental loans a priority. This is due to a change in policy at the International Development Association, which now stipulates that recipient countries should be "environmentally conscious."

The Asian Development Bank (ADB) has also been generous to China. By early 1989, the ADB granted seven loans (valued at $416 million), funded 22 technical assistance projects (worth $8.42 million), and extended a $3 million line of private sector investment equity to a Shanghai development corporation.

When the ADB resumed lending again in 1991, it funded a $4 million equity stake in a venture capital firm, $48 million to guarantee interest payments for the Nanpu bridge in Shanghai, and a $100 million line of credit to the Industrial and Commercial Bank of China for importing technology on behalf of state-run enterprises. In addition, the ADB has proposed 13 projects valued at $1.3 billion for the 1990s.

OTHER FOREIGN BORROWING

In 1988, a peak year for foreign government loans, the Japanese had set aside $6.7 billion for China for 1990–95, the West Germans $110 million, Great Britain $622 million, Canada $700 million, Australia $518 million, and Italy $300 million. Again, such loans were brought to a halt in the wake of Tiananmen.

When the passage of time showed the reform movement to be ongoing, these governments followed the lead of the World Bank and resumed loan activity. The French government, for example, granted loans of $1.2 million in 1991, much of it towards the construction of a car production plant on behalf of Citroen and its joint venture partner.

Commercial bank lending to China soared to 44% of all foreign loans in 1987, up from 21% in 1985. This increase was due in part to advantageous loan rates and also because decentralization meant local governments could now apply for such loans. Disrupted by the Tiananmen incident, commercial lending has also regained momentum. Bankers attribute this to the improving economy and the continued rise of progressive officials into the upper ranks of the central government. Morgan Stanley structured $50 million worth of credits for Sinochem International Oil in early 1991. That same year also saw Japanese syndication raise $50 million for the China International Trust & Investment Corporation (CITIC). A Euro-Japanese consortium loaned $50 million to a Shanghai steel mill.

MULTILATERAL INSTITUTIONS

China has also been a beneficiary of the United Nations Development Program (UNDP). The U.N.'s financial commitments, mainly concentrated on small-scale rural projects, totaled $217 million from 1978 to 1990. In addition, the U.N. system has contributed over 2,000 short-term experts and consultants to help in specialized training, pre-investment surveys, technology transfer, and small-scale projects in energy development, agriculture, fishing, forestry, industry, environment, information processing, and rural development.

A multilateral institution from which China would like to receive benefits is the General Agreement on Tariffs and Trade (GATT). Membership would give China a chance to increase its foreign trade earnings by strengthening its claim to most-favored-nation (MFN) status with other GATT members and entitling it to preferential export market access to the industrialized member states. It would also confer international status and respectability in the family of advanced trading nations.

| | WORLD BANK LENDING TO CHINA | | | | | |
| | TABLE 3.7 | | | | | |

| | IBRD | | IDA | | Annual Totals | |
Year	No.	Amount	No.	Amount	No.	Amount
1981	1	$100.0	0	$100.0	1	$200.0
1982	0	$0.0	1	$60.0	1	$60.0
1983	5	$463.1	1	$150.4	6	$613.5
1984	5	$616.0	5	$423.5	10	$1,039.5
1985	7	$659.6	5	$442.3	12	$1,101.9
1986	7	$687.0	4	$450.0	11	$1,137.0
1987	8	$867.4	3	$556.2	11	$1,423.6
1988	10	$1,053.7	4	$639.9	14	$1,693.6
1989	7	$833.4	5	$515.0	12	$1,348.4
1990	0	$0.0	5	$590.0	5	$590.0
1991						
Totals:	50	$5,280.2	33	$3,927.3	83	$9,207.5

In US$ millions   **Source: World Bank Annual Reports**

The unequivocal nature of GATT membership requirements are such that China would have to clearly demonstrate it was taking steps toward establishing a fully market-oriented economy. Such steps would include ending discriminatory practices, expanding market access, decentralizing import and export decision-making and licensing, and exercising full disclosure in trade policies ("transparency"). One major obstacle, the two-tiered pricing system, is being removed in 1992.

So far the Chinese government has been unwilling and perhaps unable to meet GATT's requirements. Negotiations already were bogged down in 1988; Tiananmen suspended them altogether. In the meantime, Taiwan has reapplied for membership, creating at minimum a political embarrassment for China. Positive steps in the right direction would include fulfillment of the promise made in early 1992 to join the international intellectual property rights conventions and some acceptable concessions on tariff schedules. Failure to take such steps in the near future would inevitably raise questions about the degree of China's commitment to the open door policy. The indications are, however, that China will move forward.

Organizational Structure for Carrying Out Trade and Investment

A full explanation of the labyrinthine structure set up to carry out trade and investment would require a text as long and complicated as the Confucian classics. Moreover, the foreign trade system, like everything else in China, is in flux, somewhere between the central control it left a decade ago and the market oriented system over the horizon.

This section briefly traces the development of the trade and investment structure and paints a broad-brush picture of the system as it exists as of early 1992. Because practice is so often different from theory in China, a guide to help find one's way through the system can be found in chapter 9.

EVOLUTION OF THE TRADING SYSTEM— AN EXECUTIVE SUMMARY

Generally speaking, the evolution of the trade and investment structure in the last dozen years has involved at least four broad and continuing trends, all intertwined:

1. The state-owned foreign trading corporations (FTCs), formerly controlled by the Ministry of Foreign Economic Relations and Trade (MOFERT), have been given autonomy and broken up into regional and local trading agencies.

2. China's industrial ministries have separately been granted import/export licenses and the ability to seek investment.

3. Factories also have been given the power to engage in foreign trade directly, and groups of factories producing similar products have joined together to form trade combines.

4. Investment organizations such as the China International Trade and Investment Corporation (CITIC) have been set up to develop projects horizontally across bureaucracies and vertically through the central, regional, and local decision-making bodies.

These trends, fed by reform, decentralization, and the emergence of open cities and SEZs, have created an explosion of opportunities for the foreign company. They have also created murky jurisdictional boundaries, conflict, complexity, and the need to evaluate potential business partners very carefully.

Evolution of the System[1]

Until the late 1970s, foreign traders had to rely exclusively on a dozen tightly controlled state trading corporations. These foreign trade corporations, known as FTCs, had branch offices in major cities and enjoyed sole authority to import and export goods. They traded in broad product categories. Relying on one central office, traders could theoretically conduct business throughout China. In practice, the old state-run foreign trading corporations were cumbersome and inefficient middlemen with little knowledge of the products involved, the factories making them, or the end users making the purchase.

Since 1979 China has steadily decentralized trading authority and opened new commercial trading avenues to foreigners and Chinese alike. The major shift came in 1984, when China instituted economic reforms which required a clear division between government entities and commercial companies and mandated that the latter gradually become self-sufficient.

These reforms motivated the industrial ministries to create their own trading companies. This increased the options within the trade system and initiated a newly competitive environment among Chinese companies interested in doing business with foreign firms.

Initially, these changes in policy did not have a dramatic impact. Most industrial companies (sometimes known as ministerial corporations) worked closely with MOFERT's FTCs. However, over time they have become competent competitors, and in some product areas have eclipsed their old mentors.

FURTHER PROLIFERATION

Simultaneously, provincial and municipal governments formed their own specialized industrial organizations to conduct foreign trade. Two types emerged, one specializing in specific product lines and the other, under provincial authority, trading in products that did not require an export license from MOFERT.

Further changes announced in 1988 and partially implemented in early 1989 gave large manufacturers access to foreign trade rights directly.

In addition, dozens of new companies were given the right to enter the foreign trade system. These "enterprises," as the Chinese call them, are often no larger than the owner's name card, hence their nickname: "briefcase" companies. Many facilitate deals that are legal, but not formally sanctioned. Examples are companies that trade local Chinese currency for Hong Kong dollars on the "gray" or swap market, as well as companies that serve as direct purchasing agents for Chinese firms that do not have access to foreign currency.

---

[1]Julie Reinganum contributed substantially to this section.

During 1990–91 these enterprises became increasingly active. Mainly located in southern China and the special economic zones, they import and export products and often evade taxes to central government agencies in Beijing. Many Chinese and non-Chinese are tempted to choose this route since these companies may offer quick deals on favorable terms. Caution is in order, however, as many exist simply to do one-time business (see chapter 9 for an example of how these deals can turn sour). Recently announced policies intended to limit certain loopholes in the system are likely to curtail their rapid growth.

The Trading System Today

The Ministry of Foreign Economic Relations and Trade now only controls trade in commodities critical to the state plan. Otherwise, as discussed, MOFERT's operational powers have been largely stripped, leaving it a regulatory body (it also has approval authority over joint ventures).

MOFERT's former FTCs have been cast adrift, responsible for their own profit and loss. This leaves them to sell their services as agents to domestic manufacturers and to foreign traders choosing to rely upon them for contacts and experience. More and more often, however, traders look for ways to get around them.

The trading companies under the industrial ministries have come out the clear winners. They are able to integrate manufacturing, investment, and trading activities, leaving them in a powerful position.

One of the earliest and still one of the most powerful is the China National Machinery and Equipment Import and Export Corporation (CMEC) under the Ministry of Machine Building and Electronics. This same ministry now has the China General Electric Corporation, the China Machine Tool Corporation, and the China Electronics Technology Corporation under its wing.

Other examples of powerful, fully integrated, ministerial industrial corporations are the China North Industry Corporation (NORINCO—the umbrella for companies working under the military) and the China National Electronic Technology Corporation (under the Ministry of Electronics Industry).

A variation of the industrial trading corporation is, for lack of a better term, the common interest corporation. These are factories from different localities that band together into a trading company to export their goods. Examples are the China Bearing Export Corporation and the China Cable and Wire Export Corporation.

Investment Organizations

When China's leaders opened the door to foreign investment in 1978 there was literally no organization to handle it. In a bold stroke, the government rehabilitated a group of former capitalists and called upon them for help. The result was the China International Trust and Investment Corporation (CITIC). Since then CITIC has gained respect, power, and competitors. CITIC and the other investment organizations act like merchant banks, but have wider scope. They are master builders who work with foreign companies in locating viable investment projects, then developing and even managing them.

CITIC remains one of the best-run corporations in China, with 170 mega-projects. It has also been active overseas, investing in airlines, banks, manufacturing facilities, telecommunications, and real estate, particularly in Hong Kong. There its local arm, CITIC Pacific, recently won control over Hang Chong Investment, one of Hong Kong's largest private trading companies. Some observers feel CITIC is overstretched, however. A number of their enterprises have not turned a profit, the company is burdened with debt, and it recently suffered a downgrading of its credit rating. CITIC's image was further tarnished when one of its branch directors was executed in late 1991 for corruption.

At the regional level, cities and provinces have established their own "ITICs" (Liaoning International Trust and Investment Corporation, for example). These have no direct relationship with CITIC, but carry out similar projects at the provincial level.

Another example of an international investment organization is the China Everbright Corporation. Wang Guangying, founding chairman of the company, once summed up his ambitions—and those of many other newly-minted investment bankers—in an interview with author Daniel Burstein: "One day, one contract, one million U.S. dollars. I like action. I like to get things done. It's more satisfying to me than eating an ice cream."

The most notable newcomers to the finance and investment arena are China's mega-industrial corporations. Using flagship factories as their vehicle, they threaten to eclipse CITIC and other groups as magnets for investment. The Capital Iron and Steel Works, for example, has become a commercial powerhouse, trading, buying factories and research institutes, getting involved in aviation, and engaging in international bidding. (However, a profile in *The New York Times* in late 1991 made it clear that as a state-run steel maker the enterprise was decaying into "a giant labyrinth of mismanagement.")

▼ THE NEW INDUSTRIAL INVESTMENT CORPORATIONS

An example of the new industrial conglomerates that have sprung up as rivals to CITIC is the China Electronics Industries Corporation (CEIC), established under the aegis of the Ministry of Machinery Electronics. CEIC was formed in the wake of the Gulf War, which showed China's leaders just how far behind they were on the technology curve.

China Electronics Industries Corporation has the status of a ministry, and incorporates some 1,000 factories, companies and trade and investment arms formerly under the Ministry of Machine Building and the Ministry of Electronics Industries (now merged). CEIC has inherited several dozen high-priority research institutes.

The company is led by a vice-minister and has the capability to invest, produce, do R&D work, and carry on import/export trade. As such, it already has a head start over many investment organizations in that it is already completely integrated into the economy.

▲

Foreigners have signed on to the investment bandwagon by forming partnerships with Chinese banks. In April 1991, for example, the Bank of China helped form an investment firm for fledgling enterprises called China Asset Holdings with partners Standard Chartered Bank, James Capel (Far East), and Venturetech, a Chinese venture capital company formed by the powerful Science and Technology Commission.

A similar Chinese/foreign investment company is Shanghai International Finance, formed by the Communications Bank of China, Bank of China, Sanwa Bank, and Hong Kong Bank of East Asia.

For more information on investment and venture capital activities in China, see appendix 4.

Special Economic Zones and Open Cities

In addition to specific trade and investment organizations, the third way China has chosen to implement its foreign trade and investment strategy is through a group of special economic zones and "open cities."

Five special economic zones (SEZs) were created, beginning in 1979. In addition, 14 coastal cities were given the status of "open cities," entitling them to approve foreign investment projects, offer various incentives, and retain a portion of earned foreign exchange. These cities also set aside areas for development christened Economic and Technological Development Zones (ETDZs). The first to formally open was Pudong, a section of Shanghai.

The SEZ and open cities programs have succeeded beyond many a planner's dream—or hard-liner's nightmare. In what amounts to a 12-year economic boom, the Japanese and South Koreans have set up shop in Liaoning, across the Yellow Sea. Taiwan business people are active in Fujian. Hundreds of foreign companies of various nationalities have set themselves up in Shanghai.

But perhaps the most impressive performance of all has taken place in Guangdong Province. It absorbed nearly 60% of all foreign investment, created 5 million new jobs, accounted for one-sixth of China's foreign exports, and experienced economic growth rates that exceed the best boom years in Taiwan or South Korea. The Pearl River Delta region that extends from the city of Guangzhou down to the border with Hong Kong now by itself has a population of 420 million and a gross domestic product of $240 billion.

In a country where economics and politics are inexorably intertwined, the performance of these zones and cities is richly symbolic. The Gold Coast in general, and Guangdong in particular, represent the ultimate push toward decentralization and the market economy against the pull of a leadership determined to control development through state-dominated planning. The outcome of this tug of war is not easy to predict. But huge sums of overseas Chinese and Japanese money—the smartest money around in that part of the world—is betting that economic reform will win.

SPECIAL ECONOMIC ZONES (SEZS)

That SEZs have been relatively free from excessive government interference through the years, largely because they continue to provide a healthy contribution to Beijing's foreign exchange coffers. China analyst Lawrence Reardon predicts that as they enter their second decade, the maturing SEZs will continue to be important foreign exchange generators, as well as China's major links to the two mini-dragons, Hong Kong and Taiwan. SEZ privileges are also likely to be extended to other parts of China.

As a sure signal of their future importance, Beijing announced in early 1992 that Shenzhen, the 131–square-mile capitalist development center bordering Hong Kong, would be allowed to absorb neighboring (and already flourishing) Boan County, thereby growing sixfold in size.

OPEN CITIES

In the 1990s the open cities will push to develop their infrastructure, further integrate the foreign and domestic parts of their economy, and position themselves as windows for trade and investment in the surrounding regions. Many will follow Shanghai's example and establish special development zones.

Many analysts feel that these cities will become increasingly (and disproportionately) wealthy and powerful, creating both the possibility for a replication of the city-state phenomenon seen in Singapore and Hong Kong and for the social and political problems that may accompany such growth.

ECONOMIC AND TECHNOLOGICAL DEVELOPMENT ZONES (ETDZS

One of the firmest indications that most of China continues reform even while the leadership shouts restraint is the opening of the newest ETDZ in the Pudong area of Shanghai. Pudong has the characteristics of the other SEZs, but it goes farther in allowing foreign firms to import and export goods for use within the zone duty-free (entrepôt trade). A similar free trade zone has been established in Tianjin and one will soon follow in Guangzhou.

The choice of Pudong as an EDTZ applied the special economic zone concept to a location up the coast, to a city renowned in generations past for its business and financial acumen. Unlike Shenzhen and the other SEZs which are literally fenced off from their surroundings, planners view the development as not only integral to the economic and social progress of Shanghai, but also as a way to boost the economies of the six provinces that comprise the greater Yangzi River area, home of 34% of China's population.

Trends for the 1990s

Trends for the 1990s point to continued reform and decentralization:

1. The Ministry of Foreign Economic Relations and Trade (MOFERT) will lose operational control of the few foreign trade corporations still within its jurisdiction and will become strictly a regulatory body.

2. The government is withdrawing *all* subsidies from trading organizations of whatever stripe, forcing the system to become rational. Every trading company—national, local, regional, industrial—will have to watch its own profit and loss.

3. All trading companies are being encouraged to merge with industrial enterprises. The aim is to create large multifunction

companies combining production, finance, and trading. The models are Mitsubishi, C. Itoh, and other Japanese *keiretsu.*

4. As they develop, the ministry-level industrial corporations will increasingly rival investment organizations such as CITIC. They are the ultimate "insiders," able to regroup whole factories, trading systems, and financing mechanisms under their wing without incurring a large debt up front. CITIC and the other investment organizations, on the other hand, are "outsiders," forced to buy their way in and develop businesses from scratch.

5. Several more "Hong Kongs" will be created along China's coast through the opening of a number of additional economic zones or their equivalents.

CHINA BUSINESS STRATEGIES— THE CASE STUDIES

4

Trade and Technology

Every sale that is made in China is the result of successful competition not only with similar articles made by a competitor, but with a wide variety of other things with which it would not appear to have any particular connection. . . . This introduces into the selling of goods to China complications which are measured by the geometric rather than the arithmetical progression, and adds grey hairs to the heads of sales managers.

—CARL CROW, *400 MILLION CUSTOMERS* (1937)

A half century after Carl Crow wrote these words, the China trade remains complex. China has reformed its trade system . . . but not quite. It's becoming more businesslike . . . but not really. It touts an open door policy and proclaims the ease of buying, selling, and investing . . . but with a bucket full of "ifs" and "excepts."

On the other hand, a lot of the negatives also turn out to be less than clear cut. China has a sorry human rights record and a rigid political structure . . . but its version of a market economy is benefiting millions of its citizens. Its economic policies are confusing, its laws incomplete . . . but both trade and investment are booming. Tales of business failures abound . . . but the promise of the market seems closer than ever to realization.

The shades of contrast between hope and reality, vision and frustration, expectations and fulfillment can seem confusing to evaluate. In the belief that experience remains a better teacher than analysis, the next four chapters present nearly 30 case studies that demonstrate what works and what doesn't when it comes to doing business in a place where business is done very differently. The cases cover companies large and small and demonstrate nearly every form of business arrangement being carried out. Some of the lessons are highlighted alongside the cases, but a more complete discussion of the experiences of these and other companies can be found in "The Lessons Learned" section of the book, chapters 8 through 11.

This chapter covers the basic forms of import and export trade. The thought that "If every Chinese housewife would buy one dress pattern . . ." might be regarded by Carl Crow and his modern-day counterparts as an example of wishful thinking, but McCall Pattern Company has taken a thorough look, set realistic goals, and gotten a start. The M&Ms case study shows another way to reach China's consumers.

Ibberson International sells grain and feed processing facilities with the aid of international development loans and by sustaining a sales effort at the local level. Canpotex shows that educating the market leads to larger sales.

Fluke International and Rosemount are high-tech companies which began by selling products and then moved on to solidify their position in China through licensing, technology transfer, and buy-back arrangements. Gelman Sciences tried selling, then the joint venture approach, but finally found that a technology transfer arrangement satisfied its goals.

Finally, representing the experience of importers is Monarch Import Company, which distributes Tsingtao beer, arguably China's best-known branded product.

Export Sales

■ McCall Pattern Company

There are more sewing machines in China than there are people in the United States. Aiming to take advantage of this tantalizing fact is the well known McCall Pattern Company. Starting from scratch in 1988, McCall now offers over 300 current styles for China's newly fashion conscious nation.

McCall Pattern—thanks to its consultants, the U.S. China Investment Corporation, based in Alexandria, Virginia—has proven that direct market access to the Chinese consumer is possible.

In addition to the acumen of the seller, several developments in China have made such direct sales feasible. One is that the government no longer stands in the way of getting to the consumer or end user. The second is that swapping foreign exchange for RMB has become a great deal simpler.

This case has been adapted from an article originally published in the September/October 1991 issue of The China Business Review. *Reprinted with permission of the China Business Forum, the US-China Business Council, Washington, D.C.*

McCall Pattern Company sees China as one of the final frontiers of growth for its products, given the country's rapidly rising incomes and the demand for modern, stylish clothing.

Before committing itself to the market, however, McCall conducted a market test in 1987 to gauge the sales potential of its patterns. In this test, 12 designs were placed in two department stores—one in Beijing and one in Shanghai—and sales activity was monitored for two months. Sales topped 300 units per month in both stores, prompting McCall to launch its first full-scale sales effort in April 1988.

The strategy has been to gradually build distribution and sales while vigorously promoting the use of patterns among women ages 20 to 40. McCall has registered its trademarks in both English and Chinese. Its designs are not copyrighted, but pirating is discouraged by the speed with which new designs are introduced and the large economies of scale in the printing operation.

To get the business started, McCall itself had to bring together the various Chinese organizations involved. First, an arrangement was made with one of Beijing's foreign trade corporations to become the importer of record. McCall was able to get their cooperation in part because it was pointed out to the FTC that it could earn a foreign exchange commission simply for handling the paperwork.

McCall's agent then went out and found the distributor, the Beijing Garment Research Institute. It could tell this potential distributor, a domestic state enterprise with no authority to deal in foreign trade, "Don't worry, we have the importer, all you need to do is be the distributor."

How It Works

The Beijing Garment Research Institute sells directly to department stores and fabric retailers on a consignment basis. Each store pays the Institute once a month for the patterns it has sold. The Beijing Garment Research Institute deducts its margin and pays the importer, which in turn pays McCall in foreign exchange.

The Chinese distributor is responsible for warehousing, locating and selling to new stores, shipping and filling stores' orders, ordering patterns from the U.S., fulfilling mail orders, and completing sales reports. To ensure that these tasks are performed well, McCall has hired two Americans to train Institute staff and supervise every aspect of the operation from the start.

McCall Pattern Looks at the Potential

The fundamentals of the pattern market in China look positive to McCall. Sewing machines are ubiquitous; an enormous selection of inexpensive fabrics is available everywhere. Moreover, no Chinese domestic company specializes in pattern production. The only competition is the rows of tailors who camp out in free markets; the state-owned tailor shops are expensive, carry out-of-date designs, and are very slow.

Yet sales have not exactly skyrocketed. Lack of competition also means consumers and vendors are not familiar with the product. Over the last three years McCall has had to work one-on-one with everyone from the distributor to the customer to educate them about the benefits of patterns. The Beijing Garment Research Institute's staff had no sales or distribution experience, and no professional work ethic or natural ability to deal with customers. Its leaders were skeptical until sales started rolling in.

Convincing managers of Chinese fabric and department stores was also no easy task. They initially resisted selling the patterns, claiming that since patterns were on paper they should be sold in bookstores or by stationers. To overcome such resistance, expatriate staff personally makes the first sales call to each store, meeting first with the fabric department manager and then proceeding to the store's general manager. (The contract is made between the store and the Chinese distributor.)

To clinch the deal the stores are offered start-up stock, free use of a display case and cabinet, and free posters and advertising support. Even then, many managers complain that patterns don't bring in enough money given the counter space required. Eventually, however, they learn that along with each pattern worth RMB 10, they are also likely sell RMB 40–50 worth of fabric.

McCall next works with the sales staff, giving each clerk individualized training, and standing by them on the first day to give them added confidence. Store managers are usually strict about what kind of incentives they will allow McCall to offer their staff (for fear of arousing envy among others), but among the perks found acceptable are free or below-cost patterns.

Convincing the Customer

The best clerks tend to be women who have executed McCall patterns and can relay their confidence to potential customers, many of whom are often openly skeptical about trying new things (having often had to put up with shoddy merchandise on the domestic market). To help back up their sales clerks, McCall has instituted a nationwide public relations campaign to promote home sewing in general, and McCall's products in particular. The campaign is run by expatriate representatives, based on an annual budget set by the company.

As part of the campaign, moonlighting Chinese journalists have placed hundreds of articles in local and national newspapers, covering the product from every angle. Several dozen video segments have been produced in cooperation with local TV stations. The three-to-eight minute segments have in turn been syndicated to other local stations around the country where they are shown on the local version of a prime time show for women.

On these pre-taped shows, TV personalities discuss designing clothes while thumbing through the McCall catalogue. Patterns are laid out, and a dress is made and modeled. Sometimes the host will mention where the patterns are available locally. These soft-sell ads have been very successful. The day after such a broadcast in Tianjin, customers bought 239 patterns—probably a one-day record for the company anywhere in the world. Sales in Kunming Department Store averaged over 1,500 patterns per month during a three-month series of broadcasts, making it the top-selling store in China.

Although McCall's patterns are available in some 48 stores in 38 cities, much of the potential market lies outside these areas. Hence, the company instituted a mail-order service in 1989. Currently, mail order accounts for 20% of the company's business.

Mail order is not widely accepted in China, so McCall is working hard to establish a reputation for speed, accuracy, and fairness. Staff are trained to care for each order as if it came from a friend or relative. They offer free technical assistance by mail and handle customer inquiries, though less than 1% of the customers report any problems.

To publicize the mail-order business, ads displaying best-selling designs are placed in top Chinese fashion magazines, and a 60-page color catalogue, featuring over 100 designs and a discount coupon, was distributed via book stores and by mail.

Patterns sold through the mail cost the same as those sold in stores (customers pay via postal money orders); the extra profit the distributor makes by cutting out the retailer more than covers the postage and handling charges. The Institute receives about 100 orders a day, which are processed and shipped out via registered mail within 24 hours.

A Pattern for Success

McCall's long-term view and promotional efforts have paid off. Sales per store average well above U.S. rates. The best stores are world leaders on a units-sold-per-year basis. The total number of patterns sold in 1990 hit 100,000—over three times the number in 1989. Sales for 1991 are expected to reach 150,000.

McCall's realizes the need for staying power, continued promotion, and improvements. For example, the sewing guides originally carried pictures and symbols, but no words, and there were no specific pattern instructions in Chinese. This has been corrected.

Another innovation in the works is to begin merchandising patterns in China independently of those available in the U.S. A line specifically picked for China will allow more efficient use of warehouse and store counter space, less obsolescence, and the ability to keep good sellers in stock even though they may be phased out in the U.S.

McCall also has near-term plans to expand distribution in 40 more cities and undertake more national promotions.

The Chinese government, at times hostile to other consumer-product imports, has generally been supportive of McCall's efforts, in part because use of patterns promotes use of Chinese fabric, thread, and sewing notions.

As of 1992, the company says its China operation is not yet profitable. McCall patterns retail for RMB 9.90, or about $2, only one-third the average U.S. retail price. Also contributing to negative cash flow is an investment so far of $1 million in training and supervision, sales, inventory, supplies, and promotion. Currently, McCall expects to break even in 1994, and is comfortable with its long-term view. Says Robert L. Hermann, president of McCall, and a man who personally saw the consumer market start to develop in a backward Japan in the 1950s, "He who uses a long line catches a big fish."

▼ CASE STUDY HIGHLIGHTS:
McCALL PATTERN COMPANY

• A distribution and sales organization can be built to reach the Chinese consumer, even though the product is not made in China.

• For McCall's and other companies, there are four major risks in trying to penetrate the market in this way: (a) the product might not actually sell on the market; (b) the product may have to be priced lower in China than elsewhere in the world; (c) the exchange rate may be volatile; and (d) the proper management must be available to plan and implement the sales strategy.

• While adapting them to China, McCall found that many tried-and-true advertising and promotion techniques could work in China, including demonstrations in stores and on television.

• Continued improvement in customizing the product for the Chinese market will help to build sales.

• The presence in China of the same team of knowledgeable expatriates to supervise and help manage the business is paying long-term dividends.

▲

■ Mars Candy Company

Mars, makers of M&Ms and other candies, has a unique approach to China. It sells directly to the P.R.C without benefit of a joint venture or any other type of on-site business.

M&Ms are sold directly to consumers in China through two different distribution channels: the China National Duty Free Import Corporation for its airport duty-free shops and, more significantly, key local wholesalers for distribution to neighborhood stores in Beijing, Shanghai, and Guangzhou.

This case study is a brief look at the creative use of the distribution system to reach the Chinese consumer from outside normal trade and investment channels. Company officials did not discuss how they earned the foreign exchange necessary to make this venture profitable, but some of the standard possibilities are discussed in chapter 9.

The case is reprinted, with permission, from the November 12, 1990 issue of Business China, a publication of Business International Asia/Pacific Ltd.

If more M&Ms are melting in the mouths of Shanghai consumers these days, it is because East Asiatic Company (of Hong Kong) has successfully developed a way to distribute the well-known U.S. chocolate product in the city.

In the normal distribution system, retailers are used to having to go calling on the wholesaler to try and obtain the product and then figure out a way to transport it to the store. East Asiatic has turned this old practice on its head: M&M wholesalers sell and transport their goods directly to the retailers.

Here's how it works. East Asiatic, a Hong Kong-based company has a distribution agreement with Mars for M&M candies in China. The candies are brought into Shanghai by the container-load from the U.S. or Australia or in smaller shipments via Hong Kong. East Asiatic then sells the chocolates to wholesalers/distributors in Shanghai.

The wholesaler has five vans that deliver M&Ms throughout Shanghai, either to sub-wholesalers or retail outlets. The Hong Kong agent also has a van in the city. Painted with M&M advertisements, the vehicle serves as both an advertising and distribution medium.

Choosing the right wholesalers and monitoring them closely are very important to the distribution effort's success. Besides having a warehouse for storing M&Ms properly, wholesalers must be committed to making frequent deliveries so that retail outlets receive fresh stock regularly. If a store has a quick turnover, a wholesaler should visit it once or twice a week; if turnover is slower, visits may occur every 10 to 14 days. The company works with wholesalers to select sub-wholesalers and hires salespeople directly by running advertisements in Shanghai newspapers.

The sales team visits retail outlets regularly to check displays, advertising, and inventory needs. It encourages store managers to put up M&M fliers and sometimes conducts taste tests or other promotions, like giving away trial packages of Skittles (another Mars candy) or balloons decorated with the M&M logo. Salespeople benefit from successful promotion work by earning performance bonuses in addition to their straight salary.

The Hong Kong company informally oversees and coordinates the entire distribution process—from wholesalers to sub-wholesalers to sales staff to retail outlets. It teaches all levels to sell M&Ms into the market, instead of waiting for the market to come to them, as is the traditional practice in China. Coordination is handled by the company's representative office in Shanghai, with personnel in Hong Kong visiting from time to time in order to deal with specific issues.

To select the proper retail outlets, East Asiatic set out a list of criteria and commissioned a Hong Kong market research firm that had connections with a Shanghai research firm to help identify stores in selected sales districts. At present, the distribution effort primarily targets state-run stores. Payment terms normally require settlement within one to two weeks after delivery. The Hong Kong agent sells through some private entrepreneurs in Shanghai even though they are somewhat less credit-worthy than state stores, and hopes to expand this network gradually.

The company's Shanghai distribution system went into effect in late 1989 and M&Ms are now widely available—both in large outlets and in roadside shops decorated with M&M fliers. A similar system went into effect in Beijing in 1991, boosted by a major advertising campaign in connection with the 1990 Asian Games. The firm also distributes M&Ms in Guangzhou, although the network there is not as developed. Other points in China are covered via these three cities.

A major issue for the company has been a fight to protect its trademark rights (see sidebar). Other than that, customers seem to like the chocolate (Shanghainese in particular have a taste for Western sweets), even though domestically-produced chocolate is one-fifth the price of the import.

▼ Case Study Highlights: Mars Candy Company

- Mars is teaching Chinese wholesalers a new way to serve the customer by going out to the retailer instead of waiting for him to show up at the warehouse. It also asks the local distributor to visit these retailers regularly to check displays and encourage sales.
- A wide range of creative marketing tools are used, from parasols with the M&M logo to the giving away of specially-marked balloons to children. M&Ms have also been heavily advertised, and the company has sponsored sporting events to further increase visibility.
- Rather than use its own staff, Mars has appointed a distributor in Hong Kong (but very well known in China) to serve the market.
- The Hong Kong company oversees and coordinates the entire distribution process to maintain efficiency and increase sales momentum.
- Trademarks are enforceable, although it takes diligent effort.

▼ M&Ms Stops Infringement

When Mars Company discovered that the Sanlian Food Company in Zhejiang province was damaging its M&Ms market by introducing W&W candies in Beijing, Shanghai, and Ningbo, it attempted to reach an agreement with the Chinese company.

Not only did these efforts fail, but Sanlian even tried to register the trademark W&Ws with the relevant Chinese trademark organization, the State Administration for Industry and Commerce (SAIC).

Mars successfully opposed the attempted registration on the basis of the Paris Convention for the Protection of Industrial Property.

While this opposition was pending, Mars worked with local SAIC bureaus to get W&Ws off the market. In Shanghai, where the infringement problem was most severe and the M&Ms presence greatest, authorities acted quickly. However, they required Mars to post a bond in case it eventually lost the case.

In Ningbo, home of Sanlian, Mars met with less cooperation. SAIC authorities there claimed the M&Ms trademark only applied to a particular typeset. The Ningbo SAIC went further and even threatened that the Mars trademark was in jeopardy because Mars itself used a different typeset for M&Ms than it registered. The Ningbo branch of SAIC claimed that Mars had illegally changed the mark.

Eventually, the issue went all the way to Beijing with the head office of SAIC siding with Mars. The agency issued a circular ordering its bureaus in Beijing, Shanghai, and Ningbo to cooperate with Mars in taking W&Ws off the market.

Source: Adapted, with permission, from the November 12, 1990 issue of *Business China*, a publication of Business International Asia/Pacific Ltd.

■ *Ibberson International*

Ibberson International, a Minnesota corporation involved in plant design, engineering, and construction management of feed and grain manufacturing facilities, couldn't be more different from McCall or Mars Candy. Still, all three share a fundamental strategy in selling to the Chinese—an intense effort to get close to the customer.

Ibberson made its first sales presentation in China in 1985, installed its first plant in 1986, and has since sold seven additional agricultural facilities. It has also sold many equipment packages to China.

Ibberson cites three chief reasons for its success: a long-term commitment, an aggressive pursuit of sales leads through a full time representative in China, and continued demand for feed mill systems throughout China.

This case study was contributed by P. Richard Bohr.

Ibberson's first contact with China came in 1979, when the company hosted a delegation of feed mill experts who were in the U.S. as guests of the National Academy of Sciences. This visit produced no visible results.

The next contact with a potential customer came in April 1985, when representatives from the city of Xiangfan came to the U.S. as part of a delegation of agribusiness operators. This delegation, sponsored by the U.S. Feed Grains Council, came to tour feed, rendering, and vegetable oil processing plants and asked to see Ibberson.

Ibberson played host to the delegation, and business talks began as Ibberson learned of Xiangfan's plans to build a feed mill facility in their town.

Unlike many projects in China, this one moved swiftly. By the end of the month, Ibberson had accepted an invitation to come to Beijing to meet the mayor of Xiangfan and the leader of the Chinese delegation that had talked with Ibberson in the U.S. At this meeting, a letter of intent was signed. In late June and early July, Ibberson finalized the scope and pricing of the proposed project by mail.

By early fall Xiangfan officials had received the appropriate provincial and national government approvals as well as the necessary allocation of funds. On November 12, 1985, Ibberson began the final round of negotiations in Wuhan with officials from Xiangfan, plant technicians, and representatives from the China National Technical Import Corporation. After just four days, a $700,000 contract was signed to design, build, ship, and install Ibberson's first modular feed manufacturing facility in the Far East.

A key point in this sale was that the deal was financed by a loan from Norwest Banks, co-guaranteed by the Minnesota Export Finance Authority and the U.S. Export-Import Bank (Ex-Im Bank)— a "first" for this type of arrangement.

Since that initial sale, Ibberson has gone on to sell a feed mill plant in Wuhan, an aquatic feed plant in Fuzhou, a feed plant in Jining, and a modular feed mill in Xintai. All these deals were signed in 1987 and 1988, and all were financed by the Ex-Im Bank.

The Roots of Success

Ibberson's early forays into the market made it realize that the Chinese prefer to buy from big-name American agricultural manufacturers. The company also noticed that sales often failed because the American representatives of those large companies did not, in Ibberson's words, "get down to the people."

To overcome its lack of name recognition and to cultivate buyers, Ibberson hired a young, in-country Chinese citizen as their agent. His job is to carry out the market research, locate potential buyers, and to market the company throughout the country. Ibberson feels they have a clear edge in this person, who cultivates close personal relationships with national, regional, and local contacts. Ibberson says it will continue to use Chinese nationals to do its selling in China, "as non-Chinese do not fully understand or appreciate China's different ways of thinking."

The pattern established is that Ibberson's China representative seeks out leads and begins initial discussions. As these progress, the head of the company's international division enters the picture to lead the contract negotiations. Although active in all phases of the first deal, the company president is no longer involved in the negotiations.

Ibberson's toughest competitors are from Europe and Japan, whose governments are able to offer subsidized financing to companies, giving them a decided edge. Moreover, according to the company's China rep, the Japanese have another advantage in that they send senior people to negotiate and offer the Chinese generous gifts, loans, and assistance packages. Like Ibberson, the Japanese also make every effort to stay in very close touch with the end user.

Ibberson feels its strong "local" presence plus its long-term commitment to China will yield further sales when financing for such needed agricultural projects become available again.

▼ **Case Study Highlights: Ibberson International**

• The chance to make a presentation to a visiting Chinese delegation proved to be an ideal way of getting Ibberson introduced to the China market.

• When the Chinese customer has a well-defined need, a deal can be concluded rapidly. The prospects for this sale were further enhanced by having the project on the Chinese priority list for imports and having the financing, guarantees, and other assurances in place.

• The rule of "get close to the customer" is here exemplified by a full-time sales person who is assigned to China and travels the country.

• The preference by Chinese for dealing with big names and big companies was overcome by Ibberson through the aggressive cultivation of customers over an extended period of time.

• U.S. firms are often at a competitive disadvantage with Japanese and European companies as their governments are able to offer subsidized financing.

▲

■ *Canpotex*

Canpotex is another company that takes pride in getting close to the Chinese customer, who in this case is the farmer.

While high technology sales—or non-sales—seem to capture most of the attention in the media, hundreds of companies are quietly doing a good business by selling, for hard cash, a great range of products to China. Here we look at the methods a group of Canadian fertilizer manufacturers has used to disseminate information about its product and persuade farmers to purchase Canadian potash.

This case is reprinted, with permission, from the October 28, 1991 issue of Business China, *a publication of Business International Asia/Pacific Ltd.*

Despite the "down-to-earth" nature of its business, the Canadian potash consortium, Canpotex Ltd., has acquired a reputation as a sophisticated marketer in China. Through its market development strategy, known as the Canpotex Balanced Fertilization Demonstration Program, the company has captured more than 50% of the P.R.C.'s imported potash market. In preparation for its major marketing drive, Canpotex collected extensive market intelligence on the entire range of players involved in the purchase and use of its product, rather than confining its research simply to the end users.

Although the company had been selling its distinctive "pink" potash to China since 1972, it wasn't until 1985 that Canpotex initiated a serious foray into the market by hiring a Hong Kong firm to survey more than 1,500 farmers and local agricultural technicians. From its market research and review of existing Chinese agronomic information, the Canadian firm discovered that, while the Chinese scientific community was aware of the benefits of using potash to fertilize crops, this information was not getting to the higher decision-making authorities or to local agricultural technicians and farmers.

Canpotex "needed to serve as the catalyst to move this agronomic information outwards from the scientific community," says Howard Cummer, the company's vice president of market development. The best way to do this, the company concluded, was to allow all the actors involved in potash purchasing decisions to see for themselves the positive impact potash could have on Chinese agricultural yields.

Demonstrations to Farmers

Canpotex called on the services of the Potash and Phosphate Institute of Canada (PPIC), an independent research institute with 30 years of experience in China, to establish demonstration plots in farmers' fields in cooperation with the Chinese provincial soil and fertilizer institutes. Canpotex provides funds to cover the costs of these demonstrations, which have become the foundation of the company's marketing strategy in China.

Started in 1986 in Guangxi province, Canpotex's market demonstration program has been recently expanded to include 10 additional provinces (Anhui, Guangdong, Hubei, Hunan, Jiangsu, Jiangxi, Shandong, Sichuan, and Zhejiang). Despite the emphasis on demonstrations, the company's balanced fertilization program actually consists of four main elements: demonstrations, farmer meetings, field inspections for leaders, and harvest field days.

The demonstrations, which are the heart of the program, involve the establishment of two plots side by side in the cooperating farmer's field. One plot is farmed using the scientific farming practices recommended by PPIC and the provincial soil and fertilizer institutes, while the other plot is farmed using the practices common to that area.

Having the provincial soil and fertilizer institutes run the demonstration projects with only minor assistance from PPIC and

Canpotex ensures "the scientific integrity of the experiment," says
Cummer. "You won't see our company logo 'Scientific Farming,' but
everyone still knows who funds the demonstration program."

To ensure that its ultimate customers understand the benefits
of using potash, Canpotex holds farmer meetings and harvest field
days to allow farmer groups and the larger community to inspect the
demonstration plots and learn about the recommended practices
from local agricultural technicians. Canpotex's practice of sponsor-
ing harvest field days (which include Chinese opera, cultural shows,
and a contest to guess the yield of the two demonstration plots) are
popular in the rural townships and earn the firm community
goodwill.

The company's practice of offering field inspections of the
demonstration plots to selected local, provincial, and national
leaders generates support among the Chinese leadership for increased
purchases of potash. To further get its name around, Canpotex
invites the local Chinese media to use the results of the demonstrations
for stories and articles. For instance, the company now has a slot on
the popular All-China Television Farm Show with 10 episodes on
balanced fertilization. These shows are scripted by a Chinese
producer and feature the provincial soil and fertilizer institute
people who handle the company's demonstration work. The farm
program is estimated to have an average viewing audience of 500
million people per episode. Canpotex also produces educational
pamphlets for technicians, newspaper ads, as well as radio programs
in local dialects to reach illiterate farmers.

The Results

The cost of Canpotex's field demonstration program is considerable—well over $1 million annually. While the company feels
the money has been well spent, its marketing efforts have not always
resulted in immediate sales growth. In 1985, the first year of the
demonstration program, sales of potash actually plummeted from
700,000 tons the previous year to 150,000 tons. This was largely due
to two factors outside the company's control—foreign exchange
shortages and an inefficient distribution system for potash. Nonetheless, Canpotex persevered through those tough times, and sales
have gradually risen to surpass 1984 levels. In 1991 Canpotex
expected to sell more than a million tons of potash to China.

To increase recognition of what is essentially a generic product,
Canpotex focuses on the red/pink color of its potash (it's normally
grey or whitish in color). Appealing to Chinese culture's association
of the color red with good luck, Canpotex sells its product as the
"powerful pink potash from Canada."

"Over and over we hear that Chinese farmers now associate the
color pink with potash," says Cummer. "This preference for pink
helps us convince decision-makers and buyers that buying pink is
a good business move—their customers prefer the product."

In an effort to keep in step with the progress of Chinese agriculture toward blended fertilizer rather than just single nutrient materials like potash or urea, Canpotex cooperated with the Canadian International Development Agency to build a pilot bulk-blend fertilizer plant in Guangdong. Since its opening in October 1988, the plant has been profitable.

Convinced that the Chinese market for potash will more than double over the next 10 years, Canpotex plans to continue its successful balanced fertilization market demonstration campaign for at least another 10 or 15 years. "I think even the Chinese are surprised at our tenacity," says Cummer.

▼ CASE STUDY HIGHLIGHTS: CANPOTEX

• While many companies talk "long-term," Canpotex shows its commitment through a highly visible field demonstration program.
• A remarkable level of sophistication is possible in carrying out market research.
• Canpotex cleverly made its generic product stand out by changing its color.
• Like McCall, Canpotex discovered that most of the elements necessary to create sales were already in place (peasants knew fertilizer; regional institutes knew potash), but were rarely joined together, meaning foreign company often must play the role of matchmaker (peasant, meet professor).
• The company learned the lesson that it pays to work with *all* the levels of bureaucracy involved in your business so that when the time comes, multiple levers could be applied on its behalf.

Technology Sales and Transfer Agreements

■ *Fluke International Company*

Fluke, based in Everett, Washington, is a manufacturer of electronic testing and measuring devices for the electronics and electrical industry. It began sales to China in 1973 and later developed some successful technology transfer agreements.

But sales in the late 1980s began to flag and this case study looks at some of the options Fluke is considering to improve things. It's a lesson in how a company's business assumptions must change as conditions in China change.

The case is reprinted, with permission, from the June 11, 1990 issue of Business China, *a publication of Business International Asia/Pacific Ltd.*

After a strong start, Fluke International's expanding China sales and proliferating electronic instrument technology deals began to stagnate in the mid-1980s. It, like many other foreign firms, fell victim to the foreign exchange shortage in 1986. But the company's direct sales stabilized in 1989–90, and 1991 saw sales climbing back up to previous levels. In addition, some well-structured technology transfer agreements continue to deliver profits. Rather than abandon the market, Fluke is pursuing new leads and changing some of its tactics.

Right from the start, this maker of multimeters, signal generators for the communications industry, and AC/DC calibrators has taken a long-term view, says Roland Chua, Fluke's China manager. For the first seven years of doing business with the P.R.C. (1973–80), it stuck to direct sales. Meanwhile, it was learning all it could about the market and sizing up options for deeper penetration.

That opportunity came in 1980 when Fluke entered into its first assembly arrangement with the Beijing Radio Research Institute (BRRI) to produce handheld digital multimeters for the domestic market. Nine other accords quickly followed (some with BRRI), and in 1984 and 1985 Fluke struck similar instrument assembly deals with Shanghai Electric Meter Works (for calibrators) and Qianfeng factory in Chengdu (for frequency synthesizers).

These technology transfer agreements all hew to the same basic structure. Fluke supplies CKD (completely knocked-down) or SKD (semi-knocked-down) kits, helps the Chinese partner purchase the manufacturing process equipment needed to assemble the kits, and trains Chinese personnel in manufacturing operations. The technology transferred consists primarily of manufacturing process know-how and expertise in plant management and organization.

In return, Fluke receives a "package" fee covering the purchase of capital equipment, its outlays for training, and a minimum number of kits. On repeat kit orders, the U.S. company receives a variable payment based on volume. Contracts typically range in value from around $500,000 to $2 million.

Transferring Technology

While similar to a licensing agreement in some ways, these deals fall under a "trade and technology" category of doing business, a form developed in the early 1980s when the Chinese were reluctant to pay royalties outright for technology. Fluke was satisfied with this structure since it wanted to stay away from transferring proprietary product technology that might allow the Chinese to replicate its products and compete in key markets in the future.

The agreements give the Chinese partners access to a wide range of sophisticated products they would otherwise have to import and at the same time upgraded their manufacturing skills and product knowledge. The Chinese partner in turn sells the assembled instruments domestically to electronics and computer factories, power companies, schools, petrochemical complexes, shipyards, and others. In determining what products to transfer, Fluke considers the Chinese partner's technical skills, as well as possible U.S. government and Cocom restrictions due to some products' potential military applications.

Under these agreements and through sales of both finished products and kits, Fluke's business with China peaked in 1985 at close to $10 million, accounting for some 5% of the company's worldwide sales. In 1986, when China began to restrain imports because of severe hard currency shortages, the business fell to less than $3 million. After stagnating for several years, Chinese revenue has picked up to over $4 million in 1990 and about $6 million in 1991. China now accounts for 50% of sales in a territory that includes all of Asia except Japan (about 2% of worldwide sales). Whereas business used to be divided almost equally between direct sales of finished goods and tech-transfer agreements (including kit sales), the former now account for the lion's share, while kits amount to only about 30%.

Ironically, the government's decentralization efforts are also partially to blame for Fluke's business contraction. While these policies granted local government and manufacturing units more decison-making authority, they also made them responsible for meeting foreign exchange requirements, a difficult challenge.

The 1986 foreign exchange cutback came just as the firm was broadening its horizons in China and about to embark on a series of initiatives to increase product servicing and boost sales. To help BRRI overcome foreign exchange constraints, Fluke agreed to let it export products using "key components" and the Fluke trademark to certain countries (like Japan) and to enter barter arrangements with Eastern Europe, provided the output met its stringent quality control standards. According to Chua, although BRRI output is up to snuff, the company has not yet exported anything because it does not have the needed distribution and servicing facilities in place abroad.

Fluke's attempt to establish wholly owned service centers in several parts of China also fizzled—the Chinese simply never moved on the firm's request. So Chinese-owned service centers in Beijing and Shanghai continue servicing Fluke's products.

Not all difficulties can be laid at China's doorstep. A Hong Kong subsidiary of Fluke's, which was to have supported the company's sales to China, has also suffered a reversal. It had to close down when it could not retain skilled staff in Hong Kong's labor-short market.

In 1986, Fluke was in the process of negotiating a host of new cooperation deals and exploring the possibility of licensing agreements. Today, only the assembly agreements with BRRI and Qianfeng still function. The Shanghai arrangement lapsed after a few years when the product being assembled became obsolete and the factory lacked the foreign exchange to embark on a more advanced venture. Fluke still supplies this factory with finished products for resale.

The company has recently taken a new direction that seeks to minimize its Chinese partners' hard currency outlays (while keeping Fluke's own costs down). It has entered into a consulting agreement with BRRI in which the Chinese partner designs a handheld multimeter with Fluke advice. Rather than charge a consulting fee, BRRI has agreed to buy certain parts from Fluke when the product goes into production.

As of late 1991, BRRI design and production quality is "impressive," says Mr. Chua, and the packaging is coming along. BRRI now sells these products on the Chinese domestic market, and in the near future Fluke will put them in touch with potential international customers.

Under a brand new trade and technology contract now being negotiated with BRRI, Fluke is looking to transfer its latest surface mount technology.

After a period of stagnation, business began growing again in 1991. Fluke's head count in the Beijing office went up to 16 from 10, and a Shanghai office will soon be opened. The major threat to future growth, says Mr. Chua, is not foreign exchange, quality, or the general business climate, but the deteriorating trade relationship between the U.S. and China. The firm is currently talking with four to five factories for new kit contracts, and also expects to be doing more technology transfer deals.

In the meantime, it has learned an important lesson about doing business in the P.R.C. In addition to examining the potential partner's technical qualifications and basic industry compatibility, Fluke now also looks carefully at the enterprise's access to foreign exchange and its connections within the bureaucracy.

▼ Case Study Highlights: Fluke International

• The road to success for Fluke was to start with the simplest form of doing business (in this case straight sales) before moving on to the complex (technology transfer).

• Once accomplished, the shape and form of the first business deal may be fairly easy to replicate with other partners in China, but there is a down side: when a shift in the business climate affects one venture, it will affect them all.

• Even a long-term strategy didn't protect Fluke from changes in the business climate—an evolution of the approach should be continually considered. This includes looking beyond the immediate sale to the viability and adaptability of the partner in the long run and under various market conditions.

• Fluke devised a creative way to help their partner help them, in this case to minimize foreign exchange outlays.

▲

■ Gelman Sciences, Inc.

In this case study, the area of technology is of sufficient priority that the Chinese were willing to meet Western contract terms to an unusual degree.

Gelman Sciences is a Michigan-based producer of microfiltration products. Its interest in China was based on two factors. First, the company had absolutely no market share in Asia and was facing a market already well supplied and satisfied by existing competitors in the region. The technology transfer approach, the company felt, would be the quickest and most effective way to enter the market.

Second, Eric Gelman, a vice president and principal, had a long personal interest in China. He made a personal investigation of the market (no consultants or trade organizations were used) and guided the company's approach.

At first the company tried direct sales, using trade shows as the venue. At the suggestion of the Chinese, Gelman then looked into the joint venture approach, but found that wanting as well. The straight technology transfer agreement that finally evolved is the company's largest international deal to date and offers some encouragement to other high-tech companies seeking an entry into the China market.

This case study was originally published in the July/August 1991 issue of The China Business Review. *Reprinted with permission of the China Business Forum, the US-China Business Council, Washington, D.C.*

"In China we perceived an emerging market with no established product identification or loyalty. This meant we could pioneer the market, rather than follow in someone else's path," said Eric Gelman, vice president of Gelman Sciences' international division.

The agreement that Gelman eventually negotiated involves a complicated set of technology transfer, distribution, and buy-back arrangements that took six years to complete.

The Product

Gelman Sciences agreed to sell China the technology and equipment necessary to manufacture microfiltration cartridges, used in research and clinical laboratories, health care facilities, and industrial process industries.

Four types of filtration cartridges will be produced in China. These are to be used for filtration of various fluids and fermentation of drug solution preparations. According to the firm, China will be able to absorb and assimilate the microfiltration technology "without difficulty."

Adopting the new technology will be critical to China's pharmaceutical industry, which is seeking to bring its overall manufacturing capability and quality standards up to Good Manufacturing Practices (GMP) standards, the international norm in the industry. Until these standards are met, Chinese pharmaceutical manufacturers are effectively blocked from exporting their products. Gelman Sciences estimates that China's pharmaceutical industry should be able to meet GMP standards within 10 years.

The contract with the China National Pharmaceutical Foreign Trade Corporation involves a combination of technology transfer and equipment sales agreements, a long-term supply arrangement, a distribution agreement, and a complex buy-back plan—all to be implemented between 1991 and 1998. To accommodate all the arrangements, the contract is divided into four separate agreements.

The first aspect of the contract is a technology transfer agreement, under which Gelman will transfer microporous membranes and the technology necessary to produce the cartridge filtration devices that employ them. The Chinese licensee is Shanghai's Ji Cheng Pharmaceutical Company (JCPC), which already produces similar products. Nearly all the JCPC-produced cartridges will be used in the domestic industry.

The technology transfer agreement calls for Gelman to sell JCPC the technology and equipment necessary for the Chinese company to build a plant to produce the microfiltration cartridges. Approximately 18 machines are needed to make just one complete filter; each machine performs specialized functions such as end-capping, seaming, and stamping the product. The proposed filtration plant—a 16,000 square foot facility located outside Shanghai—was under construction in 1991, and scheduled to begin full operations by May 1992.

Both technology and equipment will be transferred to JCPC under a non-exclusive manufacturing license, which is non-transferable. JCPC will make all products under its own name—the contract does not give the company permission to use Gelman Sciences' name either on the product or for promotional purposes. JCPC and Gelman's Chinese distributor have also agreed to protect from disclosure for the life of the contract all proprietary information. In a further effort to protect its intellectual property rights, Gelman will retain all trademark rights to its products, though the company has not registered its trademark in China.

Gelman is being paid a straight technology transfer fee for this part of the contract by the partner.

Other Contract Components

The second part of the agreement is a long-term supply arrangement, under which Gelman will provide JCPC filter membranes, an essential component in the microfiltration cartridge production process. For the first five years of the contract, Gelman will sell the membranes at competitive international market prices.

JCPC is to finance its purchases of the membranes and technology through scheduled progress payments. For the first year, payments are due every four to five months. They will then decrease to about one per year, ceasing at the end of the third year of the contract. Once the manufacturing process has begun, future supplies will be purchased by letter of credit. Gelman has agreed to sell any components needed to produce the cartridges should the local factory have problems manufacturing them.

A third element of the contract is a three-year distribution agreement with the Chinese Pharmaceutical Industry Corporation (CPIC). CPIC will distribute Gelman Science laboratory and process products manufactured in the U.S. to China's pharmaceutical sector. The contract does not provide for any profit sharing between CPIC, JCPC, and Gelman Sciences, but CPIC will receive commissions from distribution of Gelman products. As the expiration date of the contract approaches, each side will have 90 days to terminate the agreement; barring termination, the contract will be automatically extended two years.

The last portion of the contract, a buy-back agreement, is the most complicated—but crucial—part of the relationship. The buy-back plan will allow JCPC to sell its cartridge filtration devices, as well as other pharmaceutical products manufactured in China, back to Gelman Sciences. Gelman is obligated to purchase a specified dollar amount of products each year, and may fulfill its guarantee by buying products not produced under the technology transfer agreement, provided the Chinese agree. Gelman currently plans to meet some of its obligation by buying labor-intensive products produced outside of its contract with JCPC.

Under the terms of the buy-back contract, the Chinese can earn up to 80% of the cost of their purchases of membrane materials; the remaining 20% will be financed from commissions earned under the distribution clause. Both CPIC and JCPC will cooperate in the distribution of Gelman products—CPIC focusing on marketing, JCPC on the technical end. This arrangement will allow the Chinese manufacturer to obtain the foreign exchange necessary to continue to purchase microporous membranes from Gelman. Without a steady supply of the membrane material, JCPC would be unable to continue to manufacture the cartridges.

The agreement stipulates that all JCPC products subject to buy-back provisions must meet specified quality standards—Gelman staff will perform any necessary quality checks. Gelman reserves the right to refuse to purchase the cartridges should they not meet the prearranged standards.

Putting the Deal in Motion

Given the sophisticated nature of microfiltration technology, training is an integral part of the contract, and will be conducted in both the U.S. and China. As laid out in the contract, Gelman will provide a four-week training session at its Ann Arbor, Michigan, headquarters for nine people from JCPC. All costs for this session are to be borne by the Chinese. On-site training in China for up to 24 weeks is also included in the contract. This cost will be covered by Gelman.

The training session for the Chinese in the U.S. will include hands-on experience at the Gelman factory on a special production line. Once the JCPC people have had a chance to test it and observe production line procedures, the line will be dismantled and shipped to China.

Formal training for CPIC employees in the areas of filtration technology and product application is also part of the contract. This will allow the sales force to conduct educational seminars for Chinese. A Gelman employee in Hong Kong will backstop this effort.

Getting to "Yes"

Gelman Sciences first became interested in establishing relations with China in 1984. After several unsuccessful attempts to penetrate the Chinese market through participation in trade shows, the company decided to consider investing in a joint venture with a potential Chinese partner (not JCPC).

But a joint venture presented problems. The traditional arrangement, where a foreign partner supplies capital and technology in return for the Chinese partner's supplying of the labor, land, and facilities, did not fit a high-capital, technology-intensive business where labor is a very small component of the overall cost. Gelman felt a joint venture arrangement would have left it without a way to realize a return, so there was no incentive to invest.

After nearly two years of efforts, Gelman broke off the negotiations (which were handled by Eric Gelman, a vice-president and principal of the firm) and tried a different approach. Convinced that technology transfer was the best mode of cooperation for a high-technology company, Gelman found JCPC and started negotiating from scratch.

Progress did not come quickly. First, Gelman Sciences found that it had to scale down the size and scope of its original proposal in order for the Chinese to find it acceptable. The Chinese also insisted on manufacturing some equipment locally, rather than relying solely on imports. Other points of contention included the percent of purchases against which buy-back would be necessary, labor rates, and the amount of labor required per operation. The final contractual sticking point was the terms of payment.

Despite the wait, and the frustrations along the way, Gelman Sciences is confident that it will occupy a leading position in China's pharmaceuticals sector. Gelman anticipates revenues of $2.8 million within two years, and forecasts cumulative revenues of $5.2 million by 1997. An additional $300,000 is expected from sales of Gelman products under the distribution agreement with CPIC.

In the year or so that this agreement has been in force, Gelman has had no major problems. "We have a strong positive feeling about it," said Charles Robrecht, vice president of International Business Development. "From the beginning we made a strong in-house commitment to do everything exactly by the letter of the law as we agreed to it. And as we act this way, we find the Chinese act in kind."

Though negotiations were long and often difficult, Eric Gelman says the results were well worth the effort. "The only easy deal you can make in China is a bad deal," he says.

▼ CASE STUDY HIGHLIGHTS: GELMAN SCIENCES

• "Pioneer" deals can be done in China, but it takes insight, creativity, flexibility, and the willingness to wait until the right partner can be found.

• Complex agreements on beneficial terms for the foreign company are possible if the Chinese partner is sophisticated and the technology is sufficiently needed. An additional incentive in this instance was the Chinese pharmaceutical industry's desire to make its products conform to a recognized world standard.

• In-house China expertise proved a big plus, but the company didn't succumb to the temptation to make a deal simply so it could take advantage of it.

• The ingredients for success for Gelman included: direct involvement of top-level management, a willingness to take the time to find the right partner, a realistic but flexible business plan which was not changed simply to get a foot in the door, and large doses of patience.

▲

■ Rosemount Inc.

Rosemount, of Eden Prairie, Minnesota, designs, manufactures, and sells aerospace and industrial instruments worldwide. A division of Emerson Electric, Rosemount made its first sale to China in 1979, and used it to gain the experience and exposure needed to be able to sign subsequent agreements in different areas of their expertise—one additional contract with their first partner and four other agreements with companies in Beijing, Shanghai, and Guangdong province.

This case was provided courtesy of P. Richard Bohr.

Emerson Electric, Rosemount's parent company, initiated the first contact with China in 1977 through a Hong Kong representative hired to distribute Emerson literature and arrange product demonstrations to key ministries in Beijing.

As a result of the product demonstrations to the Ministry of Machine Building, an invitation was extended to Rosemount to come to Beijing in August 1978 and give a series of technical seminars on the company's pressure transmitter and other products. Following the seminar, the Rosemount people were invited to visit the Xian Instrument Factory, which subsequently became the licensee.

In April 1979, a vice-minister of machine building led a delegation tour of several American factories, including Rosemount. Discussions then continued in both the U.S. and China and covered both the product and the possible types of business arrangements: wholly owned, joint venture, assembly, and licensing agreements.

In most parts of the world, Rosemount and its parent, Emerson Electric, maintain 100% ownership. This was deemed impossible to accomplish in China in 1979, so even though it was not a completely satisfactory method of operation from its point of view, Rosemount selected licensing as the pragmatic alternative. It would at least satisfy one of Rosemount's chief goals in seeking entry to China: staying ahead of its competitors.

On the Chinese side of the negotiating table there was the feeling that a successful introduction of the pressure transmitter to the market would require more than simply a license to assemble. The Xian factory wanted the complete technology and therefore bargained for (and got) access to all items needed to manufacture the pressure transmitter, including documentation (drawings, procedures, purchase specifications), training, technical support, production machinery, hand tools, and assembly aids.

The chief obstacles for Rosemount involved the definition and scope of the project, the protection of the company's intellectual property rights, and the issues relating to training, equipment, and pricing. Initially, the Chinese were shopping for as broad a technology transfer agreement as possible, but Rosemount felt that the situation required a well-focused project. Rosemount also worried about its proprietary technology, feeling that Chinese engineers often share information quite freely.

The final agreement, signed in December 1979, limited sales to the domestic market and called for a Chinese investment of between $3 and $4 million dollars in addition to per-unit royalties over a period of 10 years. The concern over proprietary rights was assuaged both by the language in the contract and by the realization that while the Chinese would get up-to-date technology, the passage of time would render it less useful from a commercial point of view. U.S. government approval for the export of the technology came in mid-1980 with Chinese approval following in 1981.

Implementation

In November 1981, a Rosemount manufacturing engineer went to Xian to supervise assembly and calibration training for Chinese workers at the Xian Instrument Factory. During the same month, Rosemount conducted a technical seminar in China for individuals representing 100 potential end users of the pressure transmitters.

Production began in December 1981, using subassemblies made in the U.S. The Xian factory delivered units to 75 customers the first year, with quality standards comparable to those in the U.S., according to the company. In 1982 Rosemount gave further training to Xian engineers at the company's headquarters in Minnesota. By the end of February 1983 the plant set-up was complete and, after further on-site training, full-scale manufacturing got underway in late 1983.

Rosemount and its Chinese partners soon found that the factory was unable to meet the demand for the product. While the Xian factory had the capability of producing more units, it sometimes lacked the foreign exchange to buy the necessary parts from Rosemount.

The initial agreement had foreseen this problem and had tried to solve it by calling for the factory to gradually move towards 100% localization of component parts. This ratio was slow to develop, however, hence the need to find other sources of foreign exchange.

To supply the market and earn the foreign exchange, Rosemount independently made direct sales of transmitters to Chinese users. In 1986 it expanded its sales operation in Hong Kong and opened sales offices in Beijing and Shanghai.

Factors for Success

Rosemount's management attributes the company's success to having a good Chinese partner and then developing a strong bond of trust. The company made a point of providing precisely the technology the Chinese specified, and on terms the Chinese preferred (i.e., licensing).

The company also recognized the need to develop training programs to adapt Western management techniques to the Chinese scene, and was particularly concerned about providing skilled translators at every juncture to insure that all technical issues were adequately addressed.

In addition, the company notes, it has had to exercise the type of patience and perseverance that characterizes many such ventures in China. For example, it took the company some time to realize that the Chinese, rather than address problems right on the spot, tended to save up problems so they could be addressed in face-to-face visits with senior Rosemount management. Executives therefore travel regularly to China, beyond the contract's requirements, to facilitate good communication.

One Success Leads to More

The original agreement with the Xian Instrument Factory ran out in June 1991. The Chinese company now has a secure business and continues to produce pressure transmitters for the chemical, power, and pipeline industries. Because of the long-standing relationship between the factory and Rosemount, a second technology transfer and licensing agreement was worked out in 1991, this time for a temperature signal conditioner. As of early 1992, this contract entered the training phase.

In between the first agreement with the Xian Instrument Factory in 1979, and the second one in 1991, Rosemount was able to sign four additional technology transfer and licensing contracts in China with other partners. The contacts and negotiations for these deals were all worked out directly by Rosemount executives— the only outside expertise hired by the company was legal help. All products resulting from these additional ventures are primarily intended for the Chinese domestic market.

Summing Up the Experience

China is considered to be a "well above average" risk by Rosemount executives, but the company has been able to minimize that risk by using the technology transfer form of business rather than investment.

So far, no Rosemount deal has been a failure. The company acknowledges, though, that "some deals are better than others." It's been their experience that small deals are harder to make profitable, and that the use of royalty, in addition to up-front fees, helps partners share the risks psychologically as well as literally, resulting in increased returns.

Although foreign exchange and proprietary technology issues are important, the toughest problem, Rosemount feels, has been product performance specifications that were interpreted differently by the parties. Compromises were needed in two cases.

Despite their success with the licensing approach, the company continues to feel that licensing is not the best way to be in the market for the long term. Rosemount still prefers the joint venture option, but so far has been unable to find an arrangement that seems mutually satisfactory.

Robert Hanson, vice-president of Rosemount, has been personally involved in the China business. His view of what works and what doesn't when it comes to doing business is to do the homework and understand what the Chinese are really looking for—then see if the company can match that goal. "If you really want an arrangement in China," Hanson says, "the Chinese must first determine that the project is in their best interest. If they want something to happen, it will happen."

Overall, results have been very satisfactory for the company, but have required great patience and persistence. The new Five-Year Plan announced in early 1991, Hanson says, seems realistic and has gone some way towards making it easier to understand China's priorities. "Still, in the future, the P.R.C. must do more to encourage investment by letting foreign partners set up and manage businesses that deliver high-quality products that are price competitive and use less labor than the P.R.C. typically uses in its manufacturing plants," says Hanson.

▼ CASE STUDY HIGHLIGHTS: ROSEMOUNT

- Just as delegation visits from China can be a useful way to introduce your company, offering a series of technical seminars to end users in China can be an effective way to launch the sales effort.
- Both parties seemed determined to uncover the real interests and needs of the other and evaluate them carefully to see if they were realistic in the context of the product, the technology, and the way of doing business.
- Rosemount protected its technology by continually upgrading it so that the technology being transferred, even though state-of-the-art at the time, would be quickly rendered obsolete.
- The Chinese negotiating tactic here was to try and obtain the technology at a very low price with little up-front money and deferral of royalty payments. This approach leaves companies facing the choice of either making steep concessions, or risk having their proposals go nowhere.
- Continuity in the negotiating team paid off not only for concluding the first contract, but lent the requisite experience to facilitate the negotiations on additional projects.

▲

Importing from China

■ Monarch Import Company

*Monarch imports one of China's most popular branded
products: Tsingtao Beer.*

*Monarch was founded in Brooklyn, New York, in the 1930s,
as a wine producer. Until 1986, their facility in Brooklyn produced
Manischewitz wine. As demand for Manischewitz ebbed in the
1970s, Monarch went looking for a new product. Company
executives eventually found their way to China and the Tsingtao
(Qingdao) Brewery. Although several small firms were already
importing the beer and large firms were looking to tap Tsingtao's
potential, Monarch was chosen as Tsingtao's exclusive U.S. sales
agent in 1978.*

*Over the past dozen years, Tsingtao's popularity has
steadily increased: imports grew from 20,000 cases in 1978, to
more than one million cases per year since 1986. The imported
beer market is extremely competitive—and working with the
Chinese is reputed to be fraught with difficulty. How has Monarch
been so successful?*

*This case study was contributed by the Asia Pacific Resource
Group, Inc., publishers of* China Trade.

The Qingdao brewery, built in 1903 by German settlers in
China, is the largest of 600 operating breweries in China. Located
southeast of Beijing in the city of Qingdao, the beer is produced with
spring water from Laoshan, a mountain recognized throughout
China for the purity of its mineral water. The hops used to brew
Tsingtao beer are grown in China. Tsingtao is marketed in more than
30 countries worldwide and accounts for 90% of China's total beer
exports. It is the number one beer in China, and the leading Chinese
beer imported into the U.S. In addition, Tsingtao ranks among the
top 20 imported beers in the U.S.—it currently accounts for 27% of
the Asian beers sold.

Because the brewery is a state-run company, about half of its
annual profits are turned over to the central government. (Typically,
the better a company performs, the larger the share the state
claims.) The brewery is anxious to promote exports—which earn
foreign exchange—but the profit margin on export sales is lower
than domestic sales.

The Monarch/Tsingtao Relationship

From the outset, Monarch took the long view in China. Their successful partnership is grounded in three key principles: (1) Build a strong relationship with the brewery and Chinese management; (2) maintain a consistent, high quality product; and (3) establish solid distribution channels in the U.S.

Often U.S. companies complain about the hazards of doing business in China: bureaucratic delays, inconsistent quality, unmotivated workers. By taking the time to understand the needs of its Chinese partner, Monarch has built a productive relationship.

Since 1978 Monarch has provided the brewery with technical assistance and annually introduces new brewing technologies. The company also organizes on-site information and training seminars.

Monarch works closely with its Hong Kong-based agent, Corin International, which oversees day-to-day brewery affairs. Every two weeks, Monarch has a "summit" telephone call with the plant manager in China to discuss recent developments. It is not unusual for Monarch's vice president, Glen Steinman, to be on the telephone two to three nights a week to the brewery.

Market reports, beer analyses, and annual presentations are all produced and presented in Chinese. According to Steinman, "utilization of the Chinese language in business dealings is essential. We know the message is being communicated in the way we intend it to be."

Translations are handled by an in-house translator and reviewed by Steinman. Although translations are costly, Steinman believes that Monarch's approach to communication underscores their determination to understand their Chinese counterparts. And, Steinman notes, it pays off by creating a positive feeling between the partners. "Anyone who underestimates the importance of a close, straightforward relationship with the Chinese will have big problems."

Monarch's close relationship with the Chinese paid off shortly after the political turmoil in 1989. In October 1989, Monarch filed a trademark infringement suit against a California-based company. The Chinese authorities, including high-level trade officials, supported Monarch's action.

To maintain its U.S. market position, Monarch understands the importance of managing product quality. With Monarch's encouragement, the Qingdao brewery sets rigorous quality standards. All beer marked for export is regularly inspected by the China Commodity Inspection Bureau. In addition, the beer is regularly analyzed by J. F. Seibel Sons & Co., a top U.S. laboratory. In communicating with the brewery, Monarch underlines the importance of product quality, something the factory already promotes. Above the entrance to the brewery is a sign that says: "Quality Is Number One." The company encourages a team approach to product quality which has resulted in consistently high quality and high morale on the Chinese side.

▼ ## Case Study Highlights: Monarch Import Company

When asked what advice he might have to offer other U.S. companies thinking about importing from China, Glen Steinman, vice-president of Monarch, said:

- Take a long-term view of the market.
- Treat your Chinese partner with confidence and respect. Build your relationship with your partner by using translations in Chinese for all significant business communications.
- Be consistent in your communication. Use the telephone aggressively to communicate with your Chinese partners.
- Get actively involved in a quality program.
- Help your partner with management and technology innovations. Hold regular seminars to introduce new technologies and management innovations.

▲

5

Equity Ventures:
Part I

The decision to welcome joint ventures . . . is an exciting experiment in mutual tolerance and education, as well as profit, and in future centuries it may be seen as the measure which contributed most to bringing China and the Western world together after two centuries of mutual suspicion and conflict.

—DAVID BONAVIA, *THE CHINESE* (1980)

The 1990s begin with a world transformed. The walls traditionally marking the boundaries between us as nations—and even as companies—have crumbled about us, literally and figuratively. The destruction of the Berlin Wall, the breakup of the old Soviet Union, and the fragmentation of the bipolar world into a multipolar one, all hold profound implications for the competitive challenges of the 21st century.

China has not been left out of the pattern of historic change. The Great Wall still stands—literally and figuratively—but who among those who knew China in the 1960s and '70s ever imagined that by the late 1980s Kentucky Fried Chicken would be sold in the heart of Beijing and Avon ladies would be selling lipstick in Guangzhou?

The events at Tiananmen and a spate of books with titles such as *If Everybody Bought One Shoe* and *Bulls in a China Shop* vividly and necessarily remind us that naive optimism is perilous. So do the case studies put forward in this book. Nevertheless, David Bonavia's vision is not misplaced. Joint ventures and wholly foreign-owned enterprises are having profound impact on all aspects of the society.

This and the following chapter show some of the reasons why.

Here are companies—both foreign and Chinese—that have taken the equity plunge. They are not merely hoping, but planning on the fact that a combination of good will and mutual economic interest can bridge the cultural and developmental gap and lead to common prosperity.

United Biscuits, a British firm, established a joint venture primarily to serve its export sales, but it also sells to the Chinese market through a second brand name.

Alpha Metals is a supplier of solder to hi-tech electronic manufacturers and is building a joint venture that will supply the Chinese market. Ecolab sells cleaning products to joint venture hotels and offices as well as to the food processing industry.

Japanese companies often are seen as having a natural advantage over their American competitors in China, but, as the Hitachi Koki case study demonstrates, China can be an equal opportunity headache.

Two well-known American companies, Xerox and Polaroid, have also taken the joint venture route. Xerox is a prime example of the possibilities for localization. Polaroid started in China by selling cameras, then moved to a compensation trade arrangement, and then to a full-fledged joint venture.

The Chinese perspective is provided through a composite case study of how a Chinese factory acquires technology. To round out this chapter, a Chinese official directly involved in the negotiations sets out his perspective on a joint venture with Tambrands.

Manufactured Goods for Chinese and Foreign Markets

■ *United Biscuits Ltd.*

While the goal of many joint ventures is to sell as much as possible on the domestic Chinese market, United Biscuits, the venerable British food manufacturer, knew its first goal was to find an already established export channel for their biscuits so as to avoid any foreign exchange problems.

The solution they found involved locating a well-connected Hong Kong partner as well as a Hong Kong-based business that was already plugged into the export market and whose operations could be moved into China.

This unusual case study originally appeared in Business China *(April 30, 1990) and is reprinted here with permission of the publisher, Business International Asia/Pacific Ltd.*

United Biscuits found the right ingredients for its investment recipe after two years of trial and error. When it first started taking serious steps toward investing in the P.R.C. in late 1985, executives envisaged a fairly standard joint venture arrangement of equity partnership with a Chinese cracker maker.

By the end of 1986 they still had not found a suitable candidate. "We gradually came to the conclusion that the advantages of linking with established confectioners were outweighed by the historical baggage Chinese enterprises tend to be encumbered with," says Derek Hayes, production director of United Biscuits International. "Besides, the rules demand that joint ventures be self-sufficient in foreign exchange, yet potential partners were unable or unwilling to offer any help. They seemed to assume that foreign exchange was the responsibility of the foreign party."

The U.K. firm decided to try a new approach. In 1987 United Biscuits (Far East), its wholly owned subsidiary in Hong Kong, identified a Hong Kong cracker maker with an established local market that was about to lose its factory in the territory to redevelopment. United Biscuits eventually bought the company, Pacific Biscuits, in 1988 with the intention of moving its operations across the border to the P.R.C.

Meanwhile, United Biscuits found a Hong Kong partner that, although not in the cracker-making business, could offer P.R.C. expertise as well as equity. Owned by two Hong Kong entrepreneurs, this company, Advanced Chemicals, already had manufacturing interests across the Hong Kong border in Shenzhen.

United Biscuits signed the joint venture contract with its Chinese partner soon after it bought Pacific Biscuits, the old Hong Kong baker. It holds a 60% stake in the joint venture, with Advanced Chemicals and the Haiwan Village Development Corporation (the P.R.C. partner) sharing the remaining 40%. The partners put up cash, with the P.R.C. side facilitating the acquisition of suitable land. The joint venture purchased some equipment from the U.K. parent and a new production line. Other items came from the old Hong Kong factory. United Biscuits is paid a royalty fee based on output volume for the technology it transfers.

Once the paperwork was signed, the race against the clock began. A developer's wrecking ball was looming over the Hong Kong factory, and the Shekou plant had to be built, installed, and capable of satisfying Hong Kong demand before it was demolished. Having a P.R.C. partner with local clout helped the joint venture meet its tight production schedule. For example, the venture was able to house workers in accommodations belonging to the local partner's other interests.

Starting Operations

The factory was built in less than a year and the first cracker was baked in August 1989, just two months after Tiananmen (only one week was lost when Hong Kong workers were reluctant to cross into China). By the end of January 1990, the Shekou factory was supplying all the customers of the former Pacific Biscuits factory. The venture then introduced several product lines into Guangdong province, and supported its initial sales with heavy advertising. A second plant, increasing production to 6,000 metric tons per year, began production in 1991.

The product shipped to Hong Kong—a range of crackers and wafers—is virtually identical to that produced in Pacific Biscuit's former factory (and quite unlike what United Biscuits produces in the U.K.). Besides taste, even the wrapper designs are the same, complete with the old Pacific Biscuits trademark. Output intended for consumption within China will carry the McVitie logo, however, since this brand had been sold in China in previous years on a limited basis.

Getting Down to Business

The long period United Biscuits spent searching for a P.R.C. partner paid an unexpected dividend. The company was able to do some profitable head-hunting from the contacts made in the industry. And while taking on staff from other units proved a long and difficult process, it eventually put together a team of key technical and managerial personnel.

The training of senior personnel suffered setbacks. The vagaries of P.R.C. visa-issuing departments made it impossible to set schedules to bring people out of China for training in Hong Kong. Foreign executives supervising equipment installation had to be rotated several times, creating disruption. United Biscuits had hoped to not have to station a permanent foreign presence on site, but the venture's teething problems forced a review of this strategy. Hong Kong-based staff now serve in various executive and trouble-shooting capacities, traveling across the border regularly to do their job.

Prospects for the Future

The venture currently sources some of its baking ingredients abroad, but United Biscuits believes as much as 90% of the ingredients will eventually be sourced in China. Flour, the major ingredient in terms of quantity, has improved to the extent that most of the flour now comes from P.R.C. mills (thanks to new technology acquired by Chinese mills in recent years).

United Biscuits also found a local source of packaging materials in nearby Foshan. It found an enterprise with Japanese technology to supply the venture with the required quality and quantity of flexible packaging.

The credit squeeze in China during 1988–90 didn't affect United Biscuits as much as it did other ventures, simply because so much of the market for the products is abroad. "Constraining, but not crippling," was the way Hayes described it.

▼

CASE STUDY HIGHLIGHTS: UNITED BISCUITS

• By moving its entire factory to China, United Biscuits was able to serve both an existing market and develop a new one.
• Taking the time and energy to shop carefully for the right partner pays off.
• Creative deal-making is possible with the right partner in the right geographical area. Normally, a JV arrangement calls for the Chinese partner to contribute part or all of its equity in the form of land, buildings, and personnel. Not in this case. Here, the Chinese partner invested money, and the partners worked together to find the land, build the factory, and recruit the workers.
• A foreign presence is usually needed for management supervision even when there has been a chance to recruit and train workers especially for the venture. ▲

■ *Alpha Metals, Inc.*

Alpha Metals is a leading supplier of solder and solder-related products to manufacturers of computers, disk drives, telecommunication and electronics components. Annual sales in Asia for this Jersey City-based subsidiary of Cookson America generate 10% of the $200 million in annual sales revenue. Alpha operates a manufacturing and regional headquarters in Hong Kong and has a strong presence in neighboring Asian nations. It is building a manufacturing and marketing joint venture in the P.R.C. that will eventually supply the entire Chinese market with Alpha products. Asia Pacific Resource Group, Inc., publishers of China Trade, *furnished this case study.*

Alpha Metals has had a strong presence in Hong Kong for more than 20 years, including manufacturing, distribution, R&D, and marketing operations. According to Warren O'Sullivan, Alpha's vice president for Far East Operations, Hong Kong's major assets include excellent finance infrastructure, port facilities, telecommunications, minimal government interference and, of course, it is the gateway to China. "China is not going to throw Hong Kong to the wolves," asserts O'Sullivan.

Alpha Metals began doing business in China in the 1970s, both selling product and sourcing raw materials. In 1984 management began to consider a manufacturing operation, and Alpha sent an inquiry to the Yunnan Tin Corporation (YTC), which already had been supplying raw materials to Alpha for their solder products. YTC, China's largest producer of tin, is a state-owned corporation employing more than 50,000 workers. It is located in Gejiu, China, 100 miles north of Vietnam.

In September 1984 executives ventured to China for their first meeting with managers of YTC. A second visit, two months later, produced a letter of intent. Negotiations were tough and took several years to complete. U.S. legal assistance, with Chinese expertise, helped move the process along. The Tiananmen Square incident and the economic austerity plan that had been implemented in late 1988 had little impact on their project. Alpha considers itself an Asia veteran and was not deterred by these events—it ventured into China one month after Tiananmen.

The Joint Venture Is Established

Alpha structured a two-tiered deal. A 50–50 joint venture was established and, in addition, the company negotiated a technology transfer contract. The JV is licensed to manufacture most of the Alpha line now already being manufactured in Hong Kong and the agreement gives Alpha control over the use of trademarks and production technology.

The sale of Alpha products in China will be in RMB, with foreign exchange moving through the swap centers. A minor amount of product manufactured in China will be purchased by Alpha. Eventually, the China joint venture will handle the entire China market. On the production side, the main advantage of the joint venture is dependable, low-cost raw material. The manufacturing processes for Alpha's products are not labor intensive, and in Alpha's product line the cost of materials is relatively high. According to O'Sullivan, the most desirable location—from a marketing standpoint—would be Shanghai. But the tin is in Yunnan. To compensate for the plant's location, the partners are building their marketing organization. There will be satellite marketing offices throughout China for sales and service support.

The joint venture provides the Chinese with access to Alpha technology and the opportunity to enter the domestic Chinese market with value-added products and the prestige of having a foreign partner. For Alpha, the strategic alliance will provide them with a continuous raw material supply and a strong manufacturing and selling infrastructure for the China market.

Joint Venture Structure

The Chinese partner, YTC, contributed land, buildings, staff, and capital. The factory was built to Alpha standards and Alpha specifications. Factory design and construction supervision was coordinated by Alpha, although building construction was managed by YTC.

Alpha committed technology, training, equipment, facility design, and capital to the joint venture (Alpha declined to quantify its investment). The factory is 45,000 square feet, with 100,000 square feet of land in the compound. Maximum employment in the new facility is 110 to 120. There is one expatriate manager based in Yunnan. Chinese management will need a lot of education, not only with Alpha businesses and business practices, but also with Western-style products and services. Comments O'Sullivan: "There'll be lots to learn and lots of handholding."

In China, employees work six days with a single shift, and operations will eventually move to three shifts per day. The China factory pays a competitive wage, and there will be housing, canteen, and guest houses for the workers. One of the problems is the concept of "wages" in China. Be careful, O'Sullivan suggests, "the definition of wages is very, very different. It takes time to understand [it can include an unusually wide range of additional benefits, for example]."

The plant does not have its own power generation capabilities, and power transmission was delayed for six months. Originally, Alpha executives were told the facility would not receive electricity one day per week, but power interruptions have not been reported.

Alpha Metal's Hong Kong operation will support all aspects of the Yunnan joint venture, including both manufacturing and business operations. Training is one of the key components of the joint venture, which will be conducted principally in Hong Kong.

Alpha executives are bullish on the future. "Try to sit back and look at the big picture," O'Sullivan advises. "The Chinese are not going to do anything to upset the apple cart. . . . Watch the Japanese, they're looking long term."

▼ CASE STUDY HIGHLIGHTS: ALPHA METALS

• The company built on years of experience selling to China before exploring a joint venture possibility. Even so, negotiations proved tough and took several years to complete.

• Alpha Metals was not deterred by events at Tiananmen, and proceeded uninterrupted with the venture.

• The company sells its products to domestic end-users in Chinese currency and uses the official currency swap centers to acquire its foreign exchange.

> • Alpha provides "lots of handholding" and a range of social welfare benefits.

▲

■ *Ecolab Inc.*

Ecolab is the world's leading supplier of sanitary cleaning products for hotels, offices, and the food processing industry. For Ecolab, the opportunity in China was obvious. The tourism and business boom created rapid expansion of the hospitality indus-try. Moreover, the government had also placed priority on develop-ing the food processing industry.

The company, which started as Economics Laboratory, Inc. in 1923, changed its name and began operating internationally in 1976. It has equity positions in some 30 countries and has been the market leader in each of these since its first venture in Swe-den.

The company will not discuss specific sales figures, but published reports say it has captured a 70% market share in its core business in China and that the venture has been profitable from the outset.

This case study was contributed by P. Richard Bohr.

Ecolab's goal was to establish a production base in China, with the long-term goal of capturing the domestic market. It began negotiations in 1984 as a natural extension of its operation in the Asia Pacific region.

For a year and a half Ecolab negotiated with the Shanghai Daily Chemical Company towards a joint venture that would allow Ecolab as much access to the domestic market as possible. Because of the relatively inflexible rules about the need to balance foreign exchange that were then in effect, the Chinese partner insisted that a minimum of 25% of the factory's output be mandated for export. Ecolab wanted only to pledge "best efforts" toward this goal and, in the end, the two parties broke off negotiations.

As negotiations with Shanghai Daily Chemical wore on, Ecolab hired Alan Qian Du, a Chinese native who had received a master's degree in the U.S. after considerable experience in industrial management in China. At the same time, Ecolab also began dis-cussions with a new partner in Shanghai, the local branch of the China North Industries Corporation (NORINCO).

NORINCO is well known in China as the powerful state-run defense industry conglomerate, building everything from ships to missiles. It had embraced the concept of the "open door" with a vengeance and was actively seeking opportunities to convert some of its enterprises into civilian industrial activities. Part of its arms production involved chemical technology, so Ecolab's patented chemical processes seemed to be a good fit for NORINCO.

Negotiations with NORINCO began in August 1986. Agreement was quickly reached on some of the major points that concerned Ecolab. The Americans would have 51% ownership, a majority of the directors (four out of seven), and full power to appoint managers. All proceeded smoothly and rapidly until once again talks became stuck on the export quota issue.

NORINCO, too, insisted on the minimum 25%-of-production-for-export rule. With negotiations seemingly deadlocked, the partners went out to dinner. Philip Mason, Ecolab's vice-president for Asia Pacific operations, kept probing for a way out, and penciled in a new formula on a dinner napkin. It stated that Ecolab would export 25% of the production "which meets Ecolab export standards for price and quality." NORINCO would be obligated to supply the raw materials in order for export to occur.

This broke the logjam (the napkin, framed, still hangs in Mason's office). The deal was signed in February 1987 and MOFERT approval came a month later, just seven months after the negotiations had begun. Production started in the Minhang Development Area near Shanghai in January 1988.

Profile of the Operation

The operation was capitalized at $2.5 million, a medium-sized plant by Ecolab standards. It has been planned to meet customer needs for 10 years. With a 51-year rollover contract, planning still is on target for a second operation near Beijing in five to seven years. To date, all output has gone into the domestic market because price and quality standards for export have not been attained.

The customer base is dominated by Western-style hotels that cater to visiting tourists and business people and that are operated by foreign investors. These ventures make payment in foreign exchange. To further help foreign exchange profits, some product is exported to Hong Kong for resale back into Shenzhen and other areas.

An important part of its success, Ecolab feels, is that its contract allowed it to hire managers and staff independently. This enabled the company to hire Chinese nationals who spoke English, making it easier both to implement Western-style management systems and to easily communicate with the foreign managers of client hotels.

There are 16 production workers in Minhang and another 24 sales and service employees operating out of 12 distribution points throughout China. This ratio is about average for Ecolab operations around the world. [According to *China Trade*, Ecolab's labor costs are about 1% of unit costs, although raw materials costs are high. Some 20% of its products are sourced locally, the rest are imported with duty costs ranging between 30% and 100%].

Since Ecolab is heavily dependent upon the tourist industry, business went into a severe slump in 1989, in the wake of Tiananmen. But the joint venture managed to ride out the storm, and the company reports that business came back to normal levels during 1990.

▼ **Case Study Highlights: Ecolab**

• China can be a natural extension of a company's overall business strategy for Asia.
• Ecolab had the patience and tenacity to pursue an agreement that would fit its basic strategic plan. Although initially costly (Ecolab reportedly talked to 15 other potential partners and spent $1 million in upfront costs according to *China Trade*), it has paid long-term benefits.
• The most obvious partner didn't turn out to be the best partner. The lesson? Evaluate your potential partner as rapidly and thoroughly as possible so that, if necessary, you can explore other options.
• Ecolab made progress when it honored the principle behind Chinese negotiating points that proved to be major hurdles (in this case the then-existing 25% export rule) but continually searched for ways around them so that both sides could save face and conclude the deal.
• Ecolab retains tight control over its venture, believing that as long as profits are made and there are no major management problems, the Chinese partner will remain satisfied. Ecolab found a Chinese-born, Western-educated manager to have the right combination of attributes for the general manager position.

■ *Hitachi Koki Company Ltd.*

The Japanese were much less active than American firms in setting up joint ventures during the 1980s. Many reasons have been put forward for this phenomenon (they're doing well enough without having to resort to joint ventures, they're more comfortable dealing in more flexible arrangements, etc.), but the real reasons seem to have been practical. The Japanese were wary of what they saw as the lack of a formal investment structure, as well as issues relating to management control and local sourcing.

In the early 1990s the Japanese started to become more aggressive investors, drawn to the more secure economic climate and having had the opportunity to learn from the accumulated experience of others.

This brief case study of Hitachi Koki focuses on the three main difficulties the venture has had in becoming profitable (for other issues, see the case studies of Japanese companies in chapters 6 and 7). The venture is a 50–50 equity joint venture in Fuzhou between Fujian Investment Enterprise (30%) and Mindong Electrical Company (20%) on the Chinese side, and Hitachi Koki (48%) and Toei Shoko (2%) on the Japanese side. Min-Ri (the shorthand name given the plant) specializes in the production of six kinds of hand tools: electric drills, electric planers, compass saws, disk grinders, hammer drills, and impact drills.

This case study, originally written by Satoshi Imai, first appeared in the JETRO China Newsletter, *no. 74, 1988, and is adapted here with permission.*

Min-Ri is the only electrical toolmaker in China using foreign capital. The total targeted investment was set at $5 million, with $3.5 million of the registered capital to be spent within three years of setting up the venture.

Both the chairman and general manager of the venture are Chinese; their deputies are Japanese. The deputy general manager has responsibility for overseeing the technical side of the operation as well as for maintaining control of sales, costs, outstanding debt, and so on.

The major components are imported direct from Hitachi Koki. The rest is supplied by 47 affiliated specialized suppliers around China. Min-Ri designs adhere to international standards, so the company finds export demand high. Within two years of opening, the venture has 270 sales outlets in China and 20 overseas.

Despite steadily increasing earnings from exports ($500,000 in 1987), this income was less than half the amount required to procure the necessary imported parts. The problem was partly solved through an adjustment in the exchange rate negotiated directly with the Fujian Currency Adjustment Bureau. Vigorous efforts to promote exports continue.

The Major Problems

Min-Ri faces three major problems: lack of operating capital, lack of local content, and difficulties with parts subcontractors.

One financial problem was the sharp appreciation of the yen. This severely affected the cost of parts that had to be imported from

Japan, which had to be paid in yen and caused losses for two consecutive years. Only in its third year of operation did Min-Ri manage to make a small profit.

The most difficult period occurred in 1986 when production had to be suspended due to lack of operating capital. Before it could reopen, the factory had to get hold of additional foreign currency from the Fujian Investment Enterprise Corporation.

The second problem involves the need to adopt a localization program. Min-Ri's 47 affiliated suppliers in China complain regularly about the factory's stringent quality requirements. The obvious way to increase the use of local parts would be through introducing new technology and equipment. The merits of such an approach are obvious. They include a rapid return on limited investment, greater grasp of Hitachi technology, and self-sufficiency in key parts.

Min-Ri's third major area of concern is its difficulties with parts subcontractors. In the beginning, Min-Ri had not planned to rely on outside subcontractors. But the sharp appreciation of the yen against the Chinese currency made local procurement unavoidable. (Note the difference in approach: American companies are usually tempted to find ways to cut costs or find subsidies to solve this problem; the Japanese often will spend extra for training and other aspects of localization so as to obtain long-term competitive advantage.) One of the biggest problems with outside subcontractors is the lack of control over delivery dates and quality of components. Complicating the problem is the fact that since many of the subcontractors are owned and run by the Chinese defense industry, they are off limits to outsiders.

While efforts have been made to seek cooperation from the parts suppliers, the response so far has not been very encouraging. Some suppliers have simply ignored Min-Ri's pleas. Reliable quality seems obtainable from defense contractors, but civilian suppliers have been found wanting. The result is that all deliveries have to be examined piece by piece.

Repeated requests from Min-Ri to improve quality have led to few concrete results. This, plus the fact that the joint venture has to deal with suppliers in distant cities, supports the lesson that it will probably be necessary to invest in local production facilities that can meet supply criteria.

▼ CASE STUDY HIGHLIGHTS: HITACHI KOKI

• Hitachi has set up a clear division of leadership, with the Chinese responsible for management, and the Japanese staff responsible for sales and administration.
  • The company launched an aggressive localization program

to overcome the problems of costly imported parts. Results have been mixed: Chinese defense-related industries have the technical know-how and experience to deliver quality products, but are often unapproachable. Civilian suppliers are easier to deal with but reliability and quality have been found wanting.

▲

■ Xerox Corporation

Xerox Corporation, after many years of experience selling in China, put localization at the heart of its plans for a joint venture. It has pursued this strategy aggressively and with a surprising degree of success. In addition to transferring technology and training P.R.C. managers at its copier joint venture in Shanghai, Xerox is also heavily involved in upgrading the operations of the joint venture's multiple suppliers.

The secrets of Xerox's success seem to include a well-thought-out and supportive localization strategy, an unrelenting effort to improve supplier quality, and close cooperation with local Shanghai authorities.

This case study originally appeared in Business China (September 16, 1991) and is reprinted with permission of the publisher, Business International Asia/Pacific Ltd.

When Xerox drew up the feasibility study for its joint venture, its strategy included a plan to source 70% of the joint venture's inputs locally within five years of the start of the operation (in 1988). Four years later, the figure stands at 60%, and Xerox believes it will easily meet its goal.

The plan's basic premise was simple. The company, under a contract with the joint venture, would provide local suppliers with the technology to produce components in exchange for a fee. Frans Ryckebosch, company manager, calls this approach "good corporate citizenship," since it upgrades the technology of an entire Chinese supplier base rather than simply one Chinese enterprise. From Xerox's point of view, supporting local suppliers is a cheaper way of obtaining high-quality domestic components than producing them all locally itself.

How It Works
Through the joint venture, Xerox provides individual vendors with technical support and tooling from its engineering, manufacturing, or procurement departments. The contract with the P.R.C. supplier can be a broad technology transfer agreement or can call for certain types of technical support, assistance in securing a particu-

lar set of tools, or a combination of the above. The joint venture will either sell tools to the Chinese company outright or supply them gratis but retain ownership. (The latter course permits Xerox of Shanghai to pull the tools from an unsatisfactory supplier and maintains some control over the process.) For technical support or tools that it cannot provide itself, Xerox will put the P.R.C. supplier in touch with a foreign vendor who can.

Once a P.R.C. supplier passes muster, the joint venture agrees to purchase parts from it on a contract basis. The venture sends the supplier a purchase order with delivery schedules and provides forecast volume so that the supplier knows what to expect in coming years.

Xerox negotiates prices with reference to the purchase price of a similar product around the world. "By discussing such benchmarks, Chinese suppliers get an idea of what we want and if they can or cannot beat the price," says Ryckebosch. But here too Xerox is willing to give a helping hand. If the P.R.C. supplier needs certain imported materials, for example, Xerox will secure some of them for the vendor on consignment.

Both joint venture and supplier personnel require training to use the transferred technology. Training takes place at either Xerox facilities in the U.S. or at Xerox's established suppliers around the world. To ensure high-quality product at affordable prices, the company also educates the Chinese in materials management, materials handling, and cost accounting.

Materials management training has been particularly important for the joint venture's Chinese staff, who have had to cope with the venture's expansion from assembly of CKD (completely knocked-down) and SKD (semi-knocked-down) kits to sub-assembly using imported and locally sourced components. The whole process requires a sophisticated materials planning system to order the right type and amount of components, time their arrival, and make sure sufficient safety stocks are available in case the quality of a local part falls below desired standards.

Maintaining Quality Standards

Potential Chinese suppliers were generally unaccustomed to the high standards that Xerox expected and that are embodied in its "Xerox Quality Principles." In fact, a vendor's reaction to this program helped determine which companies would be selected to become suppliers. According to Ryckebosch: "We didn't want to do business with Chinese enterprises that weren't interested in our quality principles." He cites as a model supplier the Changzhou Electric Motor Company of Jiangsu province. This factory embraced the program so wholeheartedly that the joint venture was able to meet Xerox's quality standards on the first shipment of electro-mechanical components. Because of its good work, Changhzou

Electric has since landed a multimillion dollar export contract with an Italian buyer.

Not all Chinese vendors were as enthusiastic as Changzhou Electric. Many were reluctant to make such a large investment in upgrading their facilities, particularly when the JV was only able to place small orders with them during its first few years of production. To counter this legitimate objection, Xerox mounted a campaign to win over reluctant suppliers by pointing to Changzhou Electric's successful experience, and arguing that orders—and therefore the demand for supplier parts—would grow in volume as production took off.

But it took more than exhortations from Xerox to get the job done. The Shanghai Economic Commission (SEC) has a program to upgrade the city's supplier base and has pumped several million dollars into local companies to purchase foreign technology and equipment. Xerox became an important beneficiary of this program. Even so, SEC encouragement in some cases extended to "administrative actions" to prod reluctant companies onto the technology bandwagon.

The Shanghai authorities have been an invaluable ally to the joint venture in other ways as well. When the project was being negotiated in the mid-1980s, both Xerox and the local Chinese authorities realized it would take four to five years for the venture to generate foreign exchange through exports or other means. Meanwhile, the joint venture would have to make huge foreign exchange outlays on items such as imported kits and components. The municipality agreed to allocate hard currency to the venture during the startup years. Using this period to upgrade the quality of locally sourced components, Xerox of Shanghai is now able to earn foreign exchange by exporting its domestically produced copiers. The JV sold over 1,000 copiers in 1991, which incorporated over 40% in local parts.

The Challenges Ahead

Even after four years of working intensively with local suppliers, Xerox still has a ways to go. Although most suppliers have largely overcome the quality hurdle, they still, on the average, produce above world benchmark costs. Getting costs down would enable Chinese suppliers to export and sell to the joint venture at lower prices. The problem, says Ryckebosch, is that many vendors cannot get a handle on their own cost structures.

Another challenge facing the joint venture is to overcome bureaucratic hurdles that sometimes arise unexpectedly. As a result of central government moves to curb enterprise purchases, the joint venture is struggling to meet the sales objectives set out in its feasibility study. Copiers, which came under government purchase controls around three years ago, are now more difficult to sell, not because natural demand has evaporated, but because anyone who now wishes to purchase a copier must have government approval. The Shanghai municipal government has been instrumental in minimizing the policy's impact locally, but this artificial market constraint has temporarily affected demand outside the venture's home base.

▼ Case Study Highlights: Xerox

- Xerox was determined to produce to its own quality benchmarks and was willing to provide education (and have enough patience) to see it through.
- The company worked hard to secure the total commitment of local authorities to support the idea of the venture so it could establish a spirit of "shared purpose" from the beginning to help minimize negotiating strains.
- Substantial time and investment have been poured into providing technical support to bring the local vendor up to speed, including the involvement of China's network of university-affiliated research institutes.
- Localization wasn't a new concept for Xerox, and the company was able to draw on in-house experience by selecting an executive in Latin America, an expert on vendor development, to manage the venture.

■ *Polaroid Corporation*

Companies venturing into nonindustrialized nations often face a natural contradiction between their own goals and those of the host country. The foreign company wants an adequate return on investment and to create returns for the shareholder. The host country usually wants long-term capital investments that bring in foreign technology, create jobs based on significant value-added production and exports, and train management and workers. Polaroid's fundamental strategy in China is the same as it has been for the Soviet Union, Eastern Europe, and India: to tie the company's goals into the needs of these countries.

Polaroid has reconciled the natural differences by focusing on points of mutual advantage, namely manufacturing for export, provided there is a demand for export goods. Like other firms, Polaroid has developed its commitment to China in stages as benchmark goals were met. It began by selling, moved to subcontracting component assembly, and when comfortable with its partner, started discussions on a joint venture.

This case study focuses on the evolution of the venture and describes an important component of dealing with the domestic market—sales and marketing. This description originally appeared in Business China *(July 29 and August 12, 1991) and is adapted here with permission of the publisher, Business International Asia/Pacific Ltd.*

Polaroid has been selling directly into the China market since the early 1980s, primarily via its Hong Kong regional office marketing subsidiary. By the mid-1980s, Polaroid was ready to explore the next steps, and talks with the central government led Polaroid to initiative discussion with the Shanghai Motion Picture Industry Corporation (SMPIC).

Polaroid eventually set up a subcontracting arrangement with the Chinese enterprise. In return for Polaroid's upgrading one of SMPIC's factories, Shanghai Xianfeng, the Chinese would assemble printed circuit boards for use in Polaroid's Supercolor 635CL instant cameras.

To bring Xianfeng up to speed, Polaroid provided capital equipment, trained the work force, and upgraded the factory. As a result, the Chinese have been supplying printed circuit boards to Polaroid manufacturing plants around the world since 1989. Polaroid in the meantime had a chance to evaluate operating conditions in China, cement ties with its partner, build up the Chinese side's production skills, assess the feasibility of a larger commitment, and set the basis for a solution to the foreign exchange problem.

In mid-1990, Polaroid took the equity plunge, signing an agreement to set up Polaroid of Shanghai with SMPIC. The Xianfeng factory has since become part of this larger operation. In addition to the assembly of printed circuit boards, the joint venture will assemble instant cameras, package film, and gradually assume marketing responsibility for the entire Polaroid product line in China. So far, the camera maker, which holds 73% of the joint venture's equity, has invested close to $2 million in the project.

The transition from subcontracting and assembly to a full-fledged joint venture manufacturing operation has gone practically without a hitch. Polaroid attributes this to the evolutionary nature of its relationship with SMPIC and Xianfeng. All the camera maker had to do to get the joint venture up and running was add some new assembly equipment, introduce a detailed program for camera manufacture, and assign two expatriates to manage the project on the ground. Polaroid has also intensified training.

At first the venture assembled cameras from kits for local consumption. In 1992, it began moving toward full vertical integration of the assembly operation. Polaroid wants to source a substantial portion of its inputs locally within three years.

For the moment, sales of China-made printed circuit boards generate enough foreign exchange to meet the joint venture's needs. As the venture grows, that need will become greater, and Polaroid plans to meet it by introducing another component for local manufacture at the joint venture.

Management problems have not been severe. To help keep the 180-person work force productive, Polaroid has instituted amenities such as transportation between home and factory, new windows and lighting in the factory, and washing machines, dryers, irons, and ironing boards for personal use.

The Marketing Side

Polaroid sees sales opportunities for its instant-imaging products in China in the medical, business, and consumer sectors, and is targeting all of them.

In particular, Polaroid is targeting street photographers as well as entrepreneurs or other intermediaries who sell finished photos for passports and visas, drivers' licenses, and ID cards, and to commemorate important events. Polaroid has put on seminars for the photo studio market, showing the camera's ability to generate more business and plans to use all these outlets to spearhead efforts directed at tapping the consumer market.

Developing consumer awareness of Polaroid began several years ago when the company advertised on Chinese television in a campaign designed to broaden public knowledge of the advantages of instant cameras and photography. The company rates this and other promotional efforts as "fairly effective."

Promotional efforts are now centered around the joint venture's ability to deliver products directly to the customer (important because the JV obviates the need for an import license, something many Chinese retailers find hard to acquire). The program includes direct mail, seminars, and trade shows. Print advertisements, signs, poster boards, product literature, and point-of-sale displays will supplement the effort.

Marketing to the medical and scientific communities is concentrated on direct mail, seminars, and trade shows. Polaroid follows up any leads that come out of these events, often visiting hospitals to demonstrate the special features and advantages of instant-imaging products.

The company became one of the sponsors of the Asian Games held in September 1990, which enhanced its visibility in the consumer market. Among other things, Polaroid provided security badges for the athletes and their families, and set up kiosks around the area for local street photographers to display and store their wares.

The next step is the consumer market, and Polaroid is rethinking its TV advertising tactics to target specific cities and markets. While sales to private customers are still rare (the local currency cost of the camera is equivalent to about $100), the company is planting the seeds for the consumer market of the future.

Hong Kong Support

Polaroid's regional office in Hong Kong will continue to handle sales of locally-produced and imported cameras until the JV is ready to shoulder responsibility for all P.R.C. marketing activities. The Hong Kong office will also supervise the venture's marketing program and train Chinese customers (like hospital attendants and doctors) to use Polaroid products effectively.

Roughly seven members of the regional sales group in Hong Kong devote their time solely to supporting the company's China business and the joint venture. This includes training of the JV's sales force as they accompany Hong Kong staff on sales calls and other promotional activities.

Polaroid is now refining its distribution system and expanding its service centers to support sales in other regions of the country. The company hopes to establish a network of regional sales offices.

▼

CASE STUDY HIGHLIGHTS: POLAROID

- Polaroid took one of the basic rules of the China trade to heart: use well-established strategies that fit your business temperament. Avoid experimenting with new strategies.
- Central government assistance in finding a local partner can be helpful but is not mandatory. Polaroid found that the central government's imprimatur is not always a guarantee of success, providing the lesson that a company has to evaluate its partner carefully and continue shopping if unsatisfied.
- The gradualist approach has seemed to work well for Polaroid; it made the transition from subcontracting to full-fledged joint venture manufacturing without a hitch.
- The company has focused primarily on the professional market for product sales, but now is beginning to use a wide variety of marketing options to reach the Chinese consumer.
- Polaroid's Hong Kong office is being used for the marketing effort within China until the company feels the JV is ready to shoulder this responsibility. The Hong Kong affiliate will still train local staff and supervise the sales and distribution effort.
- Polaroid has kept management problems largely at bay thanks to a good welfare program, extensive worker training, and an effort to make all employees feel as though they have a stake in the success of the venture. ▲

The Chinese Perspective

While the foreign perspective on joint ventures is now becoming well known, the point of view of the Chinese partner must also be taken into account. Unfortunately, just as the foreign experience tends to be skewed by what Western editors consider titillating reading, so the Chinese experience is often affected by an official line that tends to exaggerate good news (at times to the point of clownishness) while ignoring the bad.

Here are two case studies from the Chinese point of view. The first looks at the process of negotiation and decision-making in a technology transfer project as seen through the eyes of a Chinese factory manager. The second is an unusually candid look at the operational problems faced by a different American joint venture in northeast China.

■ *Zhou County Number One Canning Factory*

Foreign technology in China has had an uneven impact. In most cases it is producing the results expected. But there are also computers sitting idle under plastic covers and assembly lines unused since installation. Successful acquisition, argues sinologist Roy Grow, is dependent not only on the level of sophistication of the technology and its appropriateness to the application, but on the process of decision-making by key players as well.

This case study shows the complex and time-consuming process a manager of a canning factory in China's northeast must go through in order to make a decision between two competing offers. Understanding his milieu may not make negotiations move faster, but perhaps more smoothly.

What follows is an abridgement of a case study written by Professor Grow, Chair of the Department of Political Science at Carleton College and a consultant to American and Japanese companies in technology transfer deals (for bibliographic details, see appendix 1).

Zhou County lies west of Dalian, in a region known for its excellent harvests of grain and vegetables. Central to the economy of the area is the Number One Canning Plant. Built with the aid of Soviet engineers in the mid-1950s, the plant became one of the most important employers in the region by the mid-1980s, with contracts to supply canned vegetables to four separate distributors in different parts of China.

But the plant had never been upgraded. Washing and heating were still done by hand. Machinery broke down every three or four days. Some 30% of the cans were unusable because of improper seals, inadequate sterilization, and other problems.

By the mid-1980s, agricultural reform policies had resulted in record crops, and record production for the Number One Canning Plant. But given the state of the equipment, a sense of uncertainty and vulnerability nagged at Wang Lin-sheng, the plant manager. The situation seemed clear. Unless the plant could be improved and made more efficient and competitive, business would suffer, perhaps leading to a shutdown of the plant and the forced layoff of nearly 1,000 employees.

Manager Wang explained his situation to local farmers and officials. He also talked to magistrate Lin, the ranking county official. All thought the idea of modernizing was important, but the factory did not qualify for any source of funds for such an undertaking. Foreign help was going to be the only answer. Magistrate Lin gave the necessary blessing to begin the process, and became active in trying to find a solution.

Lin and Wang first traveled to Dalian, a rapidly modernizing port and, other than the provincial capital of Shenyang, the most important city in Liaoning Province. There they visited the regional office of China's national trading corporation for cereals, oils, and foodstuffs (CEROIL). They also met people who were part of a larger, informal group of scientists, technicians, economists, and managers who had worked on a number of regional improvement projects. Scattered among various institutes, companies, and government bodies, these men shared the belief that Dalian could become northeast China's premier commercial center.

Follow-up meetings were held. Agronomists from Dalian went out to Zhou County to personally take a look. In time, Dalian officials reached a consensus. They would support the project, but only if the entire harvesting and canning process were overhauled. With this conditional blessing in hand, word was passed to the head office of CEROIL in Beijing and to regional trade and investment bodies to look for potential candidates.

Two foreign firms—Ag Midwest from the U.S. and the Hamamatsu Group from Japan—expressed interest in the project and each developed a proposal. Both were already known to the Chinese. The American firm because it had on several occasions made proposals in Beijing that had received no response, and the Japanese firm because it was already active in China.

The American Proposal
The American firm's initiative was largely the work of one man, Hank Jones, a senior vice president. His company, Ag Midwest, was one of the leaders in the industry and Jones' job was to scour the world in search of steady and reliable sources of materials for its canning operations. Ag Midwest had food processing operations in Taiwan and the Philippines, but so far talks in China had led nowhere.

When Jones heard about the project—during what was originally just another prospecting visit to Beijing—he was immediately interested, and asked to visit Zhou County. A lifelong field man, he liked nothing better than to actually go to an area scouting for good sites.

He spent several days talking to manager Wang and county officials, and walked through numerous potential fields. He found promising sites for several types of vegetables needed by his company and by the end of the visit had laid out a proposal for improved seed stock, different harvesting and storage methods, and some new transportation facilities.

Then Jones went back home to try to sell this proposal to his own company. Ag Midwest was initially reluctant, seeing China as a huge unknown. After some persuasion, they authorized him to continue the talks, but as the project proceeded Jones found himself negotiating both with manager Wang and his own management.

The Japanese Proposal

Hamamatsu had lots of experience in China, and looked at the Zhou County project as a cog in the wheel of a larger China strategy. Hamamatsu was looking for a way to replace some of its agricultural imports from the U.S. with Chinese agricultural products. As a diversified trading firm, it believed that projects such as these could also help introduce the trading arm of the company, specifically for Japanese manufactured goods and engineering and construction services.

Hamamatsu was focusing on two products, corn (for Japan's cattle industry) and fruit, particularly strawberries, to meet growing Japanese consumer demand. Hamamatsu experts had already been traveling throughout China, and found themselves looking at three competing regions: Guangdong, Shanghai, and Liaoning, each of which might serve as a location for a pilot project.

Hamamatsu's strategy was to work through officials in the provincial bureaucracies, hoping to use their leverage to introduce them to potential local partners. Working with provincial officials also allowed them to hold up one region's incentive package against another's.

So Hamamatsu heard about the project not from Dalian or Beijing, but through their contacts in the provincial government at Shenyang. Hamamatsu, in the company of provincial officials, toured Zhou County and were introduced to manager Wang's project. The Japanese, too, liked what they saw, so when they submitted their proposal for the corn-plus-fruit package to provincial officials, the Number One Canning Factory was listed as one of two possible locations for strawberry processing.

The Chinese Reaction

After Hank Jones' visit, meetings were held that included magistrate Lin, key farm families, and manager Wang. Wang was generally enthusiastic, but wanted to check on literature he had received via Beijing on two other American food processing giants. He also checked further into Ag Midwest, and found a powerful track record in advanced processing and canning technologies. As manager Wang and the others saw it, technology from Ag Midwest could become the foundation for renovating the entire range of the Dalian area's agricultural production and food processing.

Wang replied to the American company's proposal with two of his own. First, that Ag Midwest use the county as a source of vegetables for worldwide consumption, and second, that the company start a joint venture with the Number One Canning Plant so that the plant could be upgraded and be competitive worldwide.

Jones understood Wang's plans, but instead proposed a more modest relationship whereby Ag Midwest would help the county set up trial projects for growing vegetables needed by the company. It would supply the know-how, direction, management expertise, and new seed stock. It would also commit itself to buying a certain amount of the output. If it worked, Jones said, then they might consider the joint venture.

While this had its attractions, there were some worrisome aspects for manager Wang and his colleagues. Chiefly, the proposal did not offer the large integrated planting and canning operation envisioned by local officials. It was a start, of course, and if Ag Midwest was indeed the quality company Dalian CEROIL suggested, the proposal could turn into a larger project in the future.

The Hamamatsu proposal to manager Wang was very different. It focused specifically on strawberries, but it was much more substantial in scope and held out important immediate gains— permanent installations, new technologies, and an almost guaranteed market in Japan. But magistrate Lin and manager Wang also saw the downside. Strawberry growing was unfamiliar and complex. Hamamatsu's demands for water, transportation, expertise, and tight time schedules were burdensome.

There was also an organizational question: Who would manage the strawberry project? The American had focused his proposal on what manager Wang and his colleagues could do for themselves; the Japanese proposed sending in an outside expert to manage an entirely new factory.

Weighing the relative merits of each proposal was a difficult task. The initial discussions involved Wang, his staff, and those most closely involved with the canning plant's operation. County officials occasionally sat in, and sometimes experts from Dalian were consulted, but the decision was to be Wang's.

He first discussed the project within the plant. The younger technical staff people and the procurement people tended to favor

the American proposal. They favored the access to Western expertise, the chance to learn a whole range of new food processing
technologies, and the opportunity to grow and harvest export-class
vegetables. But it wouldn't yield the benefits, both personal and
commercial, that a joint venture might.

The Japanese offered the best economic package, but virtually
everyone in the plant felt the technology offered was too new and
alien, and control might perforce slip to the Japanese. Provincial
politics also entered into their thinking. Dalian seemed to favor the
Americans, Shenyang the Japanese. Could they choose one project
over the other without feeding the growing Shenyang-Dalian rivalry?

Manager Wang also held extensive talks with a range of people
whose bailiwick would also be affected by these two proposals. For
example, since the American project called for a substantial amount
of new vegetables to be planted, the local farmers would have to give
up some of their existing land. What were their views? Would they
take a risk with untried crops?

There were other problems to deal with, many of them involving
local and regional bureaucracies—water supplies, gas and oil for the
new tractors, new buildings, electricity for the new washing and
packing procedures, land consolidation permits, labor rules for
newly hired workers, permits for transportation, and more.

Manager Wang was, in effect, holding five negotiations at once.
He held talks within his plant, trying to reach a consensus. He had
discussions with farmers over their interests and wishes. Third were
the ongoing discussions with Ag Midwest over the details of the
proposal. Fourth were the delicate and complex negotiations with
both upstream and downstream users. Finally, there was the
juggling act necessary to diffuse any possible tension between the
differing interests of Shenyang and Dalian in this project.

Because of these various negotiations, Wang wanted fluidity
and flexibility in the contract details, working them out one-by-one
over time. This occasionally drove Jones to despair. His bosses at Ag
Midwest wanted a precise contract spelling out all details. They
wanted guarantees, numbers, commitments, and all the other
factors usually weighed to make a decision.

After six months or so of these discussions, a general agreement was in place. Local interests were satisfied, and so, Wang felt,
was the interest of the Americans. The agreement called for Ag
Midwest to deliver 900 pounds of new seed, show local users how to
plant and harvest the crop, pay for fertilizer and other inputs, and
take delivery of the vegetables upon harvest at Dalian.

Now at last it was time to seek higher authority. Dalian CEROIL
liked the plan, and hoped the Americans could be enticed eventually
into a joint venture that would aid other parts of the area economy
as well. The provincial authorities in Shenyang were less happy. If
Liaoning Province turned down the Japanese on their strawberries,

they might decide to take their corn business elsewhere, too. Moreover, the Americans wanted exclusive rights to the variety of vegetable they chose to grow in Liaoning Province—rights no one seemed willing to grant. Everywhere he turned for help at the provincial level, Wang heard the same answer: "We have no authority."

Two months later, and thanks to the help of his friends in Dalian, Wang found himself in Beijing, meeting with a deputy director of the cereals, oils, and foodstuffs corporation. The director was sympathetic, but was unwilling to come down on one side or the other in the struggle between Dalian and Shenyang. The best he could do was agree to a rather nebulous statement that gave the appearance (but not the guarantee) of exclusivity.

This was, from the Chinese point of view, enough to tip the scales in favor of the American proposal. But would the Americans understand this less-than-ironclad guarantee? Apparently so, for two years after Hank Jones first walked through the fields of Zhou County, an agreement was signed.

Now came the difficult task of implementing the contract. Local authorities were well aware that the track record for technology transfer projects in China was spotty. Chinese managers, they knew, could get so enthralled with the technology, and so wrapped up in making it work, that everything else—from procurement schedules to labor relations could be neglected. At the other extreme, managers sometimes got involved in technology that was way over their heads, which caused machinery to remain idle for years on end, while the principals threw recriminations back and forth.

The first steps went smoothly. Ag Midwest delivered as promised, and the company proved to be a good teacher. Manager Wang was so encouraged, he unilaterally decided to increase the amount of acreage to be seeded by 30%, hoping to earn that much more income. As harvest time approached, the reality of the international commodity markets set in. There was a glut on the market, so not only did Ag Midwest balk at buying more than it had contracted, it ended up paying less for the contracted crops than the Chinese had projected.

All this placed Wang in an agonizing position with suppliers. Didn't the Americans know they had an obligation to consider the county's welfare? Who now would pay all the costs incurred? Customers worried as well. Were they losing a reliable source of supply?

Within a year of startup, manager Wang's business relationships seemed constantly on the verge of instability. He wondered if the arrangement with Ag Midwest would hold and if it was really worth all his time and energy. He had no real clout with the American corporation if it chose to back out of the relationship.

He had discovered that dealing with Western corporations and using their new technologies created a number of ripples in his pond that threatened to tip over his old ways of doing things, and might even drown him. Then, six months later, Manager Wang's worst fears were realized. The student protests in Beijing, which had seemed so far away from his concerns, had been put down by army troops. Via radio, he heard China's new leaders talk about the need for stability, a code word for caution on all fronts, political and economic. Secondly, he received formal notice from Ag Midwest that it had been subject of a leveraged buy-out, and that a new set of executives would no longer consider China a priority.

▼ **CASE STUDY HIGHLIGHTS: ZHOU COUNTY CANNING FACTORY**

• The manager of the canning factory realized that (a) unless his plant could be upgraded business would continue to deteriorate, and (b) the only way to accomplish his goal financially and technically was to turn to a foreign partner.

• Getting Chinese authorities to accept his plan required involvement by a web of officials at the local, regional, provincial, and national levels.

• The canning factory had no direct contact with foreign companies, so it relied upon two different entities for the requisite introductions: a national foreign trade corporation and the provincial development authorities.

• The two proposals manager Wang ended up with were very different in nature. Neither one met his original goal of getting a large integrated planning and canning operation. Extensive consultation was required to see which of the two approaches offered by the foreign companies would best benefit the area.

• At one point the factory manager was, in effect, holding five different negotiations at once.

• More politics was required after the plan had been settled on; both to placate the "losers" at the provincial level and to get the needed authority to proceed from national-level authorities.

▲

■ *Shenyang Tambrands Co, Ltd.*

This second case study from the Chinese perspective concerns a joint venture established by Tambrands, Inc., the well-known U.S. manufacturer of feminine hygiene products. It was

*written for this volume by an official with firsthand knowledge of
the venture. Other than minor adaptation, no editorial changes
have been made in this refreshingly direct evaluation, which
leaves the Shenyang author's point of view entirely intact.
(Tambrands may have a different perspective, of course.)*

*One of the clearest lessons to be learned from this study is
that problems are not one-sided. For example, foreign companies
might find the lifelong employment practices of China baffling, but
the Chinese are often stunned by the way American corporations
can so quickly shuffle management around or even sell off whole
divisions, treating China as an afterthought in the name of
corporate profits.*

In 1984 the Chinese Ministry of Public Health sent a delegation
to the United States, which, as part of the program, visited the
Tambrands facilities and learned that the U.S. company was interested in establishing a joint venture in China.

One of the delegation members was an official from the
Shenyang Municipal Pharmaceutical Administration, who, upon
his return to China, helped pick the Shenyang No. 5 Northeast
Pharmaceutical Factory to be the potential local partner. Tambrands
was then invited to come to China to begin the negotiations.

Shortly after these began, however, this factory pulled out on
the grounds the project would be unfeasible due to the conservative
attitude and lifestyle of Chinese women. To save the project, the
Shenyang pharmaceutical administration turned to the No. 6
Northeast Pharmaceutical Factory. The JV was finally formed in
1986, after fairly smooth negotiations.

Establishing the Joint Venture

The venture went into operation in 1989, with a total investment of $3.4 million by the U.S. party and RMB 8.8 million by the
Chinese party. The joint venture utilized a piece of vacant land
within the No. 6 factory to build the joint venture facility. All of the
equipment was imported, together with the technology. It is believed
to be state-of-the-art equipment similar to that used by Tambrands
companies worldwide. Quality control follows the strictest Tambrands
standards, and samples are sent to a Tambrands U.S. technical
center for testing and certifying, which includes testing of both
product and packaging. Most of the raw and packaging materials are
sourced locally.

Currently, the chairman of the JV is from the U.S., as is the
general manager. Both deputy positions are filled by Chinese. The
U.S. side also has production and marketing responsibilities; the
Chinese side is responsible for finance, administration, and personnel.
The initial goals for the venture—to open up the market, stabilize it,

and break even by the end of 1991—have been achieved. In 1991, the sales volume reached 40,000 cases, 20% of which were exported to Southeast Asia, Australia, and New Zealand. The venture has balanced its foreign exchange through these exports.

Marketing

Initially, the JV used low pricing to attract consumers, and the market was quickly opened up. Ten months after introduction, a price increase of 20% was made. After seeing sales continue to rise, the joint venture then increased the price another 80%, and launched an aggressive promotion and advertising campaign. Sales continue to increase, as does profitability.

Promotion methods include: training of sales help at the retail level; distribution of free samples; and drawings for camcorders, VCRs, gold necklaces, wool blankets, and so on. Classes are also given to women to increase their awareness of the need for improved personal hygiene and of the superior quality of the product.

To increase the efficiency of distribution, the JV purchased its own container trucks to deliver products to the railroad-congested east China region.

Problems

While the story is generally positive, the joint venture is not without some serious problems. The first of which is that the location adds significantly to the cost of sales, eroding profitability. Shenyang is far from the cotton growing region. The region's concentration of heavy industry often causes power and water supply shortages. Shenyang is also distant from the major markets in central, east, and south China, and the poor transportation network makes it difficult to distribute the product through large state-owned agencies and wholesalers as well as directly to retailers.

The second major problem concerns management and is twofold: the low quality of Chinese management personnel and the withdrawal of American managers. In mid-1991 a decision was made to replace most of the U.S. management with local people in order to cut costs and overhead. The expatriate general manager and marketing manager left the company, and the vice president of Tambrands Far East temporarily took over the general manager position, with day-to-day operations in the hands of the Chinese deputy general manger.

The JV has thus been forced to practice Chinese-style management. What this means, for example, is that the budget and daily allowance for salespeople on business trips were reduced to conform to Chinese standards, which seriously damaged the morale of the sales force. Short-term thinking on marketing and sales problems has come to the fore and several key local managers have resigned because of lack of incentives.

A third problem involves the sales force, almost all of whom are young females. Their personal needs, such as marriage and pregnancy, often cause delay and stoppage in work. It is generally difficult to find a continuous supply of good quality people for hire by the joint venture.

The most critical problem, from the point of view of the health of the venture, is that the foreign party did not give sufficient attention to the training of people, especially local management people, before they pulled out the U.S. managers. This could seriously threaten the future of the joint venture.

▼ **CASE STUDY HIGHLIGHTS: SHENYANG TAMBRANDS**

- Tambrands hosted a delegation from the Chinese Ministry of Public Health which led to the initial discussions.
- The company relied upon the Chinese to appoint the potential partner, but its first choice pulled out of the negotiations, forcing it to find a second partner for the U.S. company.
- Tambrands imported all the technology and equipment to assure a state-of-the-art factory.
- Both the chairman and general manager of the factory are foreigners, but neither is involved with the venture on a day-to-day basis.
- From the Chinese point of view, the venture has some major problems, including inappropriate location, hands-off management practices, and a weak sales force.

▲

Equity Ventures: Part II

Business deals in China are always full of surprises, because, until the transaction is finally concluded and the goods or service paid for and consumed or performed, no one can ever be quite sure that all the details of the transaction have been settled, and that there will be no misunderstandings. Many authorities contend that the Chinese have a genius for misunderstanding which works to their advantage in bargains with the inexperienced.

—CARL CROW, *400 MILLION CUSTOMERS* (1937)

In China, expect the unexpected. A proposal carefully tailored to an ideal partner may unravel in the wear and tear of tough negotiations. Or, stuck in a thicket of thorny issues that seem to get only more prickly with time, a path suddenly appears that leads to a quick contract and years of smooth implementation.

What's different now from just a half dozen years ago—much less in Carl Crow's time—is that the accumulated knowledge and experience of hundreds of joint ventures and other business arrangements affords the chance to reduce the element of unwelcome surprise. Misunderstandings, calculated or otherwise, can more easily be avoided.

The case studies in this chapter point to the many different roads companies have used to achieve their strategic goals. Avon, for example, found little trouble in starting a profitable business in China, but it took 15 years and a change of partners before the company could realize its ultimate goal of selling cosmetics directly to the Chinese consumer. PepsiCo, which has some 20 ventures in China, found that establishing a business and a market was not as difficult as dealing with the human resource issues such ventures present.

Two wholly different experiences were encountered by General Bearing and Minnesota Mining and Manufacturing, in part because their goals were so dissimilar. General Bearing saw China as the ideal relocation site for a factory standing idle in the U.S. and found a partner in Shanghai eager to make, and then export, all the goods this factory could produce. Such a strong confluence of interests meant the plant was reopened within a year-and-a-half and able to bring immediate profits for both the company and its Chinese partners.

On the other hand, 3M felt that only a fully-owned subsidiary geared to sell to the domestic market could meet its goals and still bring enough benefit to appeal to the Chinese. While pioneering a venture at a time when there were few precedents proved difficult, their perseverance and subsequent success has paved the way for hundreds of other companies. One of those is Mabuchi Motors, whose perspective on the operation of a wholly foreign-owned enterprise is also included.

Convinced that China is the ultimate processing zone, Concord Camera has moved aggressively into South China, establishing a wholly owned venture and seven subsidiary JVs. In addition to manufacturing for its own needs, it is also operating an industrial estate it has set up to help other companies get established.

Of all the issues facing a joint venture, the one most ripe for misunderstanding and conflict is the relationship between foreign goals and local workers. Smack in the middle of this sits the plant's general manager. Of all that has been written about the challenges of this job, the personal account that stands out most strikingly is that of Paul Egner, general manager at Ningbo Abbott Biotechnology, whose report appears later in this chapter.

The Chinese Consumer Market

■ *Avon Products, Inc.*

Probably no two companies have received more ink in the popular press for their ventures in China than Beijing Jeep (AMC) and Avon Products. The former was used to symbolize the often overwhelming frustrations of doing business in China in the mid-1980s. Avon, on the other hand, came presented as the good news of the 1990s. Forbes magazine, for example, noted that direct selling is stagnant in the U.S., "where it has a slightly musty, 1950s aura. . . . But in mainland China, where the new lure of risk and profit is heady, this kind of marketing is a breath of fresh air."

The impending success of grass roots capitalism may be just as wildly exaggerated as the "it's all their fault" attitude of Beijing

Jeep (a great part of that problem, it turned out, was in the way AMC had structured the venture).

Avon achieved some instant success, and was able to expand more rapidly than even it had anticipated. All this is well documented in various press reports. This case study draws on such reports, but goes a step further by incorporating parts of a study of the JV done for the author by Chinese municipal officials close to the venture. It reveals not only some teething problems but the residual resentments of the foreign presence that lie just under the surface, even in such a supposedly wide-open place as Guangzhou.

Avon was already familiar with China before it approached Chinese officials with the idea of opening up a full-scale Avon-type marketing operation. For years the company had been buying gift and decorative items in China—about a $50 million business.

The company's eye was always on the prize of being able to sell directly to the Chinese consumer, and in the early 1980s Avon began to develop its strategy for the next phase. From the beginning, Avon felt that person-to-person selling would be a good fit in China, chiefly because the country has large, crowded cities, which are the right type of concentrated markets conducive to door-to-door selling.

Given that premise, the company developed a strategic plan that would let it do business its way while being flexible enough to take into account the special conditions of the Chinese market. According to a company spokesperson, these were the major objectives:

1. Develop an Avon-type direct marketing operation;
2. serve the Chinese market on a local currency basis;
3. establish its own, largely self-contained operation, from manufacturing through to final sales and service;
4. exercise management control of the business;
5. gain initial experience without major investment commitment;
6. meet the foreign exchange requirement in a satisfactory manner;
7. gain a year or more of experience before major expansion decisions;
8. proceed on the basis of reasonable longer-term profit expectations.

To implement these objectives, Avon first went to Beijing, where it tried for five years (1984–89) to convince the potential partner and the relevant government bodies that doing business this way would be feasible.

It began, however, by entering into a technology transfer contract with Beijing No. 3 Daily Chemical Products Factory. Under this more limited arrangement, Avon provided the formulas and the technology to produce a range of cosmetic products for the local market (mostly perfumes).

After four years, Avon felt it was ready to move to the next step: expand the project into a full-scale joint venture and thereby establish the first direct marketing company to open in China since 1949.

No Flexibility in Beijing

The Beijing authorities responded cautiously to this plan, fearing the impact should anything go wrong. Many of the concepts behind direct marketing were alien to the local population. Officials couldn't conceive of selling the product anywhere except foreign hotels and friendship stores. "Where do we get the people?" was a typical objection. Hire them part-time, came the answer. Impossible, came the reply, all workers belong to an organization and this would conflict with the interests of their work unit.

After many rounds of discussions and debate, the Beijing government turned down the project. Retaining confidence in its plan even while losing it in its Beijing partner, Avon began shopping elsewhere. The company shifted its focus to Shenzhen, Dongwan, and Buo Luo, all in the Guangzhou-Hong Kong corridor and all known for their receptivity to a wide range of foreign investment. Avon also had decided it would prefer to establish a wholly foreign-owned manufacturing company to avoid the restraining influences of a Chinese partner.

These explorations were unsatisfactory. Finally, Avon was advised by David Li, CEO of Hong Kong's Bank of East Asia and a member of the company's international advisory board, to give up the idea of establishing a subsidiary and work out a partnership with the Bureau of Light Industry (BOLI) in Guangzhou. Mr. Li introduced Avon to its prospective partner, and an agreement followed within a year.

BOLI immediately saw the practical advantages. One of the 140 factories under its jurisdiction had a product range similar to Avon's and needed modernization. The factory was already planning a move to a new location, so the existing factory site could be converted for the new JV.

From Avon's point of view, the people of Guangzhou seemed intuitively to accept the direct marketing concept. In Guangzhou, for example, many people have additional sources of income, and part-time work in second jobs is regarded as a sign of capability.

The Guangzhou Joint Venture

Negotiations began in September 1988 and a letter of intent was signed after only one month. The final contract was approved 14 months later, and trial production began in September 1990. Along the way, Avon was impressed with the ability of BOLI to arrange the necessary meetings with relevant municipal authorities, and with the open, pragmatic attitude of officials.

The deal is structured so that Avon has 60% equity, and the right to appoint a majority of the directors. The Chinese own 35% of the venture, and David Li 5% (his willingness to invest reportedly gave the Chinese a greater sense of confidence). The Avon investment amounted to $1.28 million, including $896,000 in cash and a bank loan for the remainder. Avon also agreed to provide cosmetic formulas, technical expertise, and sales and marketing programs. The duration of the JV is 30 years. For its technical contributions and trademarks, Avon receives a modest royalty.

Management is firmly in Avon's control. The general manager (a slot over which Avon retains control) is a Guangzhou-born Hong Kong Chinese with 12 years experience in the company. The contract also stipulates that Avon has the power to decide which staff to hire from the old Guangzhou factory, and to require training of all candidates.

On the Chinese side, the capital contribution is in the form of facilities and equipment. The Guangzhou Cosmetics Factory will lease most of its plant to the venture, and will upgrade and expand it. This gives Avon the advantage of inheriting a well-established company (20 years in business), a trained work force of 150, and a plant with most of its utilities, infrastructure, and machinery in place. "Upgrading" was the operative word, not starting from scratch.

The scope of business as stipulated in the contract includes production and sales of cosmetics, personal care products, and related cosmetic packaging materials, fashion jewelry, and gifts and premium items. The production target was set to reach 9.5 million pieces of cosmetics a year by the fifth year. The first year target was 750,000 pieces.

The JV is basically a sales operation. The Guangzhou factory initially is importing the ingredients and then packaging them. "At the moment," says Barry Wang, general manager, "there are no local ingredients we can use. Maybe there will be in the future."

Because it can only sell its product on the domestic market for local currency, the venture must generate foreign exchange by exporting cosmetics and other products it manufactures. Some of these finished products will be sold back to Avon. According to *Business China*, Avon negotiators were able to avoid a commitment to export a fixed percentage of sales, opting instead for a general balancing of the venture's foreign exchange requirements by exports and other means (such as use of the swap centers).

Business Development

Since the start of marketing in November 1990, the JV has launched over 80 products in five categories (skin care, skin cleansing, facial cleansing, make-up, and beauty aids). The sales revenue in the first four months reached RMB 4 million. In view of market demand, the JV board approved the establishment of its own retail outlets in major cities in Guangdong Province, and Avon increased its investment by $1.12 million. An additional, even larger investment, is expected in early 1992.

At the start of the JV there were about 50 employees. Now the management staff number 120, production staff 50, and sales managers or support staff 78. In addition, the JV has over 10,000 direct salespeople (including seasonal workers), comprised of "FDs" (sales assistants) and "ALs" (Avon Ladies).

Avon has adopted the market approach it successfully used in the Philippines. Sales people do not go door-to-door but make presentations to friends, relatives, neighbors and, especially, co-workers. Merchandise is not delivered to each salesperson but is distributed at special depots to avoid problems with tangled communications and transportation. Seminars on skin care and other beauty "secrets" are held, and the whole effort is supported by advertising and printed materials. Avon has translated its brand name as "Ya Fang," meaning "exquisite fragrance."

Any doubts about Chinese Avon Ladies' ability to understand the concept of direct sales quickly faded. After just four months of operation, the top saleswoman earned more than RMB 30,000 ($5,600) in commissions alone—200 times the average yearly income of a Chinese worker. Says John Novosad, Avon's vice president for Asia, "These people are not only beauty oriented, they understand business. This is the first place in the world where the local representative told us to double our prices. And here we were worried about teaching them how to calculate commissions."

The venture has gone so well that first-year sales amounted to about $4 million. By 1995, Avon projects sales of $50 or $60 million and the venture has embarked on its expansion plans ahead of schedule. Sales networks will be set up in two additional cities in the province within the next couple of years.

Some Problems

Despite its huge and well-advertised success, the JV is not without problems. Missing among the "gee whiz" stories in the mass media are points such as these:

1.   Growing pains have led to management problems, including loss of control and improper training. The lack of training for the women who carry out the direct sales has resulted in poor quality of service to customers. Pricing chaos has been created by Avon representatives who cut prices on their own initiative.

2. Because the JV is still basically an assembly operation rather than a manufacturing facility, it is dependent upon imported raw materials and packaging, creating a foreign exchange problem.

3. Finally, and perhaps more ominously, Avon has been the subject of hostile publicity from powerful officials who point out that those who work for Avon get distracted from their regular jobs, putting themselves and their desire to make money ahead of the needs of their regular work units. Even in progressive Guangzhou, officials are worried that this venture is polluting people's minds with Western-style values.

▼ **CASE STUDY HIGHLIGHTS: AVON PRODUCTS**

• Avon did not come out of the blue to set up its historic door-to-door sales efforts—the company had been doing business in China since the early 1970s and had experience in importing as well as with a technical cooperation agreement.

• Unable to achieve its long-term objectives through its original partner, Avon shopped for a different partner in a different part of the country until it found one who could provide not only an operational fit, but one of the right "attitude" as well.

• The company was able to draw on powerful connections—in this case, through Hong Kong companies—to achieve its aims.

• The case demonstrates the types of flexible arrangements, in size, scope, and finance, that are now feasible in Southern China. Yet, as "modern" as these arrangements are, traditional political and cultural values still act as powerful restraints on the venture. ▲

■ *PepsiCo, Inc.*

Various divisions of PepsiCo have been buying and selling in China since the mid-1970s. The company's first direct investment was in 1982, when it opened a joint venture bottling plant in Shenzhen. Since then this maker of snacks and soft drinks has developed 20 different ventures in China, including:

- *seven Pepsi Cola plants (JVs)*
- *five Kentucky Fried Chicken restaurants (JVs)*
- *one wholly foreign-owned concentrate plant*
- *one JV concentrate plant and R&D facility*

- one Pizza Hut franchise operation
- one JV for manufacturing toys for export
- one JV for exporting spices
- one fish farm JV, and
- two PET baby bottle manufacturing plants.

These various ventures are located in Beijing, Shanghai, Fuzhou, Nanchang, Guangzhou, Guilin, and Shenzhen.

PepsiCo has found creative ways to convert the local currency it earns on its drinks and food outlets into the foreign exchange earnings needed to make them profitable. For example, RMB earned from its KFC outlets might be used to buy mushrooms, which are purchased in dollars by its Pizza Hut chain. Another outlet for RMB is the joint venture it has with McCormick & Co. to package herbs, spices, sauces, seasonings, jams, and other food products.

Because PepsiCo employs more than 1,500 people in its various ventures, this case study focuses on the recruitment of local labor. Lai Kim Yin, area vice president for Pepsi Cola International once told an audience: "China provides one with a lifetime of learning experiences that is enough for many lifetimes." Some of the labor issues Lai cited in his speech are presented here.

Each PepsiCo venture has its own human resource issues, but some broad general themes emerge from more than a decade's worth of experience.

The key individual is the chairperson, who is usually the chief Chinese contact during the negotiation period. In one JV, the chairperson was also the Party secretary of the factory, which greatly aided in the recruitment of good personnel.

PepsiCo tries to influence the selection of key personnel, particularly the general manager, but sometimes finds the choice is imposed upon them by the Chinese partner. The company has learned that qualified managerial personnel are somewhat easier to find in the advanced cities and zones than in the secondary cities. Day-to-day management of its joint ventures is left largely in the hands of the local Chinese partners.

Once the management team is in place, the next step is to focus on finding a reasonably competent team of middle managers. Normally, the number of key managers to be supplied by the Chinese partner is limited to six, and the remaining managers are hired from outside the venture. To accomplish this, PepsiCo advertises open positions widely, administers written examinations to all candidates, and then personally interviews leading prospects.

PepsiCo uses training as a method for both selecting and retaining staff. Training also provides a means for terminating employees or returning them to the Chinese joint venture partner when individuals cannot complete such courses satisfactorily.

For its restaurant JVs, PepsiCo uses expatriates for the position of general manager. Initially, the Chinese partners resisted this policy, and PepsiCo found it extremely difficult to get the partners to pay the full package of salaries and benefits required to attract qualified general managers. Once these expatriate managers are in place, however, PepsiCo feels that its Chinese partners realize their value. Currently, the manager of the Kentucky Fried Chicken outlet in Beijing is from Taiwan, and the Pizza Hut general manager is a Malaysian Chinese from Australia.

The wholly-owned venture had different personnel problems but, in general, they were easier to solve. Recruitment and selection for the Guangzhou concentrates plant was left entirely in PepsiCo's hands. The venture set its own salary scale and benefits package (substantially better than what the JV allows) and thus was able to recruit a well-qualified staff. The general practice has been to recruit a few technical and finance managers from Hong Kong, and the rest of the management team from the local region (Guangzhou).

For all ventures, PepsiCo faces the issues of worker mobility, which severely crimp the recruitment of the best talent. Workers in China are not "independent." They have traditionally worked for state factories, and those factories provide many of their necessities. Moving from region to region, therefore, jeopardizes their housing, children's education, spousal income, and medical benefits. They must also give up their local registration card and work permit. This means not only that the foreign-owned venture is burdened with the replacement cost of the housing and social services but, for the employee, that once their contract expires they effectively cannot return to their home city. This trend particularly works against those who are being asked to move from big cities to work in smaller, more isolated, inland ones.

To show how micro-managed most people's lives are in the traditional Chinese economy, PepsiCo once wanted to hire 17 salespeople who had driver's licenses. The workers were found, but their employer would not release them. If they resigned, the workers would lose their driver's licenses, an action the employer (not the government) has the right to take. Only after a compensation fee was negotiated did the employer agree to let these men keep their licenses after their release.

Wages and Incentives
PepsiCo, like all other foreign investors, finds itself continually involved with issues regarding wages and incentives. The State Labor Bureau now monitors JV wages closely, restricting them to about twice the size of those of state-controlled enterprises, and allowing wage increases only when JVs are profitable. The trend is toward more government control on wages and wage levels for fear

that the growing disparities within JVs and also between JVs and state-controlled enterprises will trigger more social discontent.

Incentives remain the key to performance and, PepsiCo finds, cash isn't necessarily king. The company found that under the Chinese system cash rewards must be shared equally amongst employees, regardless of their position. The board of directors of one of their JVs, for example, voted the general manager a bonus of RMB 16,000—three times his annual salary—for his outstanding work. But the money was divided among all employees under a point system, leaving the general manager with RMB 300.

Successful incentives, PepsiCo found, included "study trips." In 1990, the company arranged incentive tours for the employees and their families after one of their plants achieved its target. Workers were taken to Hainan Island and key managers of the venture were able to go to Australia. The general managers of this and other plants have received trips to the U.S. The company also takes along local city officials on such trips, since the venture is so heavily dependent upon their support.

One incentive that has not seemed to work well has been to assign dollar values to achieving targets and subtracting them if the target is not achieved. Over time this seems to become expected and routine, and loses the flavor of a special incentive. This fate also befell the 13th month pay scheme (paying an additional month's wage as a bonus at the end of the year).

PepsiCo has followed the advice of others to stay away from the "contract system" of incentives, in which the general manager sets targets on a contract basis with workers and middle managers. From what the company has observed, this system appears to invite "creative" management practices such as substitution of raw materials, short cuts on production, and lower quality.

The Major Problem: Work Ethics

Of all the frustrations encountered, PepsiCo worries most about workers who continue to ignore instructions or otherwise refuse to cooperate. Some of these conflicts may surface as negotiation tactics, but PepsiCo feels most are old habits difficult to break. The problem, PepsiCo people say, is a system of work ethics—or lack thereof—rooted in the old Communist Party system where underperformance and lack of accountability were the norm.

On the more positive side of the ledger, PepsiCo believes it and other investors are benefiting from the 1988 "Personnel Opinion on Further Implementation of the Right of Autonomy of Joint Ventures" issued by the State Council. The Opinion allows JVs to conduct their employment affairs independently and in accordance with international practices. This means that PepsiCo does not need central government approval to recruit from other regions, that it need hire only those employees it wishes, and can dismiss them on its own criteria. This Opinion also makes it easier to transfer employees among various ventures because it forbids Chinese organizations to charge high fees or to impose administrative restrictions.

Despite such laws to protect joint ventures, PepsiCo still finds it very difficult to manage human resource issues, particularly in recruiting qualified labor, non-compliance with company regulations, and, of course, ubiquitous bureaucratic politics.

▼ **CASE STUDY HIGHLIGHTS: PEPSICO**

- Labor problems are fewer in the coastal regions. Personnel tend to be better educated and more qualified. Moreover, the bureaucracy is more fluid, and creative ways can more easily be found to either work with or around government bodies (i.e., a regulation may state one can't hire certain types of workers from certain types of Chinese companies, but a way to do so can often be found nevertheless).
- PepsiCo has paid a great deal of attention to recruitment and training practices.
- For ventures dealing with both local and JV labor, solutions must be found to the potentially divisive problem of differentiated wage and benefit scales.
- Cash incentives have begun to play a less important role in certain locations in China and are being replaced by other rewards, such as trips abroad.
- Work ethic issues remain a major barrier to the rapid growth of these and similar ventures in China.

Export Platforms

■ *General Bearing Corporation*

In the midst of China's political turmoil in 1989, General Bearing Corporation (GBC) became the first foreign bearing maker to establish a manufacturing facility in China. GBC is a privately-owned, $60 million dollar company based in Blauvelt, New York.

Under the terms of its joint venture agreement, GBC is entitled to receive the factory's entire production of tapered roller bearings, raw forgings, and finished bearing rings. The major portion of the JV's output feeds into General Bearing's finishing and assembly operations in the U.S. with the balance going to the company's primary customers. These include automobile companies and manufacturers of heavy equipment. In 1991, the com-

*pany imported $5 million of tapered roller bearings from the joint
venture.*

*Several features of this JV stand out. It utilizes entirely
reconditioned, used equipment, and has no expatriate management. Both elements cut cost significantly. Moreover, the JV
qualifies for preferential tax and customs treatment because it
has been designated a "technically advanced" enterprise and
100% of production is geared to the export market.*

*In 1991, the GBC joint venture was investigated for alleged
dumping of bearings in the U.S. market—the first time a U.S.
venture was probed. The Department of Commerce has since
announced that General Bearing was not involved in dumping
practices.*

*This case study was provided by Asia Pacific Resources
Group, Inc., publishers of* China Trade.

General Bearing is a ball and roller bearings manufacturer
with four subsidiaries and 340 employees in the U.S. In 1987 the
company acquired the assets of Hyatt Clark Industries as the result
of bankruptcy proceedings. Among the assets was $5.5 million
worth of production machinery, designs, and tools. This equipment
became the basis for establishing the company's joint venture.

The original joint agreement between General Bearing and its
Chinese partner, the Shanghai Roller Bearing Factory, was reached
in record speed—only 70 days elapsed between the signing of a letter
of intent and the execution of the joint venture agreement. The
venture produces tapered roller bearings (2 million annually at full
production in 1991), raw forgings, and finished bearing rings. To
house the project, the Chinese began building an 86,000 square foot
factory including office and manufacturing departments for hot-
forging, assembly, cold-forging, turning, grinding, and heat-treat-
ing.

The JV exports 100% of its production to hard currency
industrial countries. The project fits the ideal profile for the Chinese,
who are anxiously looking for businesses that will earn foreign
exchange. For GBC, the export orientation of the venture makes it
less dependent on what it considers to be an unpredictable Chinese
economy.

Chronology of the Venture

Here is a schedule of how the GBC deal came together:

April 17, 1988: GBC signs a letter of intent with executives of
the Shanghai Roller Bearing Factory (SRBF) with an initial capital
investment of $4.95 million. Construction of one building has been
completed, and construction of two other buildings is well under
way.

June 11, 1988: The Bureau of Mechanical and Electrical Industries Administration (BMEIA) of the Shanghai Municipal People's Government approves the overall plan for the JV.

June 15, 1988: An independent consultant, commissioned by the BMEIA, completes a feasibility study and submits it for official approval.

June 25, 1988: BMEIA approves the feasibility study. The contract for the joint venture is signed by representatives from General Bearing and SRBF, as well as representatives from BMEIA and the Shanghai Foreign Investment Commission.

July 26, 1988: A delegation of 24 workers from SRBF arrives in New York to begin the transfer of equipment to Shanghai.

August 4, 1988: GBC and SRBF sign a letter of intent to increase the joint venture's capital to $9.9 million. It's approved by the Shanghai authorities (BMEIA) in November.

September 1, 1988: The first shipment of machinery leaves the U.S. for Shanghai. It arrives at the end of October.

September 8, 1988: The joint venture receives an operating license from the Shanghai Bureau of Industry and Commerce.

October 15, 1988: The fifth shipment of equipment leaves the U.S.

December 1, 1988: Construction is completed on the second and third buildings.

April 30, 1989: Foundations for the largest and heaviest equipment (1,600-ton press, 800-ton press, and hot-forging machines) are finished.

June 1, 1989: Utility connections are completed for water, power, and compressed air. A month later, the grinding department begins initial operations.

August 22, 1989: Equipment installation is complete.

October 30, 1989: Official opening of the joint venture.

Strategic Considerations

The Shanghai JV gives General Bearing a production base in a low-wage country from which it can service customers worldwide. It has kept the entry cost low by contributing its capital in the form of the 300 pieces of used equipment. (The Chinese partner rebuilt and upgraded the equipment by adding microprocessor controls made by other Chinese companies under license from the Japanese. GBC estimates that rebuilding costs were one-tenth what they would have been in the U.S.)

An added advantage is that with a strong Chinese partner (the Shanghai Roller Bearing Factory is highly regarded) General Bearing is able to leave the operational management of the venture to the Chinese without worrying unduly about quality.

The management of the JV has been assigned to Joseph Hoo, a vice-president of GBC. Instead of relocating to China, however, Hoo travels there about once a quarter. This has allowed General

Bearing to save the cost of an expatriate manager, an estimated $100,000 annually.

To increase the stability of the venture, GBC has added Chinese partners who contribute directly to the project. A steel company supplier and the Municipal Government of Shanghai have come in as partners. Originally a 50/50 venture, GBC has now reduced its share to about one-third. This change helps insure the venture a steady stream of steel and electricity.

The venture predicts sales of between $24 million and $30 million in 1991. At full production, it will employ 500 people operating in three shifts.

 ### CASE STUDY HIGHLIGHTS: GENERAL BEARING

• The company found that Chinese officials often talk about the need for new technologies and equipment, but a venture that provides used equipment and a guaranteed export market is almost irresistible to many factories in China.

• An idle U.S. factory was moved lock, stock, and barrel to China and made operational there within a matter of months.

• General Bearing was able to find both the technical sophistication and the low-cost production it was seeking. At the same time, the Chinese could upgrade their production capabilities and reap the rewards of foreign exchange profits.

Wholly Foreign-Owned Enterprises

■ Minnesota Mining and Manufacturing Company (3M)

Minnesota Mining and Manufacturing (3M) pioneered the wholly foreign-owned enterprise in China. Its success in doing so was based on a solid track record in China that began in 1973.

For its first seven years in China, 3M sold finished products and purchased some Chinese raw materials for its own use. Then, in 1980, John Marshall, who had all along been responsible for 3M's presence in China and who had become a well-known figure there, was given the task of investigating and evaluating the desirability of establishing a 3M company in the P.R.C.

More than four years later, 3M announced that China had issued the license and that manufacturing would begin in 1985.

Although such ventures are now becoming more common, and the atmosphere in general has changed for the better, a look at 3M's experience carries a number of lessons about the development of company strategies and the techniques of negotiation used to implement them.

In 1980, a senior 3M executive attended a conference with a group of other businesspeople and became convinced that Deng Xiaoping was firmly in charge and that his reform program offered solid potential. In a subsequent conversation with John Marshall, 3M's China representative, this executive suggested that the company move beyond its well-established trading relationship and try and establish a formal 3M presence in China.

A number of guidelines were established:

1. The venture should be a wholly owned subsidiary.
2. It should offer China what it wants in terms of technology and product.
3. It should be a manufacturing operation, but initially modest in size to minimize risk.
4. Products should be for the local market rather than for export.
5. Earnings could be reinvested for some years.
6. John Marshall, as 3M's China representative, was to have full authority to draw on various divisions within the company as necessary and to negotiate the agreement, including site and partner selection.

There were no consultants, no major investigations, no company conference, no presentations to and votes by the board of directors. (Of course, 3M already had accumulated a great deal of in-house expertise on China.)

First came the decision on what products should be made in China. After internal discussions with various divisions and with contacts in China, Marshall chose electrical and telecommunications products because managers of this product group already had a lot of international experience, including in the Far East; the products required only a small front-end investment, and the line was good for expansion as conditions might warrant; and, a clear case could be made to Chinese officials that these products were essential to the modernization program and thus needed to be available locally.

3M's experience in China made site selection rather simple. Shanghai was chosen because it was the biggest industrial area in China and had long exposure to Western firms. It also came closest to approaching Western standards with respect to its infrastructure and business and social amenities.

The Negotiation Process

3M started in Beijing, with Marshall making the first of the 50 trips it would take to complete the contract negotiations. Somewhat to his surprise, the Ministry of Foreign Economic Relations and Trade (MOFERT) was open to the proposal, although the format fell outside its experience and outside the existing regulations governing foreign investment.

The proposal was left with the ministry, and 3M developed a technique for pushing it beyond the scratching-of-heads stage. At the end of each visit, Marshall would review whatever conclusions had been reached and then set a specific time for a return visit to seek answers and move forward. For a time, little was achieved. But, after continued urging, MOFERT pushed 3M's proposal up to the State Council level.

In early 1981, MOFERT told 3M that approval had been given and suggested the company next work with a specified partner—the Shanghai Electrical Machinery Company (SEMC). This company, directly under one of Shanghai's key municipal bureaus, operated 40 plants, one of which was the Shanghai Insulating Plant, with which 3M later dealt at length.

3M was shuffled from one set of bureaucracies to another, but, although frustrating, this process did allow the proposal to move from the hypothetical stage to actual negotiations. At SEMC there was an attitude of acceptance and helpfulness, but also the feeling that what 3M's proposal demanded was a good deal of work and trouble without much direct payoff. "Why did you come?" and "What's in it for me?" seemed to be unspoken questions. Unwilling to take the initiative on their own, Shanghai officials kept referring decisions up to Beijing, and Beijing would defer back to Shanghai. Key questions were passed back and forth, and Marshall found himself shuttling back and forth as well, pushing Shanghai and pulling Beijing.

Chinese objections revolved around several points. At the time, an independent enterprise was ideologically suspect. To get around this, 3M did its best to sell itself as a company that operated "locally" wherever it did business.

A second sticking point was SEMC's insistence on an export quota. 3M did not want such a commitment. The Chinese kept pushing the company to accept even a very general pledge, but 3M felt that any such vagueness might later be subject to unfavorable reinterpretation.

Then there was the foreign exchange issue. 3M pushed hard to get the Chinese to accept the principle that in this case, precious foreign exchange would not be spent outside the country, as it might be were they to purchase the same products in Europe or the U.S. In the end, 3M agreed to keep an overall balance of foreign exchange, without committing itself to specifics.

As a gesture of goodwill, 3M invited key Chinese players to come to North America in 1982 to visit plants and become acquainted with 3M's corporate culture. A visit to a subsidiary in Mexico, which was operating successfully despite a general climate in which joint manufacturing facilities established by other multinationals were being shut down, made it clear that 3M could operate a self-sustaining business that served the needs of the local market, and with a management style that was similar to the one proposed for Shanghai.

To John Marshall's surprise, a meeting at the end of the tour resulted not just in a favorable impression but a verbal commitment to the 3M proposal. The negotiations then began to move quickly—until a newspaper report quoted a Shanghai official close to the venture as saying: "We call them the 3-No company: no joint ventures, no exports, no technology transfers." This story made the rounds among top officials in Beijing, where it raised a lot of red flags. It took Marshall six months of explaining before things moved forward again.

By this time it was 1984, and with preliminary approval out of the way, the detailed tasks of assembling a work force, putting together the distribution system, and developing the financial and management plans had to get underway. There was still inertia. Officials at the factory said it was pointless to do X, Y, or Z until there was permission to start. Those in charge of permissions, on the other hand, said that no approval would be forthcoming until X, Y, and Z were accomplished. Marshall could only push.

In June 1984, all seemed ready and the final documents were prepared for signature. But there was to be one more impasse—the name of the venture. 3M wanted to use the word "China" in the name, but the Chinese felt it would undermine their sovereignty. The signing ceremony was called off. It took another trip to Beijing before authorities granted the company's request. At last, on November 10, 1984, 3M China was inaugurated.

According to *The Wall Street Journal*, 3M hasn't had any regrets. The paper quotes the general manager of the venture, Ronald Harber, as saying, "It's extremely difficult to blend two very different management styles. But when I walk into my office, it's 3M—the procedures and layout pretty much match our style anywhere." The added bonus, according to Harber, is that the operation is profitable.

▼ CASE STUDY HIGHLIGHTS: 3M

* 3M had a long and substantial track record in China before deciding to embark upon the effort to pioneer a wholly foreign-owned venture.
* Clear strategic goals were laid down before starting the negotiating process.
* 3M found itself negotiating with national and local officials as well as its local business partner. While all were enthusiastic, a major stumbling block was the willingness of relevant officials to take responsibility for approving the project. Preliminary approval served only to set off the next round of meetings, consultations, and negotiations.
* Final negotiating roadblocks involved not only business issues but political ones such as the name of the venture.
* The venture has become profitable, and, except for continuing efforts to blend Chinese and American management styles, the company has operated without major hitches.

■ *Mabuchi Motor Company*

Mabuchi, a Japanese company specializing in the manufacture of a type of micromotor used in video cassette recorders as well as for the automobile industry, set up a wholly foreign-owned production facility in the Dalian Municipal Economic and Technology Zone in October 1987.

Total investment was around RMB 5 billion, and the company started with an initial payroll of 540, which is expected to rise to 4,000 in 1992. Output upon opening was about 35,000 units a day, moved up to 100,000 a day in the late 1980s, and is planned for about 120,000 a day at peak production (140–150 million units per year).

Mabuchi's case study first appeared in the JETRO China Newsletter (no. 76, 1988) and was written by Satoshi Imai of JETRO's Beijing office. It is adapted here with permission.

Mabuchi began overseas production in the mid-1970s, setting up its first overseas plant in Taiwan. Between that plant, one in Hong Kong, and now the one in Dalian, only 2% of the company's output is produced in Japan.

Mabuchi decided to set up shop in Dalian for a number of reasons. One was the supply crunch in micromotors in 1987. The second is that labor rates in China began to compare favorably to

Taiwan. Dalian also offers a port close to Japan, a large expatriate Japanese presence, a good business climate, and a pool of technical workers.

The company decided to set up a wholly owned subsidiary after fact-finding studies indicated two potential problems with joint ventures. First, the company found, not all joint ventures work out smoothly. Second, they made the judgment that the strict production management practices required by their industry would be difficult to put in place in a joint venture.

The agreements signed by Mabuchi with Dalian allow it to sell up to 10% of its output in the Chinese domestic market. With the exception of cartons for packaging, all raw materials and parts are imported, including the wrapping material used in packaging.

Labor and Management Issues

All top management staff of the Mabuchi venture are expatriate Japanese. Seven are there on a permanent basis; five on a temporary assignment. The highest-ranking Chinese on the staff is a division head. Mabuchi does assign Chinese staff the responsibility for handling most of the company's local concerns, such as telephone, water, and other matters.

Workers are recruited through lists of those seeking jobs with foreign companies provided by the Dalian Economic Development Zone, through the Dalian Municipal Labor Office, and through classified ads in local newspapers.

One problem that surfaced is the staffing difficulties created because workers are not always free to join Mabuchi, even when the company has made an agreement with the worker's old employer. The understanding in Beijing had been that this would be feasible, but at the local level some units wait two to three months before giving workers permission to leave. This has created staffing difficulties. On the other hand, job stability is good and Mabuchi has experienced few resignations. A number of workers were laid off because of conflicts and absenteeism.

Labor quality is satisfactory, according to the factory manager. They are able to select 200 workers from a pool of 1,000 applicants. Productivity is not yet up to the level of their plants in Hong Kong and Taiwan (the difference is 10%), but the defect ratio is under 1%, more or less the same as in Hong Kong and Taiwan. There are three regular shifts and workers alternate between them for a week at a time. Mabuchi has found that Chinese workers are generally not eager to put in overtime.

Mabuchi's company philosophy is to let Dalian solve the problem of housing for the workers. The lack of such housing has sometimes discouraged technical staff from joining the venture. Without alternative housing they were not prepared to give up the living quarters provided by their existing work units.

Another related problem is transportation, because of the hour-long commute from the urban area of Dalian to the economic zone. The company provides a bus service for the commute, although it is pressuring Dalian city officials to provide this themselves.

Other Issues

Mabuchi would like to start selling its products on the Chinese market, but finds that the operating restrictions on a wholly foreign-owned structure work against them. A Chinese manufacturer wanting Mabuchi Dalian micromotors, for example, must pay import duty, which artificially pushes up the price. If the micromotors were a joint venture product, the Chinese buyer could purchase them duty free.

Technology leaks are not of great concern to the venture. Experience has shown Mabuchi that even if Chinese enterprises introduce new plants and equipment, they are not necessarily able to make the same products. Manufacturing, says the deputy general manager of the venture, is very much a "national product" in the sense that quality has a lot to do with technology levels in related fields and China is missing these technology levels. Another deciding factor lies in management know-how, which also seems to be missing.

In the past, according to the deputy general manager, Chinese authorities believed that by acquiring the latest in plants, technology and equipment, they would be able to produce exactly the same goods as foreign manufacturers. But there are many plants around China with the latest equipment that don't function properly because the engineers lack the know-how to handle advanced equipment.

Case Study Highlights:
Mabuchi Motor Company

- The company has almost 100% of its products made abroad and views China as the low-wage alternative to its present factories in various other Asian countries.
- Mabuchi chose to set up a wholly foreign-owned enterprise instead of a joint venture because it felt it could have better control of all aspects of the operation. The chief disadvantage of this is that the company has found it difficult to sell its products domestically.
- Labor quality is satisfactory, but the company has had some problems recruiting the staff. It also finds itself negotiating with the city over who has responsibility for workers' housing and transportation.

> - Technology leaks are not seen as a major problem because the general manager believes China does not have the context in which to apply it.

▲

■ Concord Camera Corporation

A New Jersey company, Concord Camera has expanded its manufacturing operations in South China to include the development of its own industrial estate. In addition to assembling its cameras, Concord leases industrial space to foreign computer and high technology companies interested in manufacturing in South China, providing foreign companies a unique "turn-key" manufacturing service. The Concord industrial and residential complex is located in Baoan County, north of Shenzhen.

This case study of Concord's aggressive strategy for South China was provided by Asia Pacific Resource Group, Inc., publishers of China Trade.

Concord designs and manufactures cameras and other photographic products in the Far East through Dialbright Co., a wholly owned subsidiary in Hong Kong. Concord began manufacturing operations in South China in 1982, but a failed joint venture led Concord to buy out its Chinese partner and to go it alone. In 1984 Concord reestablished its operations in the form of a wholly owned facility in Henggang, just north of Shenzhen.

The initial operation involved 10,000 square feet of manufacturing space and 50 employees. In five years, the operation had expanded to 240,000 square feet and 1,500 employees during peak production months. (In camera production there are two peak periods: April to June and August to November.)

In July 1989—one month after the Tiananmen Square incident—the company signed an agreement with local authorities to spearhead the development of a huge industrial and residential complex in Henggang. Concord's plan was to provide a cost-effective and efficient site for other foreign companies interested in manufacturing in South China. Concord currently rents out 50,000 square feet in this complex to a NYSE-listed company making precision computer components.

In July 1991 Concord's activities expanded further. The company announced plans to invest an additional $12.8 million in advanced production and printing equipment, bringing its total investment in Henggang to $18.6 million. Under the expansion, fed in part by rapid internal growth (in May 1991 it had acquired Keystone Camera), Concord will add 176,000 square feet of production space to house precision metal stamping operations, screening and printing equipment to upgrade the company's printing capability, lens-making equipment to produce telephoto lenses, and plastic injection moulding equipment. The company anticipates building an additional 250,000 square feet of space in the future to expand its OEM consumer electronics division.

Manufacturing Operations

Components are shipped to Henggang from Hong Kong, where Concord has nine JVs. These parts are then assembled in production lines stretching 250 feet, with approximately 160 workers per line. Concord's facility is organized with the following departments: management office, training area, production engineering, inspection, production, incoming parts quality control, material control, in-line and off-line quality control, and packaging and shipping. Concord has its own internal security staff to protect raw materials.

There are three inspection stations per line, staffed by Chinese engineers. (In contrast to U.S. assembly operations which have inspection and rework stations located at the end of a line, Concord has found that inspection stations must be located alongside assemblers.) Completed cameras are sent back to Hong Kong by truck-in containers.

Concord's Industrial Estate

In 1989, Jack Benun, president of Concord, outlined the logic behind Concord's plan to develop an industrial estate: "We believe many manufacturing companies worldwide would like to take advantage of the quality work, favorable rent, and low labor costs that China affords."

Its agreement with Wan Kong Economic Development Corporation of Henggang gives Concord the right to lease up to 60 million square feet of industrial space in Baoan County for a period of 25 years. Concord's plan has been to market the industrial space to computer and high-technology companies interested in low-cost manufacturing. Concord can provide companies with different services, including political risk insurance and "turn-key" operations. Depending on the type of building, the rental cost on the estate is about U.S.$3.00 per square foot. The cost of labor is U.S.$90.00 per worker per month.

Concord has had some difficulty marketing this space, especially in light of the political problems surrounding China. But Benun remains optimistic. "I am still confident that China's strong fundamentals—cheap labor, low-cost production, and access to the Asian market—will eventually stand out."

CASE STUDY HIGHLIGHTS: CONCORD CAMERA

- Concord has aggressively sought various types of business in China, including joint ventures, technical cooperation agreements, and a wholly foreign-owned venture.
- The company firmly believes in the long-term future of its activities, signing an agreement to develop a major industrial and residential complex just one month after the Tiananmen Square incident. This project has since been expanded.
- Not just content to manufacture, Concord Camera has set itself up as a consultant/developer/landlord for foreign companies wanting to come to China and step into a ready-made industrial park rather than having to create their own from the ground up.

The Perspective of the General Manager

■ *Ningbo Abbott Biotechnology, Ltd.*

Ningbo Abbott Biotechnology is a joint venture between Abbott Laboratories, the American pharmaceutical firm, and three Chinese partners. Negotiations for this JV began in 1985, some 12 years after Abbott was among the first American firms to visit China in the wake of "ping-pong" diplomacy.

Instead of tracing the history of the venture, however, we focus here on the experience of Paul Epner, who was appointed general manager of this joint venture in 1989. Before becoming general manager, he served as project manager during the venture's negotiation phase. Epner says, "There are three key factors for the success of any venture in China: people, people, and people."

This case has been adapted from an article written by Epner, published in the July/August 1991 issue of the China Business Review. *Reprinted with permission of the China Business Forum, the US-China Business Council, Washington, D.C.*

The experience of a general manager of a JV manufacturing diagnostic reagent in China reveals that the key to success lies not only in finding the right individuals, but in molding them to the Western company's needs and then maintaining their effectiveness as the business and work environments change. There is no unique method for managing Chinese employees. Common sense and paying attention to a few simple rules will produce the best results.

Recruit the Best

The first rule is so basic it is often overlooked. Find the right people. This can be a time-consuming task given the shortage of skilled labor in China and the bureaucratic obstacles involved in hiring them, but it cannot be overemphasized. The people hired will probably be there for the life of the venture, so they must possess the talents and skills needed. The general manager should play an active role in the recruiting and hiring process, as ultimately it is he who is responsible for shaping the staff into a productive unit.

Keep in mind the following factors when hiring Chinese staff:

• *Avoid taking too many employees from any one source.*

People with similar bad habits may tend to reinforce each other. In addition, one inherits the power and social structure of the previous organization, which will compete with the environment being created for the new venture.

Although recruiting from the outside is much slower, involves many bureaucratic hurdles, and may require the JV to provide even more training, it is best to accept these costs. Try to position the investors to tolerate a slow initial growth rate—finding the right people will pay off over the long term.

• *Be patient and flexible.*

It will take time to find everyone needed. Ease the search by distinguishing which positions clearly require previous experience and by accepting applicants with less experience for the others.

When considering employees, focus on intelligence, motivation, work ethic, and curiosity. If an unusually good candidate appears, hire him even if a suitable position isn't available immediately. At the same time, be alert for the candidate who is looking for a one-way ticket to the West. It's routine to receive applications from researchers who think a JV will be a panacea for their problems, but who are not really committed to profit and manufacturing objectives.

If operational needs force one to fill some positions with candidates who do not meet the requirements, downgrade the position. Keep focused on the long-term needs rather than the organizational chart.

• *Resist the temptation to over-hire.*

China's interest is to increase the number of people hired out to joint ventures. But too many employees encourage low productivity and conflict will result as underutilized departments protect their territory.

• *Find a confidant.*

One person in the management staff should have maturity, experience dealing with the bureaucracy, good people and business instincts, and complete trustworthiness. This person plays an essential role in instilling Western business practices.

Building a Nurturing Environment

Once the staff has been hired, it's time to create a corporate culture that reflects a Western management style yet is comfortable for the Chinese staff.

It begins with selecting a general manager who can be a role model, and who creates a flat organization structure that allows him to have his hand on the pulse of the company at all levels. To reduce the impact of such traditionally important Chinese cultural characteristics as the fear of responsibility and the need to find one's identity through the *guanxi* system (the web of relationships—see chapters 8–10), the general manager must clearly explain what is expected of the employees and support them as they adjust to a new value system.

This can be accomplished in several ways:

- *Provide detailed job descriptions.*

But also recognize the limitations of such descriptions. Many will use their job description to justify their actions—or their inaction. The job description becomes a training tool to help staff understand their responsibilities and place in the organization. Expectations of results and accountability should be clearly explained to management staff.

- *Integrate training into daily operations.*

Work closely with the management team from the outset. The venture's corporate culture can be established only through actions and contact, not through speeches and memos. Introduce concepts of responsibility, accountability, budget control, forecasting, etc., as part of the agenda of staff meetings, so the concept can be simultaneously learned and applied to a real problem.

- *Stress accountability.*

To achieve innovation, reward creativity and tolerate failure. Provide a nurturing environment for risk takers by establishing a system of checks and balances for big decisions, while letting people make mistakes in areas that do not threaten the staff or operations. Treat every bad decision as a learning opportunity.

- *Expand time horizons.*

Since command economies rarely force people to plan ahead, many Chinese may have trouble recognizing future cause and effect relationships, a necessary skill if they are to manage proactively instead of reactively. To address this void, teach management staff how to set goals by requiring them to turn in a monthly report indicating what they plan to do in the coming month, what they have done in the past month, and whether they have attained the previous month's objectives. This routine not only gets them to anticipate future needs, but the feedback loop—with which the general manager should be involved—helps improve forecasting skills.

Dealing with the Bureaucracy

Many general managers are overwhelmed by the demands of meeting their head company's expectations while coping in a foreign, at times mysterious, environment. They are afraid they will be accused of insensitivity to the native culture or branded as having little respect for the "laws of the land." The result is that they frequently accept bureaucratic requirements that are not in the best interests of their venture.

All general managers must learn how to deal with the Chinese bureaucracy if they hope to be able to manage their operations effectively. Though many foreigners find the workings of China's business environment hard to fathom, the system becomes easier to comprehend if it is viewed in the context of a large corporation—a point made by Roderick Macleod in his book *China, Inc.* If Chinese ministries are likened to corporate divisions and the municipal organizations to matrix site management teams, many of China's business practices—parochialism, inter-ministerial hiring difficulties, and power politics—no longer appear so strange.

Viewing the bureaucracy in this way makes it easier to operate in the system and challenge it, which is occasionally necessary if the general manager is to be able to control both the venture's business and internal environments.

▼ **Case Study Highlights: One General Manager's Advice to Another**

Paul Egner, general manager of the Ningbo Abbott Biotechnology has some further advice to fellow general managers:

"The job of a general manager is to give middle management the tools to do their jobs without you. Force them to stretch. Don't let them come to the office with problems unless they have recommendations about how to solve them. Be sensitive to their needs and backgrounds, but not to the point that the effectiveness of business is challenged.

"Stay involved, but give them room to innovate and make mistakes. Work with them behind the scenes so that they can build credible Western-style management techniques they can use in front of their subordinates.

"The reward will be an efficiently operating business that enables the general manager to devote his efforts to creating a long-term vision for the venture."

▲

7

Other Business

When an export manager comes to China to bestow the representation of his products on some deserving agent or distributor, he is usually rather shocked at the lack of enthusiasm with which his advances are met. Of course, if his product has been on the market for a long time and has a well-established sale, he will have plenty of agents to choose from, but if his company is unknown it is usually quite disillusioning to him to learn how completely and thoroughly it is unknown and what an entire lack of curiosity there is about it.

—CARL CROW, *400 MILLION CUSTOMERS* (1937)

Getting established in China is a challenge not just for companies buying, selling, transferring technology, or investing in an equity venture but for hundreds of firms in specialized niches.

This chapter looks at companies involved in what might broadly be called the service industry. Two of them are joint ventures—an auto shop and a hotel. The other two are American consulting companies that work for both foreign and Chinese clients.

The Sanlian Automotive and Olympic Hotel case studies are real-life versions of the "boot camp" tales old China hands like to share among themselves and with newly arrived recruits. They speak volumes about what can go wrong with workers, with partners, and with bureaucracies. They also highlight a phenomenon common to ventures of all types. Contracts may be signed in an atmosphere flushed with pomp, circumstance, and optimism, but those left to carry out the agreement can find themselves saddled with problems never imagined by the CEO comfortably back home in his corner office, getting reports indicating the deal is on track and making money (or not). This dissonance of perceptions can be damaging to the venture's success.

Included in this chapter as well are examples of the work done by two types of consulting companies. A. T. Kearney is a large international management consulting firm working on behalf of clients in China and multinationals operating there. The case study discusses the company's approach to management consulting in China and the Greater China region.

Pacific Rim Resources is a specialized China/Asia advisory service providing consulting, investing, trading, and market development services. Its case study demonstrates the type of work these companies can do on behalf of their clients.

Service Industries

■ Sanlian Automotive Technical Service Company

The case studies recounted so far have touched on problems, but in a general way. None match the bare-knuckle tactics experienced by Jardine Matheson in the operation of its foreign car repair and service center joint venture. Jardine has 150 years experience in China, and is one of the most prestigious trading houses in Hong Kong. Yet it not only walked into this joint venture, but continues to operate it despite the problems. The reason? It's very profitable.

Here Peter Po, director and manager of Jardine Matheson (China), recounts in unusually blunt terms the experience of Sanlian Automotive.

This case appeared in the December 10, 1990 issue of Business China, *and is reprinted here with permission.* Business China *is a division of Business International Asia/Pacific Ltd.*

Jardine Matheson is one of the most enduring names in China trade. But even after a century and a half of experience, the company does not always have an easy time. At the top of the list of complaints are a dishonest deputy general manager, two law suits, and two workshop break-ins.

While China has passed joint venture laws and other commercial legislation that have improved its investment environment, doing business in the P.R.C. can still be rough going, says Peter Po. One of the most crucial factors in the smooth running of a joint venture is picking the right partners. If both sides are cooperative and considerate, then all the problems can be resolved, he says. "If it's the reverse, simple matters can become very complicated."

Jardine's experiences in its venture, Sanlian Automotive Technical Service Company, prove that even profitable partnerships can be unpleasant.

A History of Troubles

In November 1985 Jardine set up the car maintenance joint venture that—despite making profits from day one—has provided endless headaches. Jardine and its two Chinese partners each hold a one-third equity share in the RMB 4.6 million venture.

The Chinese deputy manager, who was well connected to the president of China National Automotive Industry Corporation (CNAIC) [a ministerial-industrial corporation of the type described in chapter 3], started causing trouble right from the start, according to Po. He was uncooperative and Jardine soon suspected him of conspiring with the contractor to defraud the venture on the construction of the new workshop. The workshop's original construction budget of RMB 600,000 leaped up to RMB 1.5 million, yet the building was so poor that it failed to pass quality inspection. Lamps dangled precariously from the ceiling, roof and walls leaked in the rain, and windows were not properly sealed.

Convinced that the deputy general manager and the contractor were in cahoots, Jardine told its Chinese partners that the deputy general manager had to go. They agreed and sacked him, but made the mistake of underestimating his connections—he appealed to his friends at CNAIC, who in turn dismissed the joint venture's chairman and all the directors without further notice. (As the official "sponsor" of the JV, CNAIC had this power.)

The dispute lasted over a year, despite support for Jardine Matheson from the Ministry of Foreign Economic Relations and Trade (MOFERT) and other organizations. The case was finally resolved by going end-around to China's top authorities. They put pressure on CNAIC and eventually the original JV chairman and directors were reinstated. Although Po cannot be sure it was because of the Sanlian case, the head of CNAIC was also dismissed.

What did Jardine take away from this episode? "It was a disaster, but we learned the lesson that if we want to invest, we should try our best to renovate an existing facility—not to start construction from scratch. It just took up too much time," says Po. In subsequent China ventures, Jardine has indeed used existing buildings and been satisfied with the results. "You can find shops that are set up nicely—they just need some renovation. And with so many idle, prices are quite reasonable," he says.

It's Not Over Until It's Over

The next dispute at Sanlian concerned pricing policies. The JV charges the standard rate of RMB 50 per hour for service, following its Hong Kong luxury car manufacturing subsidiary's time budget for each task (wheel changing, carburetor cleaning, etc.). This was deemed outrageous by an official at the price bureau in Beijing. The bureau accused Sanlian of breaking the law, saying that each person-hour should be charged at only two RMB.

Sanlian tried to explain that its way of calculating was quite different from the Chinese method. "For Chinese car maintenance, they probably charge 50 hours for changing a wheel. But we say it's half an hour regardless of how long it takes," says Po. The price bureau wasn't convinced and the authorities verbally told the venture it was going to be fined. Sanlian asked for a formal, written notice. Two months later the venture received a telephone call from the Bank of China's Beijing branch and learned that the price bureau had summarily penalized Sanlian RMB 200,000 and had simply ordered the money drawn out of Sanlian's account.

That was back in 1987 and, again with MOFERT's support, Jardine has taken the case as high as the State Council. According to Po, China's legal authorities are currently examining whether the law was properly executed and have issued an internal document stating that the fine was incorrect. Even so, the price bureau has not repaid the money.

And Still It's Not Over . . .

Then there was the dispute with the former leaseholders of the Sanlian site. When Jardine established Sanlian, it agreed to lease the land for the venture from the original work unit on the site. The unit, Po says, was bankrupt. Sanlian razed the old building that stood on the site and built the new workshops.

On top of paying rent for the leased land, the JV gave the unit a quarter of the new buildings and an interest-free loan of RMB 400,000 to be used for setting itself up in another line of work. Sanlian gave them 10 years to repay it.

The unit was satisfied with this arrangement until it saw how much money Sanlian was making, Po says. It then claimed it had been cheated and that the venture owed it millions of RMB in lost revenue.

The argument festered until the beginning of 1990, when unit members twice broke into Sanlian's factory, occupied the workshop, ripped out electric wiring, and threw out tools and equipment. To prevent physical confrontation, Po told the JV staff to go home. But he could not interest the authorities in taking action. "We called the local Public Security Bureau—everybody we could think of in Beijing. Nobody gave a damn," he says.

Finally the Public Security Foreign Affairs Office of the city put some pressure on the local branch bureau, whereupon the jealous work unit brought suit against Sanlian. A Chinese court official advised the JV to countersue, saying that the other side would lose without question. As of early 1992 the case was still waiting to be heard. According to court officials, the venture can expect another two to three year wait since there are so many other economic cases before it.

Sanlian repaired the damaged workshop but took the precaution of videotaping the ransacked premises for the record. The JV also signed a contract with a newly established security guard service to watch over its facilities. The service is working out very well, says Po. Even so, Sanlian's six Hong Kong expatriate employees have left the venture and are unwilling to return.

Despite the seemingly endless succession of serious problems, business at Sanlian is going well. Thanks to strong technical back-up from one of Jardine's luxury car subsidiaries in Hong Kong, the venture is popular with top party officials. It mostly services Mercedes-Benz and Japanese-made sedans. Customers are willing to wait their turn for Sanlian's services because it is the only plant in the area that does bodywork and repairs in addition to servicing.

"Sanlian is still making a good profit, with an annual turnover of about RMB 10 million. It's crazy, but we can't close down something so profitable," says Po.

▼ **CASE STUDY HIGHLIGHTS:**
SANLIAN AUTOMOTIVE

• Even a company very experienced in China can get burned: choose your partners *very* carefully.
• In retrospect, starting from scratch might have been better than buying into an existing venture. Sanlian found ongoing labor and management problems, compounded by corruption and the fact that everybody minds everybody else's business and intrudes without hesitation. These negative factors made it difficult to get the cooperation of all those affected by its venture.
• The company also found that when things go wrong, there is little short-term effective legal recourse—solutions are often negotiated or paid for.
• Sanlian has needed guts, patience, money and leverage to keep operating. Concludes Peter Po, director of China operations for the foreign company, "It's crazy, but we can't close down something so profitable." ▲

■ *Olympic Hotel*

Speaking of problems . . .
In the following case study, three out of the four partners involved all had extensive experience in negotiating, developing, and managing joint ventures in China. But when it came to

actually building The New Century Hotel and Office Center, the rookie partner—All Nippon Airways—found that even its more experienced colleagues couldn't shield them from the capricious nature of China's administrative regulations and the ugly reputation of the building trades (which had also bedeviled Sanlian). On top of that, there were problems among the partners.

Now renamed the "Olympic," the project started out as "The New Century," a 60/40 joint venture between Xiyuan Hotel (itself a JV) and the Bank of China on the Chinese side, and All Nippon Airways and C. Itoh on the Japanese side. The venture was set up in January 1987 with initial capitalization at $19 million and a total investment of $92 million. The period of the JV was set at 18 years, including a four year construction period. Completion was slated for late 1990, prior to the opening of the Asian Games.

Though foundation work was finished on schedule in 1988, delays began to creep in due to a shortage of raw materials and workers. The upheavals of 1989 did not help. The hotel and office complex did open in 1990, but as of mid-1991 many of the facilities (pool, etc.) had not yet been completed, victims of money and other shortages.

This case study focuses on the problems encountered in the first year of construction. It is adapted, with permission, from the article "Beijing New Century Hotel," by Satoshi Imai in the JETRO China Newsletter, no. 80, 1989.

The hotel/office venture was conceived in 1984, three years before the inauguration of All Nippon Airway's (ANA) Beijing-Dalian-Narita service. Shopping for the right location and partner in China began in 1984, with a delegation to the scenic city of Hangzhou. Some 15 similar missions to various Chinese cities followed in the ensuing two years but suitable conditions or partners were not found.

Then, in the spring of 1986 and independent of ANA's efforts, Chinese authorities asked a third party—C. Itoh, the venerable Japanese trading firm—to approach ANA to see if there would be interest in building a parking lot and other facilities near the Metropolitan Stadium, site of the 1990 Asian Games. ANA saw this as an opportunity to introduce its idea of a hotel and office complex. All parties soon agreed, and a contract was signed by October 1986. The business was registered in January 1987 and construction began in February 1988.

The Japanese partners chose this project for several reasons. The Xiyuan not only runs an international hotel of its own, but is itself a JV. The Bank of China is well versed in international ways of doing business and was helpful in breaking a number of deadlocks (like convincing Xiyuan of the importance of following international business practices). Both parties had strong ties to the Beijing municipal government. Moreover, the Japanese thought that having two Chinese partners would reduce the direct conflicts.

Problems

That an agreement was reached in so short a time seemed auspicious, but problems soon came up during the actual construction phase.

First were changes in the investment situation and government policies that added greatly to the cost of the project. In late 1986 the State Council issued a circular requiring major electricity users to purchase electricity bonds. The hotel's share came to $2.16 million, with 25% up front, and 38% prior to opening.

The next surprise came when the Beijing Municipality notified all foreign joint ventures that users of the "four utilities," (cold and hot water, gas, and sewers) should shoulder development costs. This added an unexpected $1 million to the escalating costs.

Then the municipal construction company wanted a .3% fee for registering the plans (eventually negotiated to half that), and $400,000 for construction "quality" certification. It didn't stop there. A new regulation in 1988 assessed the project $210,000 for stamp tax. Then came non-contractual extras such as compensation to residents for the building of a parking lot (which originally had been the responsibility of the Chinese side), as well as the cost of building roads, providing a bus service, and more.

Administrative fiat cost the JV another $1.5 million as Beijing authorities insisted it accept the more expensive bid from the local interior decorator ($5 million) over the lower Hong Kong one ($3.5 million).

These and other problems forced the investors to raise the investment capital to $92 million from the original $77 million, severely eroding the potential for profitability.

Bureaucratism

Other problems can be put under the label of "bureaucratism."

1. The Beijing government (not a partner) was an active proponent (they wanted to see the facilities in place before the Asian Games). On the other hand, the Xiyuan, which was a partner, was less than enthusiastic. They dragged their heels on every occasion, apparently worried about competition from another JV hotel just a few blocks away from their own facilities.

2. Active support by the local authorities also meant active interference. They had "national" goals in mind and wanted to see them implemented even though others were paying the bills. Other abuses that cost the venture money and frustration included the insistence on a particular local construction company and the insistence on domestic elevators and other Chinese-made items.

3. The JV found a myriad set of rules and regulations governing every contingency—but some were "internal" and hidden from view and most others were open to divergent interpretations, depending on the official in charge. For example, materials imported for JV use are supposed to be exempt from import duty, but while a generator entered free, its parts and peripheral equipment were taxed (some shipments simply got "lost" when going through customs, says the venture).

The biggest problems the Olympic had during its start-up phase were with the contractor. Unlike the situation in Japan, where the contractor is responsible for obtaining building materials, the contractor in China put on the JV the burden of finding the supply of building materials (such as cement, timber, and steel). It also did not pay any attention to the work schedule, or the quality of the job. The contractor didn't feel it a responsibility, for example, to consider the effects of its work on future operations.

Cultural and organizational differences also reared their head. From a Japanese point of view, Chinese work morale suffers from the tendency to avoid responsibility, an inability to distinguish between private and public prerogatives, and a lack of company loyalty. Closely related was the issue of corruption. The JV found that almost invariably some sort of payment was necessary when it tried to acquire things in short supply.

The Future

After two years of work, the Japanese partners had some pointed advice for their colleagues. First, they said, the Chinese partners and workers should accept that they have a lot to learn and get on with it. They cannot absorb the know-how and experience of the foreign partners if they insist that this and that foreign approach "won't work in China."

Second, the Chinese should understand that, in a budding service industry like hotel operation and building construction, they need the more experienced expatriate managers to show them the way things are done and they should welcome their presence.

Other lessons are contained in the accompanying sidebar.

▼ Case Study Highlights: Olympic Hotel

Mr. Imai, who wrote this case study for JETRO, draws a number of lessons from this venture:

• Build human ties with local counterparts to stave off misunderstandings and willful distortions. Many problems can be avoided if a channel for consultation is in place before actual difficulties arise.

- Lay down concrete rules governing every possible situation, from the use of company cars, to everyday work matters, accounting procedures, and recruitment requirements.
- Keep informed as much as possible about unpublished regulations that leave the foreign partner with little choice but to accept.
- In times of real difficulty or when the attitude or behavior of the Chinese side becomes unreasonable, it sometimes helps to drop a few words in the ears of responsible officials or members of relevant government organs.

Consulting

Surveys show that more than half the American companies investing in China rely upon the services of some type of consultant. There are many firms and individuals providing such services and the key question to be posed to all of them is, can they deliver both China expertise and the ability to serve the foreign company's business interests? Simply speaking Chinese or having a good "connection" will not cut it in the business environment of the 1990s.

Two very different companies which both clearly meet the test are A. T. Kearney and Pacific Rim Resources. There are others, too, of course, and they can be found through the China information and support network discussed in chapter 8.

■ *A. T. Kearney*

China is a "frontier market" for any professional services firm. This is particularly the case for management consulting, which is just beginning to take hold in the most advanced industrial countries of Asia.

A. T. Kearney is a management consulting firm with a 65-year history and a reputation for strength in manufacturing operations and logistics. Its earliest contacts with China occurred in 1944, when President Roosevelt named the founder of the firm, A. Thomas Kearney, to head a special mission of 23 leading industrialists to China. In modern times, the firm first became seriously interested in China in the early 1980s, when the development of "beachhead" joint ventures by some of its major clients coincided with its own drive into Asian consulting markets.

In October 1985, Kearney CEO Fred Steingraber addressed a business conference in Beijing and from that flowed several assignments, including one on behalf of a Chinese manufacturer of electronic equipment. Since then, Kearney has undertaken

World Bank-funded industrial restructuring projects as well as investment strategy projects for multinational corporate clients. Also, in collaboration with the International Trade Research Institute of the Ministry of Foreign Economic Relations and Trade, it produced the influential investment guide, "Manufacturing Equity Joint Ventures in China."

This case study of A. T. Kearney's approach to China was written by Dr. Kim Woodard, the firm's director for China.

The challenges facing A. T. Kearney in the China market are similar to challenges faced by business, in particular service companies, in frontier markets around the world. Local enterprises in Third World markets such as China are not prepared to carry the cost of professional services that were originally designed in the context of a commercial corporate client base. Frontier market entry must therefore be viewed as a long-term investment strategy, not as a short-term source of revenue. Investment in a market presence must be made carefully and in a highly targeted manner.

Kearney's investment strategy balances public and private sector clients in selected locations and industries. Our assignment slate rests on four main pillars:

1. Small marketing projects for local Chinese enterprises in key industries, such as auto parts and electronics.
2. Research projects focused on market trends and foreign investment trends, often published in white papers.
3. Industrial restructuring projects funded by the World Bank and other international lending agencies.
4. Marketing, investment strategy, and operations projects for major multinationals in our traditional client base.

Of these four pillars, the first three tend to require net investment by the firm. Only the fourth generates net revenue on a project-by-project basis. The growth objective, therefore, must be to expand assignments for our major corporate clients. In the long term, as the reform process takes hold in China, local enterprises will gain sufficient foreign exchange and competitive strength to need commercial consulting to assist them in achieving world competitive standards in quality and customer responsiveness.

Operational Challenges
The most important challenge to a firm working in a frontier market is to reach across the barriers of culture and ideology and induce productive change and tangible results for the local client. Creating "common cause" and good communication with the client is difficult. In China, creating and sustaining a sense of shared identity and common objectives faces deep-seated client resistance for a number of reasons:

1. The competitive ethic and the drive to be "number one" in quality and market position are unfamiliar to industry leaders schooled in communist economics and socialist ideals.

2. Involvement of the consultant in the implementation of recommended change is often viewed as subversive of national prerogatives and objectives.

3. Management consulting is an unknown profession that remains largely unaccepted by enterprise managers who are poorly trained and inexperienced in modern management practices, leaving them unable to utilize fully the consulting resource.

4. Rapid and effective decisions by the client are difficult to elicit, both at the contract stage and during the consulting process.

5. Fee and cost structures that are common in international consulting appear exorbitant and extractive in the context of local costs and salaries.

The net impact of these perceptions is to greatly lengthen the consulting process and to temporarily focus on management education rather than the achievement of tangible results.

A secondary challenge to firms working in a frontier market is to contain operating costs. Particularly during the early years, as the firm moves up the learning curve, operating costs tend to outrun revenues. To help contain costs, A. T. Kearney keeps professionals and support personnel dedicated to China to a minimum. There are currently a number of highly experienced consultants firm-wide who are bilingual and have a background in China. Just a few serve full-time in the China practice. The others work in diverse geographic and functional consulting markets, ready to be brought into the China operation on a project basis.

A. T. Kearney has just one quality standard for our consulting services: service that exceeds client expectations on every assignment. At the end of each project, excellence of service and tangible results for the client must be the primary objectives. There can be no compromise and no double standard of quality in services provided to China or any other frontier market. This means putting the best available people on each assignment for as long as is required to finish the project at the highest standards of quality with the maximum results for the client. This commitment to China and the other frontier markets where we are active is the reason why Kearney views participation in these markets as long-term investments, not as short-term revenue opportunities.

Building for the Future

The professional service market in China is entering what promises to be a rather extended intermediate growth phase. The 1980s, a decade of dramatic opening of China's markets and of very rapid growth in China's domestic economy, are over. The promised land of industrial modernization, full market reforms, and integration with the world economy, still lies many years, perhaps decades into the future.

The intermediate phase of China's development is characterized by a mixed economy, thick government red tape, continuing domestic market barriers, weak but growing local enterprises, the rising commercial influence of Hong Kong and southern China, and growing foreign investment. For professional services firms, China will continue to be viewed as a difficult frontier, where operating costs are high and market opportunities scattered and variable. China will continue to have a reputation as "too large to ignore but too difficult to be profitable."

The "Greater China" area (the mainland, Taiwan, and Hong Kong) increasingly functions as a single commercial supermarket, regardless of political barriers. Hong Kong provides the combined forces of large-scale finance and global trade. Taiwan is a platform of advanced technology and manufacturing management. China has the resources, the people, and above all, the market to absorb capital and products from the other two. Driven by this dynamic, the economic power of Greater China in the Asia-Pacific region will rise in relative as well as absolute terms. By some estimates, the real growth of GDP in the Hong Kong-South China region is currently about 12% per year, which may make it the fastest growing economic region in the world.

Future investment strategies for China for the professional service firm will seek to tie the mainland market back to operations in Hong Kong and Taiwan. Service firms are likely to choose a single office location that is suitable for access to all three pieces of the Greater China market. It is also likely that the range of services provided in the China market will broaden and deepen during the 1990s. Banks will move from offering "investment services" to a much higher volume of commercial lending. Law firms will broaden their services to provide a wide range of commercial legal services to both local and foreign clients. Management consulting firms will focus less on World Bank work and market studies and more on investment strategy and operational efficiency.

Service firms will slowly decrease dependency on expatriates and will cultivate talented and highly motivated local professionals. During China's intermediate development phase, professionals will increasingly be recruited from the Greater China region for service in the mainland market.

As part of our drive toward globalization, A. T. Kearney is committed to long-term growth in the China market. During the past five years, we have achieved initial success in the mainland consulting market. During the next five years, our objective is to establish a leading position in the Greater China market for management consulting services and to continue our high growth in the Asian region.

▼ **CASE STUDY HIGHLIGHTS: A.T. KEARNEY**

- There is a market for China-related professional management consulting services in the U.S., in the P.R.C., and among international development institutions such as the World Bank.
- The market for such services within China is limited, however, due to culture-based resistance to concepts such as competitiveness, rapid decision-making, and the paying of high-cost fees for consulting services.
- The cost of operating and maintaining a full-fledged China division within a company can be high, so relevant personnel should be able to assume other roles within the organization as well.
- The "Greater China" market holds more immediate promise for management consulting services.

■ *Pacific Rim Resources*

Specialized China consultants have become an integral part of the China trade. Some companies find they prefer relying on their own resources (see the case studies of Gelman Sciences, 3M, and Ibberson International, for example), but others have found great value in a consultant who can help evaluate the opportunity and assist in implementing the necessary strategy to exploit it.

To show the role a consultant can play, this case study traces the history of InkFont Technologies as it tries to take advantage of the growing demand for computer printers in China. Based in Canmore, Canada, InkFont had a long-standing relationship with a Hong Kong partner on whom it initially relied for its China venture.

The example used here was provided by Julie Reinganum, managing director of Pacific Rim Resources. The name of the client company has been changed.

InkFont Technologies is a Canadian company that has helped revolutionize the world of computer printer technology by developing an ink for inkjet printers that will not smudge, fade, or shrink on Chinese papers. As mundane as the process sounds, it offers Chinese officialdom the opportunity to shift from the laborious process of using a Chinese typewriter to the computer age.

InkFont Technologies (IFT) had been selling to the Asian market for some time through a Hong Kong partner. In 1984, this partner suggested a joint venture in China that would serve the largest potential market in the world for computer printers. Because of the type of cartridge, ink, and paper used by the Chinese for official documents, all other inking cartridges had not done well. IFT had the technology and could deliver it in a printer priced well below any competitor's.

IFT readily agreed to its partner's proposal. Shortly thereafter a joint venture was formed giving roughly equal share to the Canadian, Hong Kong, and Chinese partners. The contribution of the Hong Kong company was in the form of capital, machinery, maintenance, and the introduction to the Chinese partner (who would manufacture the cartridges and make the ink from the raw materials supplied by IFT). The Canadians contributed capital as well as the technology and raw materials required for manufacture. They were paid a technology transfer fee and expected continued profits through the sale of raw materials, which the JV bought in foreign exchange.

The Canadians anticipated a tremendous marketing opportunity. Over time, however, they found that the sales of raw materials were not only small, but diminishing. This didn't make sense to them—the Chinese seemed to be enthusiastic about the product, and the Hong Kong partner was assuring them that they were not only the first, but the only inkjet manufacturer in China. InkFont Technologies asked questions at the annual board of directors meeting, but never got satisfactory answers. The Hong Kong partner, whom IFT relied upon as its sole source of information, blamed it on the lack of foreign exchange in China, and the product's lack of popularity.

It didn't ring true, but the company had no independent reference point to find out if everybody had to do business this way in China. Finally, in 1988, they realized something was wrong and turned to Pacific Rim Resources (PRR) to help find the answers.

The Consultant Steps In

Pacific Rim Resources began by asking questions at IFT's headquarters in Canmore, then went to China to talk directly to the Chinese joint venture partner (PRR principals are fluent in Chinese). They also talked to the JV's sponsor (the Arts & Crafts Corporation) and the ministry to whom the sponsor reported. They then talked to customers all over China.

What they found was that there were by now not one but 70 to 120 factories in China making the inkjet cartridge and using Japanese-made ink refill kits sold through a Shenzhen-based trading company.

The Hong Kong partner, it turned out, had also been selling machinery to the new rivals of their own JV, a far more profitable enterprise than selling IFT's inkjet cartridges. Their position as screen between IFT and the Chinese partner (among other things, the Hong Kong company always supplied the interpreter) allowed them work this way for four years.

During the process of investigation, which took place over a period of about two years, PRR also learned that the Japanese ink was not only being sold at a tremendous mark-up, but was inadequate. (The ink would dry much too slowly, especially in the humidity of South China. When it did dry, it cracked. These problems made it unsuitable for official use.)

Pacific Rim Resources then made a series of recommendations to InkFont Technologies:

1. On the basis of quantitative information, there was a market in China for IFT's products, and it was continuing to grow. IFT should therefore sell an inkjet cartridge similar to the Japanese one and undercut the market for this product. This would allow InkFont Technologies some income as it explored its other options.

2. Even though the Japanese had usurped the market, their product was not considered ideal technology. If IFT's R&D department could come up with a product that better met market requirements, there would be an opportunity to re-enter the market with a new product under a new name.

3. The present JV should be shut down, not only because of the actions of the Hong Kong partner, but also because the Chinese partner had lost both clout and interest.

4. A new partner should be found that could fulfill the objectives of making two grades of ink used by the inkjet factories of China. One would be the lower grade of cartridge that would compete with the Japanese, and the other would have the new, superior ink which could be used both in China and, on a limited basis, abroad.

The job now turned on PRR's ability to line up a new partner. The qualifications the company was looking for had less to do with the prospective partner's production capability or its location than with its understanding of the market and its all-important access to distribution and sales channels. Criteria also included the potential partner's access to foreign exchange, its ability to invest in the new venture, and the *guanxi* (relationships) it had.

InkFont Technologies and PRR (which, in addition to its fee, will take an equity position in the new venture) are in discussion with two potential partners. One is in an economic zone in a major port city, the other is a manufacturer of printer ribbons. While the latter has no inkjet manufacturing capability, it does have the advantage of knowing the market and having the sales and distribution network in place. The potential partner located in the economic zone has no experience in this business, but has money to invest and is actively demonstrating a willingness to get into the business.

PRR expects to structure a JV with a strong tech transfer component. A tech transfer fee is to be paid up-front and this fee is likely to be a significant portion of InkFont Technology's equity share. The venture should be up and running by the end of 1992.

▼ **CASE STUDY HIGHLIGHTS:**
PACIFIC RIM RESOURCES

• Specialized China trade consulting firms can play a useful role in all phases of China business, from strategic planning to partner selection.
• Appropriate technology must be matched to appropriate partners, who in turn must be matched to the appropriate markets.
• China need not be mysterious, let alone opaque. Solid business intelligence is now readily available and should be used both to do proper market research and find the best partner.
• It may sometimes be better to start with a company new to the market but demonstrably willing to both learn and invest than with a company that knows the market but may not be willing to adapt to the demands of the Western partner.
▲

How to Approach the China Market— the Lessons Learned

8

Solid Planning

The first question to ask is not how big is the market, but "What does my product and/or technology do for China?" The customer's need is to know how to improve the quality and quantity of his production, increase yields, save material, reduce waste, save energy, and improve communications and transport. Chinese consumers may love Coke, Pepsi, and Kentucky Fried Chicken and that's why the companies want to be there. But that's not how they got there. They got there because the authorities they had to deal with wanted Coke's and Pepsi's water analysis and purification technology and Kentucky Colonel's technology for food preparation and preservation.

—RODERICK MACLEOD, *CHINA, INC.* (1988)

The case studies in the preceding four chapters carry a wealth of lessons. Chief among them are the need for solid planning, sound positioning, and effective negotiating. These, combined with realistic evaluation and healthy doses of patience and persistence, form the basis for a sound trade and investment strategy.

Of these points, preparation is perhaps the most essential, yet the easiest to overlook. Homework is not exciting. It takes time. Nonetheless, a China trade and investment strategy is only as good as the research that has gone into developing it.

Strategic Issues

Some corporations have gone into China on the strength of the personality and insights of one man, as in the case of John Marshall of 3M, or Hank Jones of Ag Midwest. Other companies, such as P&G, have sent platoons of scouts in relay to assay the territory. What the

two approaches have in common is that they are not improvised—
both fit within the overall strategic plan that the company has laid
out for international business in general, and China in particular.

Here are some of the questions companies such as these and
other successful businesses are likely to have asked themselves
before starting out:

1. Does China fit into our overall strategic plan, or is the main
reason for going simply because "everybody else is doing it"? Do we
want to be there simply because we don't want to be left out?

2. Have we had experience in other parts of Asia or at least in
developing countries, or will this be our first foray, making the
learning curve more challenging?

3. Can we accept a moderate degree of economic risk and a
fairly high degree of political risk? Are we comfortable enough to
operate in an atmosphere of bureaucratic regulations, uncertain
policies, and chronic lack of money? And in a place where the track
record of foreign involvement is just being built?

4. Must this business show results within the first few quarters? Must there be a return on investment target that is etched in
stone? Or are we willing to look at broader measures of performance
such as new sourcing, larger marketing network, better competitive
position, or greater market share?

5. Can we commit the staff and other resources to a China
project for as long as reasonably necessary? Are these available and
if not, is it viable to hire the required expertise, either directly or in
a consulting capacity? Will the effort have visible and consistent
high-level support? Is there one person in the company who can be
identified with our China effort over time?

6. Is the company philosophy, or that of the people who may
be assigned to China, one of "It'll be done this way, or it won't be done
at all"? Or can there be creativity and flexibility as long as the overall
objectives are being met?

7. Will the form of business under consideration be at least
somewhat familiar, or will the company have to pioneer a whole new
way of doing business, either for itself or for the Chinese?

These questions—and their answers—will take on a different
emphasis for different kinds of business, of course.

Small and medium-sized companies trying to trade with China
may have to focus much more directly on the bottom line—which
doesn't mean they shouldn't be in China. Experience shows such
companies do well in China, and may sometimes even have an edge
over their bigger brethren in that they are likely to have simpler
management structures (faster decision-making), greater flexibility
(when the Chinese change course, they can do so quickly), and a
more personal touch (highly regarded in China).

Those investing in China—which includes small companies as well as some of the biggest and most powerful companies in the world—have to adjust their sights to more long-term goals. For example, many of the companies successful in China mention the word "collaboration" as often as "bottom line." In other words, they have a high level of commitment to the process that allows them to become insiders over time. (The Chinese, of course, will play the "think of the long-term, Mr. Jones" theme to the hilt, seeking every ounce of pre-profit commitment they can. This is all the more reason to develop a sound strategic plan that includes realistic benchmarks for assessing progress.)

In the end, what counts in China is less the size or type of business than the ability to accurately evaluate the market's potential and make the necessary commitments in time, people, and money.

Looking at It from Their Perspective

Having looked in your own back yard, next look in China's. One of the lessons offered by experienced companies is that many CEOs—particularly of companies that are seeking to invest in China—overlook the fact that the objectives of their potential Chinese partner may be different from their own.

The foreign investor may want entry into the vast domestic market or may be looking for a low-cost production base. The Chinese, on the other hand, may see it as a chance to gain advanced technology, create further export opportunities, and get an infusion of badly needed capital.

The foreign company with technology to offer may be looking for a simple fee plus royalty arrangement. The Chinese, on the other hand, may want not just the technology, but help in finding a way to pay for it through a joint venture, licensing agreement, or other arrangement.

In general, the Chinese tend to look for companies that:

• can help them earn immediate foreign exchange—whether through outright purchase, countertrade, or export-oriented joint ventures;

• are willing to supply intermediate technologies and equipment that will help China's long-term export requirements; preferably, this technology and equipment will be provided within the context of a compensation trade, equity venture, or other flexible arrangement;

• have well-established products (as importers or exporters) with a worldwide reputation and strong market position and seem willing to commit themselves to long-term partnerships.

The point is that to minimize the clash of expectations, carefully investigate the real motives and objectives of the Chinese counterparts, and explicitly state your own.

Flexibility May Be Required

The case studies as well as the experience of others show that various levels of flexibility may be required, depending upon the business being pursued. For example, a company with broad international experience in sourcing raw materials, commodities, or labor will likely find China a relatively easy fit. The same can be said for importers who buy off-the-shelf or custom-produced products.

A somewhat greater degree of flexibility may be needed for those seeking to establish some type of countertrade or processing and assembly operation in China.

Sellers of technology or those wishing to sell directly to the Chinese domestic market may well find that a high degree of flexibility is required. For example, news stories have enthusiastically reported that Kentucky Fried Chicken sells more chicken in its Beijing outlet than anywhere else in the world. Yet KFC hasn't been taking out a dime of profit in foreign exchange. How feasible is that for your company? (PepsiCo, KFC's parent, uses profits to buy mushrooms, spices, and other products in China, which in turn are provided to other divisions such as Pizza Hut.)

Flexibility may be required in other ways as well. Several companies—such as Coca-Cola—have found it necessary to literally help invent the infrastructure required to support the venture. A foreign company might itself have to find refrigerators for its distributors, the electricity needed to run the plant, or the transportation required to get assembled parts to the closest port.

The most relevant question of all raised during the planning process often becomes, "Just how far are we willing to stray beyond business as usual?"

With these considerations in mind, the process of market research and lining up the required support network can begin.

The China Information and Support Network

Market research should be carried out long before trying to bang one's head against the Great Wall. As any of the executives involved in the projects discussed in the case studies can attest, there is no shortage of information available about China. But it won't be found by sitting in a hotel room in Beijing waiting for the phone to ring.

The main methods of research are little different from those that apply to other international ventures. Evaluating the information once it's gathered can also be done with relative ease, thanks to a sizable group of experienced analysts in business, trade organizations, and academia on both sides of the Pacific. Whether importer or exporter, small or large firm, a little homework will pay big dividends.

An introduction to the China information network begins with the basic China business library found in appendix 2. Several excellent business magazines and newsletters are devoted exclusively to China, including *The China Business Review*, *Business China*, *JETRO China Newsletter*, and *China Trade*. One can also keep current on China-related information in newspapers and business magazines through a number of databases (listed in appendix 2).

There is a great deal of institutional expertise in organizations ranging from professional associations (machinery, music, chemicals, aerospace, importers, etc.) to those that are China- or Asia-specific. The latter include the U.S.-China Business Council, National Committee on U.S.-China Relations, Asia Society, and so on. The American Chamber of Commerce in Hong Kong has a China Committee which has long been active, and there's now a chapter of the Chamber in Beijing. These organizations all offer seminars, luncheon meetings, private briefings, publications, business introductions, and more. Contact information for these organizations may be found in appendix 3.

Another tier of information in the U.S. starts with the International Trade Administration of the Department of Commerce and its branch offices in various states (information, trade leads, exhibition opportunities). There is also the Department of State's China desk and its embassy and consulates in China. The commercial section of the U.S. Embassy in Beijing is a particularly good resource.

Several states have excellent world trade organizations, some of which have nurtured China business through delegation visits, exhibitions, and more. Some groups publish specialized directories. New York State, for example, publishes a directory called "Global New York."

There is a great deal of expertise in academia. A number of universities have formal area-study centers on Asia or China (e.g., Harvard, Columbia, Michigan), and there are China experts with hands-on experience scattered throughout the country (the National Committee on U.S.-China Relations, noted above, is one source for locating such individuals).

China itself releases a flood of information. Extensive trade, investment, and general economic figures are available from the State Statistical Bureau and the Customs Administration. Although they're often one-dimensional, Chinese publications such as *China Daily*, a newspaper, and *Economic Reporter*, a weekly newsletter, are often found in corporate, academic, and institutional libraries (e.g., the U.S.-China Business Council).

Publications and reports put out by Chinese government ministries and other organizations often find their way to Hong Kong, which is itself a gold mine of information. Banks, industry groups, trade promotion organizations, and academic institutions all provide detailed and up-to-date reference information about the People's Republic. Standard Chartered Bank, for example, publishes an excellent newsletter with contributions from the legal firm of Baker & McKenzie as well as a Hong Kong-based China trade consulting firm.

▼ **Who Used What as Information Sources**

	Small Firms(%)	Large Firms(%)	All Firms(%)
U.S. Firms			
Department of Commerce	61.9	72.2	63.4
U.S.-China Business Council	42.9	71.4	53.6
Private Consultants	52.4	61.1	53.6
State agencies	52.4	53.6	51.2
Chinese government agencies	57.1	50.0	51.2
Regional/local China organizations	47.6	55.6	48.7
Trade associations	52.4	44.4	46.3
Chamber of Commerce	33.3	38.9	34.1
International accounting firms	28.6	30.9	31.7
Other	13.8	5.6	7.3
Japanese Firms			
Ministry of Int'l Trade and Industry	85.7	94.1	90.3
Banks	78.5	94.1	87.0
Ministry of Finance	78.5	88.2	83.8
Trading companies	71.4	94.1	83.8
Other firms	71.4	88.2	80.6
Trade associations	57.1	76.4	67.7
Chinese government agencies	42.8	41.1	41.9
International accounting firms	21.4	23.5	22.5
Prefectural agencies	14.3	5.8	9.6
Private consultants	0.0	5.8	3.2

Source: Roy F. Grow, from survey data. The survey question read: "Check the sources you used and evaluate the usefulness for the information they supplied."

▲

Getting Professional Help

Inhabiting the third tier of the information network are companies that specialize in market research or other types of consulting. Examples of the category include management consulting companies, law firms and accounting firms, as well as a handful of experienced China-trade consulting companies.

In addition to the types of firms mentioned above, specialized China expertise can be found in public relations firms, translation services, banks and financial institutions, and of course agents, distributors, and freelance sales representatives.

In addition to American firms, hundreds of Chinese companies, many attached to ministries or other government organizations, have established offices in Hong Kong and elsewhere abroad to facilitate contact. Many have hung out their shingle as consultants. Firms report mixed results in using them. Some are narrowly framed, unprofessionally staffed, and serve as a disguise for bringing business to their client ministry or company. Others, such as China United Resources (New York City), have their sponsors, but are quasi-independent and have been able to build a good track record of successful cooperation with well-known American firms.

Whether from a Chinese or American company, consulting help is not for everybody. Some companies—Procter & Gamble and Chrysler, for example, use them advantageously. Other companies don't believe in them. Again, it's a matter of knowing your own strengths and weaknesses.

Listings of agents and consulting companies can be found through trade groups (the U.S.-China Business Council, for example), and other organizations, such as those listed in appendix 3. An analysis on the use of specialized China trade consultants can be found in the sidebar.

▼ ## Use of China Trade Consultants

Whether you call them consultants, "helpmates" (Roderick Macleod), or "China craftsmen" (Nigel Campbell), there are people available who have the specialized China skills to help in all phases of a business. Over the years, their roles have changed. In the 1970s, they generally knew more about China than business, carrying out basic logistics, helping to educate a company, and speaking for the Chinese. Today, as both logistics and contacts in China come more easily, the handholding role has become secondary. The best of them act more like traditional management consultants, able to understand and facilitate the business requirements of both parties. Many also act as agents and traders.

A qualified consultant can:

• help carry out market research and identify the right companies and enterprises to talk to in China.

• define the limits of what a Chinese (and American) partner can and cannot do, and ascertain the *real* goals of the Chinese partner and help determine whether they mesh with the foreign company's strategies and objectives.

• Move quickly when a business opportunity has been identified.

• Facilitate communication by acting as a translator, by assisting in cross-cultural understanding, and by serving as a third-party facilitator who can conduct informal negotiations in the hall, dining-room, or office where the real deal is often structured.

In evaluating the abilities of the consultant, look beyond language ability and the promise of a "contact." Whether the person is an Anglo- or Chinese-American, language skills are no substitute for business acumen, and a "close friend" may mean a relationship that needs to be preserved rather than one that can be critically evaluated and exploited.

The best consultants are realistic and put their client's interests first. In other words, they are understanding but tough. Caution flags should go up at easy cynicism, or the promise of special "inside" connections. Good intermediaries— and the companies that employ them—know they are just that: they facilitate but do not become substitutes for sound strategic planning and effective relationship-building.

To summarize, excellent publications, helpful organizations, and special consultants are available to help you find the right way to enter the market and to keep you up-to-date with the ever-changing environment. The next step is to find the right way to make contact.

Finding Entry Points and Establishing Ties

Ties with China are established in dozens of ways. These range from cold calls on Chinese factories in far-off provinces to private parties with high government officials in Washington townhouses; from brochures provided as part of a government catalog show, to a CEO with a phalanx of aides descending on Beijing in a private jet for a banquet staged at the Great Hall of the People; from providing all the traffic police in Beijing with colorful logo-imprinted sun umbrellas to responding to a cold call request by a Chinese delegation to come and visit your plant or showroom in downtown Des Moines.

There is no *one* way to establish contact. A survey done by the Manchester Business School (U.K.) found that out of the 29 joint ventures surveyed, 11 started because the companies were already doing other forms of business in China, another 11 started through the use of middlemen, and six were launched because the Chinese approached them. Three came about because they searched out the opportunity on their own.

China will also take the initiative. A survey of small and medium-sized companies carried out by the China consultant Robert Engholm found that 59% of the firms had entered the China market after the Chinese solicited them directly. This usually happens when China is in search of a very specific piece of required technology, or trying to find new markets for their exports. In such cases, they consult embassies and trade offices abroad, use the networks established by branch trading or consulting companies operating in a foreign country, and comb industry directories and trade publications.

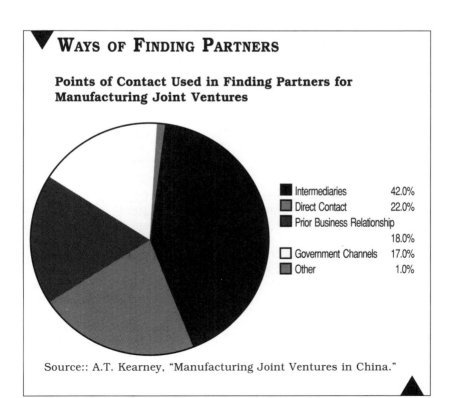

▼ WAYS OF FINDING PARTNERS

Points of Contact Used in Finding Partners for Manufacturing Joint Ventures

■ Intermediaries	42.0%
■ Direct Contact	22.0%
■ Prior Business Relationship	18.0%
□ Government Channels	17.0%
▨ Other	1.0%

Source:: A.T. Kearney, "Manufacturing Joint Ventures in China."

For those not wishing to wait for the mountain to come to Muhammad, a range of contacts in China are usually required to start business there. No single person, ministry, or organization controls the foreign trade and investment network. An importer looks for the trading corporation, agent *and* factory—then decides which is suitable. A seller looks for different potential end users in different parts of China as well as bureaucracies that oversee them. A joint venture involves a host of Chinese contacts in agencies at all levels, including officials in the relevant city, province or national bureaucracy.

Introductions and Contacts

Nowhere has the "who you know" syndrome been raised to so fine an art as in China. Close personal relationships (*guanxi*) are formed through kinship, schools, institutions, and long-term familiarity with business associates. The importance of *guanxi* is hard to exaggerate. It's the key to getting things done in China—from arranging a train ticket to a complex joint venture. (The use and abuse of *guanxi* in its various forms is a theme woven throughout this and the next few chapters.)

Introductions into the *guanxi* network can be accomplished through a wide variety of people and organizations, often used in concert with each other:

1. Important political figures (Henry Kissinger, Edward Heath) or well-known business personages (chairmen and CEOs of multi-nationals, heads of professional associations) who are "old friends" of China.

2. National, state, and local government officials who often lead business delegations to China as well as officials in the U.S. embassy in Beijing or consulates in various Chinese cities.

3. The trade and other organizations listed earlier in this chapter.

4. Executives from companies already in China as well as hired intermediaries—Chinese, foreign, and Hong Kong-based— who act as consultants, agents, representatives, distributors, and so on.

Business Delegations and Technical Seminars

An excellent method of getting introduced to potential partners is via business delegations and technical seminars. These take several forms.

High-level government delegations (governors, mayors, ministers, planners) often come at the invitation of semi-official exchange bodies, such as the U.S.-China Business Council and the National Committee on U.S.-China Relations in the U.S. and the China Council for the Promotion of International Trade or relevant Ministries, State Council bodies, and cities or provinces on the Chinese side.

General interest business delegations are also popular and have been organized by trade promotion groups, state and local governments, and other umbrella organizations on both sides. The Hong Kong branch of Standard Chartered Bank, for example, sponsored a series of "China Business Insights" tours in 1992. These visited joint ventures, met with officials, saw special trade zones, and were accompanied by consultants and experts. Such delegations are a useful way of getting to know China's priorities and business procedures, and a good method of building initial contacts.

More substantial business missions, which might be called "professional" or "technical" delegations, are commonly organized by Western professional societies (machinery, analytical instruments, water conservation, and so on). Their main agenda is usually the presentation of technical seminars (or in the case of Chinese delegations, specific shopping lists) which address end users and other personnel who make the basic decisions about adopting technology.

Finally, there's what might be called the "grand tour" seminar where top level Chinese government bodies sponsor or co-sponsor very expensive programs intended to lure top-level U.S. executives for some highly visible hobnobbing (see sidebar). These have abated since Tiananmen.

▼ SOME HIGH-LEVEL HOBNOBBING

Before Tiananmen made many top-level executives shy of being seen shaking the hands of China's leaders, the China International Trust and Investment Corporation, one of China's most powerful investment organizations, sponsored a gala event in Beijing. Its co-sponsor was the America-China Society, a group founded by Henry Kissinger and others.

At the conference, some specific investment projects were put forward, but the meetings were kept very general. Ron Yiren, CITIC's president, gave a speech which concluded that "Sino-U.S. relations have made gratifying progress." Not to be outdone, Dr. Kissinger said, "China is making an unprecedented transition from a centrally-planned economy to a socialist market-oriented economy."

Sixteen senior executives from 15 American companies attended (Xerox, American Express, Union Carbide were represented). None expected immediate business results, but all wanted to cement their ties to the *guanxi* network.

▲

Not all delegations or seminars are equally useful, but many can provide solid personal introductions that lead to business opportunities. Specific business is usually not undertaken at seminars, but they can help a company make strategic assessments and can supply contacts for future business discussions.

Exhibitions and Trade Shows

Exhibitions and trade shows offer an effective way of introducing a company to the market.

For exporters, there are now so many formal exhibitions that they border on overkill. In the spring of 1991, for example, there were four electronics shows in various parts of China within the space of two months. The problem is not the availability of venues as much as the need to carefully select the most appropriate ones. On the other hand, China held its first U.S. consumer goods fair in April 1992, which drew companies selling on the domestic market, including Pabst Brewing, Mars, Procter & Gamble, Campbell Soup, RJR Nabisco, and Nike.

Small and medium sized companies often start with catalog-only shows organized by the U.S. Department of Commerce or the world trade organizations of various states. Larger companies find taking a booth on-site effective to varying degrees. The Association for Manufacturing Technology, for example, served as the umbrella group for 30 U.S. companies participating in the China International Machine Tool Exhibition in Beijing in September 1991. According to the association, the companies brought a total of 13 containers of equipment and virtually all of the machines were sold.

That, plus the chance to meet relevant end users, is the reason many companies cite for participation. But it's also easy to find critics of these shows, who argue that there are too many (decentralization has meant more and more groups are authorized to hold such shows), that they do not always deliver the end users promised, and that fees, charges, corruption, and lack of buying power can make them unsatisfying. One participant in the Electronics China '91 exhibition ended up selling his equipment for RMB—useless to him, at least for now—to avoid excessive packing and return freight charges. "It just seems they do things that don't promote good relations. They are money hungry," he said.

▼ **EVALUATING AN EXHIBITION**

The U.S.-China Business Council surveyed a group of exhibition organizers and participants and came up with this valuable checklist for evaluating an exhibition.

• *How good are the organizer's credentials?* To judge this, look for timely and accurate China market information in the brochure, experience in holding exhibitions in that sector in China or other Third World countries.

• *Has the show been held before?* Request the post-exhibition report from the organizer to review the results, and talk to past exhibitors to hear their reactions.

• *Is the exhibition certified by the U.S. Department of Commerce?* Companies generally find Commerce's certification a reliable indicator of quality.

• *Who are the Chinese sponsors and how much money do they have to spend on purchases?* Exhibition firms often try to get support from one of China's ministries, since a ministry that endorses an exhibition also sets aside state funds to spend there. If the endorsing organization is merely a department within a ministry, less money will generally be available. And local support means only local funds will be spent.

• *Does your own market research confirm the organizer's figures? Are China's end-users ready to buy the equipment being exhibited?* Try to do some of your own market research. Good sources of information include the US-China Trade Council, relevant professional associations, and the Department of Commerce.

• *How much customer contact will there be?* Ask what the Chinese attendance promotion plan will include, and check to see if there will be adequate time to meet with key prospective customers. This contact can take place in meetings, private presentations, or banquets. Also, ask the organizer if you can invite people who are not on the official attendee list.

Source: Priscilla Totten, "Exhibitions at the Crossroads," *China Business Review,* July–August 1987.

▲

Chinese Export Fairs

For would-be China importers there are frequent and wide-ranging Chinese product shows held both within China and abroad.

Decentralization, specialization, and the loss of the monopoly held by MOFERT's foreign trade corporations has led to the staging of special fairs in all parts of China. Sometimes these are for specific commodities (down jackets, silk clothing, carpets, leather products). At other times, they are group events staged by individual cities or provinces to show off the export capability of a range of local factories.

Permanent showrooms and traveling trade shows also are to be found in the U.S. and other countries as China makes an effort to push forward its export strategy.

The grande dame of all Chinese trade shows is the Chinese Export Commodities Fair (better known as the Canton Fair). This event draws tens of thousands of traders, particularly overseas Chinese and other Asians. Held twice a year, the Canton Fair is China's main export window and an ideal venue for foreign buyers to be introduced to China's exports as well as its ways of doing business. The Fair is generally not for foreign sellers, although many long-time China traders attend simply to keep up with old contacts and the latest news.

While the Fair is an excellent and convenient opportunity to see products from every region, and an experienced staff is ready to help, there are some serious shortcomings. Trade fair reps no longer have control over production, so they have no record of other commitments and there is no way to determine the ability (or desire) of the manufacturer to supply this product. The Chinese often will not take seriously a buyer who does not visit the factory, which means orders placed at the Fair can remain in limbo unless personally followed up. Finally, prices at the Fair tend to be 20–30% higher than through local foreign trade corporations or direct from the factories.

▼ RECENT MAJOR EXHIBITIONS IN CHINA

Exhibition	Location	Organizer
China Science & Technology Fair	Shenzhen	Glahe International
Industrial Trade Fair '91	Shenzhen	Coastal International
Consumertech China '91	Shenzhen	Glahe International
Consumer, Gifts & Housewares	Shenzhen	Chinese Domestic Producers
21st INTERMED '91	Zhengzhou	Goodwill Trading
Hardware China '91	Shenzhen	Glahe International
Semiconductor China '91	Shanghai	Cahners
Water & Electric China '91	Shenzhen	Glahe International
Food China '91	Shenzhen	Glahe International
International Shoes & Leather	Guangzhou	Top Repute
Instruments China '91	Beijing	Adsale
Electronics China '91	Beijing	Adsale

Exhibition	Location	Organizer
22nd INTERMED '91	Hefei	Goodwill Trading
MICONEX '91	Shanghai	SHK International
Clock, Jewelry & Optics	Shenzhen	Chinese Domestic Producers
China Food '91	Shenzhen	SHK International
Textile & Leather '91	Shenzhen	Glahe International
Textile, Fashion & Garment Accessories	Shenzhen	Glahe International
Medical '91	Shanghai	Top Repute
Shanghaitex '91	Shanghai	Adsale
Medical China '91	Beijing	CIEC Exhibition
Intermedia China '91	Tianjin	Glahe International
China DIDAC '91	Tianjin	Glahe International
4th National Litchi Festival	Shenzhen	Glahe International

Establishing a Representative Office

It may seem as if the establishment of a formal representative office in China is the ultimate means of entry into the market. Even though a number of offices were shuttered in the wake of Tiananmen, the beginning of 1992 saw a record number of nearly 3,000 foreign representative offices in China, ranging from official bank branches to those kept by consultants.

Few, if any, companies have found success by *first* opening the office and then scouting the territory for business. The problem is not the availability of space (there is now a glut) or the lack of welcome. It is instead the cumbersome bureaucratic requirements involved, the great expense (upwards of $150,000 per year for an expatriate plus one local staff person), and the difficulty of hiring qualified local help.

In the opinion of many analysts, a representative office becomes justified only when it can offer substantial logistical support for ongoing business. Even then, many companies large and small choose to base their China office in Hong Kong. It's often less expensive to fly people in and out on a regular basis than to station them within the country, and communications and accommodations are far superior in Hong Kong.

Dealing with Corruption

For as long as humankind has been doing business, it's been inventing ways to "facilitate" it. Many feel the process has been perfected in Asia. In recent years China has moved from being a country where such practices were strictly outlawed and not carried on to one where everything imaginable seems to be tried—often without the subtleties that characterize the practice elsewhere.

Some companies report little problem with graft or corruption, others have had to cope with severe cases of it every step of the way. Almost all should be prepared to deal with it on both major and minor levels.

Experience shows it's best to be prepared for this contingency well in advance. Establish a well-defined policy, announce it loudly and consistently, and then stick to it no matter what the pressure.

Gifts

Before launching a discussion of corruption, it is worth pointing out that in China gift giving is often done voluntarily and with a genuine sense of sharing. Officially, Chinese government officials and employees are allowed to receive only token gifts. Unofficially, it gets infinitely more complex.

Pens, office items, appliances, consumer electronics, lavish banquets—the ladder of acceptable gifts has been continually extended. It all depends upon the manner of the giving. Automobiles cannot be accepted personally, but many have been given to companies, institutions, or government entities, making the present free from stigma. There is obviously a fine line here, and those found trespassing may get punished. The government has even executed trade officials for soliciting such gifts.

A gift in the form of a trip abroad is widely accepted provided the American company can offer it and the Chinese officials can accept it in the context of business. It has virtually become a prerequisite to negotiating a sale or a joint venture that the Chinese side expects to make a personal visit to the foreign company's facilities, not just once to inspect the technology and equipment first-hand, but perhaps several times. Extras are often thrown in— shopping expeditions with the company picking up the tab, or a side trip to Hawaii, Paris, or the Barrier Reef and, of course, a mandatory stopover in Hong Kong on the way home.

Perhaps the ultimate gift is education. The Chinese government actively encourages professionals (young and middle-aged) to gain further education abroad. Since neither the individual or his unit can afford the expenses involved (air fare, living allowance, tuition), many companies have sponsored individuals whom they met in the course of business negotiations.

Westinghouse Electric has sent more than 500 Chinese engineers to the U.S. for advanced schooling. AT&T brings critical contacts for its future business to the U.S. and involves them in its "Tomorrow's Leaders" program. Because a range of logistics and permissions are involved, the foreign company can be assured that this type of gift, when accepted, has official blessing.

The gift of education can also be established within China's borders. Joint ventures have found the recruitment of qualified talent to be one of their most severe challenges. They have turned to leading Chinese universities and institutes for help in identifying potential junior managers. As part of this effort, several foreign companies have established scholarship or other programs at these educational institutions to promote the development of talent. This kind of gift, too, is warmly welcomed.

Corruption

When is it a gift, and when is it corruption? A decade of experience in the "new" China gives no clear guidelines. In some ways American traders have an advantage in the Foreign Corrupt Practices Act. This act, while itself confusing, at least provides a legitimate reason for refusing overt solicitations such as the demand for an off-the-books fee just prior to the signing of the contract. Unfortunately, such principled stands do not solve the complex web of corruption that has engulfed China.

Money talks. Everything seems for sale. And foreigners can pay. These are the attitudes widely reported by companies doing business in China in the early 1990s. Side deals to import-export trade are so manifold that money parked outside the country may reach tens of billions of dollars. According to unofficial estimates published in *Business China*, in 1990 foreign exchange earnings on exports were to surge by $20 billion. Actual reserves grew only $11 billion. The rest, traders say, is in third-country accounts.

China has committed great resources to combat corruption. Four ministries, employing more than 360,000 people, regularly devote the majority of their efforts to controlling graft, says *Business China*. In the past few years, thousands of companies have been audited, including large and powerful enterprises such as CITIC. One of them, Kanghua Development Corporation, was shut down. Trading companies run by relatives of top government leaders also have been shut down. All in all, the late 1980s saw 537 companies closed and 3,975 others forcibly separated from their ministry associations.

Despite these efforts, corruption flourishes, and seems to go farther and deeper every time yet another crackdown ends. There are many reasons, including low salaries, bureaucracies wielded as personal fiefdoms, the inefficiency of normal business procedures, and much more.

As long as decisions continue to be based more upon personal power than economic choice—in other words, based more upon *guanxi* than merit—traders and investors are likely to have to face corruption without letup.

TYPES OF CORRUPTION

There are probably as many types of corruption as there are types of tea, but they fall into some general patterns.

Payments to facilitate, maintain, or improve business

In international bidding, a winner may be decided even before the bidding starts because of special under-the-table payments. People with purchase orders shop around and begin negotiations. Suddenly the deal goes to someone else and all they're told is that the reasons are "technical" or "commercial" or "political." In fact, the deal has gone to the person "savvy" enough to have offered a kickback.

A variation occurs during joint venture negotiations when, just as everything seems completed, the Chinese side asks for a kickback on part of its equity contribution.

By far the most common form of corruption is the solicitation of trips abroad. It's one thing to offer trips and the extras associated with them as gifts during the negotiations or as incentives for good performance. On the other hand, reports abound of Chinese enterprises demanding such favors *as a condition* of the negotiations or the contract.

Trips abroad may seem a marginal case in the current environment. Many other requests are not. Direct requests are made for support for the education of the children of officials, cars, and more. Some exporters have found contracts made out for 1–10% above the negotiated price with the factory. The difference, the understanding goes, is to be deposited in a company or bank outside of China by the foreign company.

Greasing the wheels of the bureaucracy

The partner will not be the only one with his hand out. He is caught in the web of a larger system, and the other actors want their share.

Ministry officials sometimes pass the word to favor one particular Chinese trading company or consulting company over another. Customs officials hold up shipments until they are taken for a day of shopping at the foreign exchange store, an evening banquet, and a night at a plush foreign hotel. The black market offers inspection certificates used by the Commodity Inspection Bureau, complete with signatures and seals, for $200.

Quotas for restricted goods can be circumvented by a Hong Kong company whose representative office in a port city is staffed by "public relations" girls to "make friends." After a night on the town, the morning sees a flurry of contracts.

The ever-popular trips abroad are requested not only by the Chinese partner, but by the people with whom he has to do business.

One large American joint venture partner regularly brings officials from the Tax Bureau, the Commerce and Industry Bureau, and other in-country agencies to Hong Kong to "discuss problems." No money is passed out in this case, but it's an all-expense-paid trip, with lots of entertainment and gifts.

One report told of a Letter of Credit (L/C) for the sale of some spare parts to a chemical factory that was continually postponed. Finally, the Chinese customer suggested to the foreign company that it should invite some bank officials overseas for an inspection tour. A week after the invitation was extended, the bank issued the L/C.

Being held up for fees and favors

The outstretched hand seems everywhere. That can be the case in any part of the world, but it can often seem more aggressive and intrusive in China: the taxi driver who demands his cash off the meter as a condition of the ride; a Chinese business associate who asks you, just before you enter the negotiating rooms, to exchange his RMB for your foreign exchange certificates or dollars so he can buy a VCR on the export market.

In trading companies and joint ventures, relatives of officials need a little extra help. Payrolls suddenly expand to include a dozen more people.

Then there's the institutional corruption. Foreigners are forced to pay double or more for airplane and train tickets, food, and any and all business services. Fees, levies, and charges come up for reasons known and unknown, obvious, and obscure. They are just as likely to appear during the process of hiring local employees as they are when making airplane reservations.

COPING WITH CORRUPTION

Some estimate one-third to one-half of all deals now signed in China involve some form of obvious corruption. But while corruption is a factor in many deals, it certainly is not so for every one.

Many companies clearly state their policies against such practices. If well-known and big enough, they don't need to get involved. This is especially true in joint ventures, where the partners are supposed to live with each other for a long time and the operations are pretty much in the open.

The biggest danger comes in one-time deals, where buyers, sellers, and middlemen can get in and get out quickly. The attitude often seems to be, if one can get away with it, why not?

Does one fight it, or join it? Every company must provide its own answers and set its own standards. The important thing is to let those standards be clearly known to all involved in the negotiations, both Chinese and foreign. If they are violated, say so at the time, and say it clearly and explicitly. There's a good chance the Chinese side will back off from the demand (or get more creative about soliciting it).

If the Chinese partner persists in trying to break the standards you have set, the advice from experienced China hands is to withdraw, for moral, legal, and business reasons. Once the cycle starts it's hard to break, and a "just this one time" can sound mighty hollow.

✦ ✦ ✦

Having developed a sound strategic plan for entering the market, it now becomes important to position the company properly within the system. This is the lesson offered in chapter 9.

Sound Positioning

*The way China is organized for administrative and eco-
nomic purposes can be described in terms of Western
corporate organization: every economic unit belongs to and
reports to a higher unit of a huge conglomerate [known as]
"China, Inc." This provides a familiar and orderly framework to help Westerners organize information about their
Chinese counterparts—not only where they fit into their
organizations, but what they are doing and why they do it.*

—RODERICK MACLEOD, *CHINA INC.* (1988)

After good planning comes good positioning. This is the second
major theme to emerge from the experience of companies successful
in China. Faced with a bewildering set of choices, the ability to
choose the right place and pick the right partner within the
conglomerate that is China, Inc. is an essential component of the
business strategy.

Charting A Course Through The Trade Maze

The picture drawn in chapter 3 of the foreign trade and investment
structure in China is idealized. While it may look clear on canvas,
actual experience reveals it to be more chaotic. Order will emerge
through the making of two key decisions: (1) which form of trade is
best suited to your business plan, and (2) what organizations can
best fulfill the plan's goals.

Forms of Trade Revisited

If the business arrangement is limited strictly to buying or
selling, then all that's left to decide is where to enter the structure
(see next section). But for those considering various types of flexible

trade arrangements, such as countertrade and compensation trade, some evaluation is in order.

Countertrade (also known as counterpurchase), for example, has been promoted by the Chinese in theory, but has been difficult to orchestrate in practice. Unless the foreign company is experienced in this field, the complications can become enormous.

The vertical nature of the Chinese bureaucracy creates natural obstacles to working horizontally across the other ministries or trade entities that typically need to become involved in a countertrade deal. Reform-induced decentralization and the growing independence of factories and their trade reps makes the job of coordination even more difficult. Add the lack of an effective national countertrade policy and a central mechanism to facilitate it, and there remains more enthusiasm than incentive.

Compensation trade, on the other hand, has had a good track record. It provides some of the advantages of an equity venture (access to an inexpensive labor pool and direct control over the production process, for example) without the attendant legal, financial, and other entanglements. Indeed, many companies use this approach as a stepping stone to a joint venture. It allows them to learn how to operate in China as well as the chance to thoroughly evaluate the competence of the potential partner before expanding their commitment. (See, for example, the Xerox and Polaroid case studies.)

Hurdles such as lack of efficiency, quality, and other management issues apply to compensation trade arrangements, of course, but the biggest drawback for some might be the expectation on the Chinese side that a healthy amount of technology transfer will come with the deal. Given both the cultural legacy (chapter 10) and the overall principles that govern trade and investment (chapter 3), the Chinese will try to avoid deals, which, in their eyes, ask them only to be someone else's sweatshop.

Priority in compensation trade deals is therefore given to foreign companies willing to undertake the technical revamping of existing enterprises and provide the advanced technology needed to make export-oriented products. This holds equally true for light industrial projects, such as the assembly of hair dryers, and for technology-intensive industries such as aerospace. Having decided on the type and form of business to be done, the next step is to chart a course through the maze of trade organizations.

Charting the Course[1]

Whether buying, selling, or engaging in some form of countertrade, a basic decision on where to enter the trade structure must be made. This section evaluates the relative merits of dealing

---

[1] This section is largely the work of Julie Reinganum, President, Pacific Rim Resources.

with the various types of foreign trade corporations (FTCs), industrial corporations, and other entities in the system.

Decentralization, reform, and the explosion of foreign trade corporations have thrown all the neat organizational assumptions of the early and mid-1980s into confusion. No longer can the foreign importer or exporter identify potential suppliers or end users by working exclusively with officials of well-delineated foreign trade corporations. No longer does the physical location of the customer or supplier provide a guide to the selection of the trading partner.

Now the foreign trader must understand both the current formal trade structure, the history of each trading company, and the backgrounds of the individuals who manage these entities. Buyers must decide whether it is better to approach the central FTC in Beijing or the local FTC branch . . . or go directly to the manufacturer . . . or work with industrial trading companies . . . or hook up with one of the new foreign trade enterprises not formally linked to anybody.

Sellers must decide whether to try to work directly with the end user, rely on an FTC or industrial trading corporation as a sales agent or distributor, or use an entrepreneurial independent third party.

Each option has clear advantages and disadvantages, and the trader must understand them all in order to shape the most workable and advantageous deal.

OPTION 1: THE CENTRAL FTCs

Going to the head office of a foreign trade corporation offers the convenience of working with a single, experienced central organization that has an established infrastructure to deal with foreign buyers and sellers. The national-level FTCs can also do legwork for foreign traders, contact provincial and municipal FTCs, and scout factories around the country to help find desired products or customers.

Buying

Relying on the national FTCs to purchase Chinese products has some strong points. The government still gives these trading companies major allocations of certain products, particularly raw materials and commodities. Moreover, factories new to the export market sometimes turn to the FTCs because they have a wide customer network.

On the other hand, dealing with a national FTC may also involve significant risk in terms of reliability, sourcing, quality, and delivery time. Often factories give FTCs the lesser quality products they cannot sell themselves and the trading corporations may not have access to the desired products or end users. Scarce products, for example, are often sold only by the manufacturers or local FTCs. A national FTC that formerly handled most of China's exports of vitamins A and E, for example, had only a 25% share of the export volume in 1988, and none the following year—all were handled by factories or other trading companies.

Another drawback is that the national FTC, which must contract with the manufacturer, may not be well acquainted with the product's technical specifications, meaning traders may not get what they ordered.

The FTCs demand a premium for handling the sale of export products. Sometimes their high prices reflect what they think is world demand. Most often, they're trying to cover their operating costs, now that the government no longer subsidizes them.

Dealing with the national (as well as regional) FTCs can also present an administrative risk. The government is spinning these organizations completely out of MOFERT's orbit, leaving them to sink or swim on their own. Experience suggests that in many cases their bloated bureaucracies may not survive the pressures of the market.

●●●●●●●●●●●●●●●●●●●●●●●●●●

SCORECARD: Buying through the national FTC network

+	Experience
+	Access to products nationwide
+	Access to government allocations
+	Telecommunications and translation facilities
−	Inflexibility
−	Expense
−	Less dependable quality and delivery
−	In transition

▼ **Sometimes, They Can Get It for You Wholesale**

There may be a hidden and little-known benefit in buying from a national foreign trade corporation. For example, a company looking for graphite might initially turn to a JV that produces it. They're quoted a good price, since they've been dealing with this JV for some years. Yet, catching wind of these negotiations, the local branch of the state trading corporation (in this case the

China National Metals and Minerals Corporation) tells the foreign company they can get the same graphite from the same source at a 20% discount from the JVs best price.

Too good to be true? Not in China, where finding ways around the system is elevated to an art form. Here's how it works. Lesson One: FTCs buy product in RMB, which they borrow from the bank. They then sell the product abroad for foreign exchange. To encourage such exports, the government gives the FTCs an important incentive—bring in the foreign exchange, and you can claim a tax rebate. This rebate becomes the FTC's hidden profit.

In this case, by offering the discount, the FTC is subsidizing the sale by giving up their profit. Why would it be willing to do this? Lesson Two: FTCs exist because they are given allocations. Say they had 500 tons to sell this year. If they sell only 400 tons, then the government will give them no more than that next year, figuring someone else can do a better job of selling it. The FTC doesn't want to lose the allocation, so to make quota they will offer a discount equivalent to the tax rebate.

Of course, in the vast majority of cases, they've sold their allocation well before the end of the fiscal year (January–December), but sometimes there's a window of opportunity. The smart foreign buyer will get the best price possible from the source, then check with a national or regional FTC handling that product just in case the price they can get from the middle-man is better than the price from the source.

▲

Selling

Historically, the national foreign trade corporations have played a major role in the procurement of chemicals and other commodity products imported into China. In this capacity, the FTCs often will supply information on requirements, and they may be called upon by a variety of different Chinese organizations to fill spot purchase requirements.

Despite this important liaison function, the national FTCs have never been the best way to sell product to China. Because the end user is screened from the seller, the foreign company gains little insight into what the customer requires and little feedback on how well the product is received. (This is also a disadvantage to the buyer, of course, and hence the reason so many factories, institutes, and other entities will try their best to deal directly with foreign suppliers.) In addition, if the FTC locates a less expensive source of supply, it will switch suppliers with little regard for factors that differentiate products.

●●●●●●●●●●●●●●●●●●●●●●●●●●●●●●

SCORECARD: Selling through the national FTCs

+	Major purchasing agent
+	Information source
+	Purchasing authority
+	Overseas offices
–	No direct budget
–	Rarely initiates purchases
–	Little or no familiarity with Chinese customer requirements
–	Little loyalty to foreign or domestic customers

OPTION 2: LOCAL FTCs

Working with a local FTC promises some of the advantages of working with a national trade corporation, along with the added benefit that a local FTC has a closer relationship to the manufacturer. In addition, a local FTC's ties to a broad range of hometown suppliers may enable it to help local manufacturers obtain the scarce raw materials, resources, and utilities needed to satisfy production requirements.

Buying

If you know which cities or provinces produce the items you want, the local FTC can be very helpful in introducing you to specific factories. Proximity also gives these organizations more influence over the production process, giving the buyer a more direct and effective role in solving problems.

●●●●●●●●●●●●●●●●●●●●●●●●●●●●

SCORECARD: Buying from the local FTC

+	Effective troubleshooting
+	Access to raw materials
+	Ability to get scarce local products
–	Inexperience
–	Parochialism
–	Lack of nationwide access to products

Offsetting the advantages of proximity, local FTCs may have problems related to their small size and relative inexperience. The local FTC is unlikely to have access to producers in other regions, for example, and many local FTCs are new to the export business and may lack experience handling international financial arrangements, contracts, and transportation (this is more true of inland FTCs than those based in large cities such as Shanghai).

Selling

Foreign companies wishing to sell to China will find that local FTCs tend to be less active in signing foreign product contracts. This is because they rarely have access to the foreign exchange necessary, or contact with potential foreign exporters. Chinese buyers

● ●

SCORECARD: Selling through the local FTCs

+	Close to customer
+	Understands local conditions and requirements
+	Industry knowledge
+	Technically competent
–	Lack of overseas presence
–	Does not make volume commodity purchases

usually work through the national FTCs for these reasons. A local FTC can be useful, however, in that once the sale is made, it can provide a link to the domestic distribution network, which in turn may provide further sales leads.

OPTION 3: INDUSTRIAL TRADING CORPORATIONS

Industrial ministries and bureaus now also administer trading corporations that have the authority to work directly with foreign traders (see chapter 3). Working with these entities assures a thorough understanding of the products being traded. In most cases, the staff of these corporations have technical experience in either product research and development or manufacturing. Such knowledge provides thorough and easy communication between the trader, the industry bureau, and even the factory itself.

These ties can be either an advantage or a drawback. If there is a longstanding dispute between factory and bureau, for example, it may affect business. It is therefore important to understand the relationship between the industry bureau and a specific manufacturer as quickly and thoroughly as possible.

Although technically competent, the industrial trading corporations (ITCs), like the local foreign trade corporations (FTCs), generally do not have access to products outside their geographic location, and they are also new to the foreign trade game. Still, many traders prefer ITCs to FTCs because the ITCs have a greater knowledge of the industry and are rapidly gaining experience in foreign trade.

Industrial trading corporations are only beginning to build a track record of purchasing foreign equipment. But because of their sophisticated product knowledge and because the government is encouraging these corporations to become Japanese-style *keiretsu*—trading companies encompassing manufacturing, trading, and investing—their overall importance in the foreign trade picture cannot help but grow.

OPTION 4: DEALING FACTORY-DIRECT

●●●●●●●●●●●●●●●●●●●●●●●●●●●●●

SCORECARD: Dealing with ITCs

+	Product and industry knowledge
+	Sophisticated technical background; familiar with purchasers' requirements
+	Administrative relationship with producers
+	Growing clout on the foreign trade scene
−	Lack of access to producers in other industries
−	Lack of access outside own geographic locations
−	Lack of experience

Dealing with a factory is of course the most direct way to buy or sell in China, but there are pitfalls. FTCs have been known to recommend factories without a track record, leaving the trader to provide the necessary education—an expensive and time consuming process. Independent research (through directories such as the *China Directory of Industry and Commerce*, or representatives of industries or provinces stationed abroad, for example) is recommended, as is the use of an experienced foreign intermediary.

Buying

Buying factory-direct is advantageous because it allows a direct working relationship with the producer. Product changes, delivery schedules, and other adjustments can be made much more easily, since the factory representative has a better understanding of the production process than the FTC as well as direct control over schedule and quality.

On the down side, the manufacturer may have even less experience than the local FTC when it comes to the mechanics of foreign trade. Also, the manufacturers have little clout in getting raw materials from other factories, and in certain areas of short supply they may have to pay more for the material than a central FTC, which has a state-allocated quota.

Local manufacturers are just learning to implement transactions with the help of the FTCs, so there may be few, if any, support services (telecommunications, interpreters, and so on).

●●●●●●●●●●●●●●●●●●●●●●●●●●●

SCORECARD: Buying directly from the factory

+	Flexibility in production
+	Technical understanding of the product
+	Better quality control
−	Inexperience
−	Lack of communications, translation facilities
−	Lack of access to raw materials

Selling

As more factories become familiar with overseas purchasing practices, directly approaching potential customers for your products is gradually becoming a viable business practice. The end user generally is best informed on product requirements and can contact the other entities required to conclude a purchase contract. Working with the end user also provides the trader with information needed to put together a realistic proposal for product sales.

Unfortunately, the end user does not usually have control of the foreign exchange budget, nor does it have final decision-making authority. Before entering negotiations with factories, find out who has the budget and who else is involved in the purchasing decision. Then include them in discussions as appropriate.

●●●●●●●●●●●●●●●●●●●●●●●●●●●●

SCORECARD: Selling directly to the factory

+	Understanding of production needs
+	Understanding of the regulatory environment
−	Lack of access to required foreign exchange
−	Lack of familiarity with purchasing procedures
−	Lack of clout with government apparatus

OPTION 5: INDEPENDENT ENTERPRISES

By far the most entrepreneurial—but also the most risky—companies dealing in foreign trade are the independent enterprises that have been authorized to handle trade. Such enterprises usually stand out because of their high degree of staff motivation, flexibility, and ability to solve the maze of foreign trade riddles. Highly personal, they can be very well connected and can move within the bureaucracy much faster than the FTCs.

The reliability of these enterprises, whether subsidiaries of central government trading companies or private companies funded on a shoestring, is very difficult to assess. Their success or failure often depends solely on the capabilities of one individual and his *guanxi*.

One such company in Shenzhen, for example, was able to work out an arrangement with a Hong Kong company to import feed additives on behalf of a Chinese customer. The end user did not have access to foreign exchange. The Shenzhen company accepted the local Chinese currency payment and made arrangements to bring in the product. So far so good. But the Shenzhen company imported the products before they had been properly registered with the Ministry of Agriculture, which disallowed entry.

●●●●●●●●●●●●●●●●●●●●●●●●●●●●

SCORECARD: Dealing with "briefcase" companies

+	Strongly motivated; willing to solve problems
+	Good connections with key bureaucracies
−	Inexperience and lack of reputation
−	Lack of communications, translation facilities
−	Difficult to evaluate credibility
−	Short-term oriented; can disappear quickly
−	No recourse in case of defects or other problems

Although attractive for a one-time sale, this option may be costly in several ways, and not in the long-term interest of the foreign seller. The government tends to clamp down regularly on these so-called "briefcase" companies.

▼ **A "BRIEFCASE" DEAL GONE SOUR**

Making a quick deal through an entrepreneurial middleman can be tempting, but, as a large agricultural processing firm found out, also risky. The company, which had had long experience in China, needed a blend of two grains grown in China's western provinces. The deal was worth over $2 million.

The company's resident representative in Beijing was approached by a Chinese individual who represented himself as a former ministry employee now out on his own. He seemed intimately familiar with the product as well as the producers and assured the company he could fulfill the contract exactly to specifications—a mixture of at least 80% Grade A, and no more than 20% of Grade B.

The arrangements were made and a payment transferred. When the first third arrived, however, it was only 40% Grade A. Angry with this violation of the contract, and unable to use this mix, the foreign company held the Beijing trader to account. Without flinching he told them that there was no more supply of Grade A and that they'd have to make do.

The foreign company was enraged. It complained loudly and publicly, and started a lawsuit. But all they had was this man's business card, which, they later found out, had an address of a small lane in Beijing. The foreign company had tried a shortcut from which they had absolutely no recourse. Lesson: Investigate your partner. ▲

Which Option Is Right?

Before choosing a Chinese trade agent or arrangement, answer several questions for yourself about the products being traded.

For Buyers

Does the product's quality need to be consistent? Products easily purchased in China have many potential sources, but quality often varies greatly. The best protection is to deal with the factory, since FTCs have had the habit of promoting products based on considerations other than quality. Of course, if you or the factory have had a long-standing relationship with an FTC, use it.

Are raw materials required to make the product? If the products or materials to be used in the manufacture of an export item need to be imported from abroad, it's best to work with local, regional, or national FTCs (which have the needed expertise as well as the authority). If these raw materials are available domestically, a local enterprise will be more helpful in finding supply.

Is there a local price for the product? When the FTCs were still subsidized, they had the flexibility to make the export price competitive with the local price. With the removal of such subsidies, it's best to work with local enterprises, since they themselves can do all the acrobatics involved in getting the product out at a reasonable price. Of course, there are always exceptions, as shown in the sidebar "Sometimes They Can Get It for You Wholesale" in this chapter.

Is a Chinese export license required? If so, the FTC system is better qualified to arrange such deals, since MOFERT sets and implements trade policy and oversees the approval process.

Which company has historically handled the product? In the past, FTCs would command factories to produce a specific quantity. Now the system has been turned on its head and it's the factory tells the FTC how much of its product it is willing to allocate and to whom. Talk to the people who make the product, since they now control the source. Do realize that factories that have exported their products successfully through a particular channel (whether or not it is an FTC) will be loath to change that channel.

For Sellers

Is the product purchased on a commodity basis? Since FTCs have traditionally played a strong role in this area, they will probably be valuable sources of information. Commodity products are often used across a range of industries in China, but are purchased centrally. If this is the case, it may be useful to work with both the FTC and an industrial trading corporation from the start.

Does the product require technical support? Industrial trading corporations, new enterprises, and end users are always eager to learn about product specifications and will be a receptive audience. They may also provide a good base for uncovering future distribution channels in the broader Chinese market.

Does the product need to be registered? Many commodities must be registered with the appropriate Chinese ministry. For example, pharmaceuticals must be approved by and registered with the Ministry of Public Health. In these situations, working with industrial trading corporations may expedite the approval process.

Does the product require an import license? If so, checking with an FTC is a good first step. Although it may not be the entity that buys the product, the FTC can provide information on the regulations.

Sorting through the trading options can be laborious. If done correctly, it can also be profitable. Doing your homework at this stage helps to avoid problems later and permits a strategy that uses the strengths of each of the entities involved.

The general rule of thumb is: Work with the partner closest to the product's source whenever possible and evaluate the entity carefully.

Charting a Course Through the Investment Minefield

Investment in China has been the subject of much negative reporting. Yet surveys show that despite real problems and many frustrations, most companies are satisfied. Some are very happy indeed—although for competitive and other reasons, they choose not to say so publicly.

The U.S.-China Business Council determined that about half of the 50 American ventures they contacted in early 1989 (a psychological low point for investors, see chapter 3) were profitable, at least in local currency. Most others were satisfied with their market position. Chinese officials claim 85% of all equity ventures in China are profitable.

Part of the road to success is finding the form of investment most suited to a company's China strategy. The rest is the ability to navigate around a number of key issues.

Investment Forms Revisited

Investment in China has gone through two phases and is entering a third. During the first phase, from 1979 through 1985, joint ventures were primarily geared to those that could earn foreign exchange—hotel and real estate ventures, provision of oil and equipment services, and some light industrial processing for export. The excellent report, *U.S. Investment in China*, issued by the U.S.-China Business Council, makes it clear that during this period China did not generally welcome and did not facilitate manufacturing investment projects that would compete with China's own enterprises for customers.

The next phase, 1986 through 1988, saw China liberalize the rules to encourage broader forms of investment; the country also took steps to help solve the issue of foreign exchange repatriation (for example, by the creation of currency swap centers). Manufacturing companies could now enter the "import substitution" market, allowing them to sell product on the domestic market as long as there was no comparable Chinese-made product available or when the product qualified as "technically advanced."

Consumer giants were even welcomed. Among the American

▼ THE LEGAL ENVIRONMENT FOR INVESTMENT

China does not share the West's history of legal tradition. Since opening the doors to foreign investment, however, it has made a systematic if incomplete effort to safeguard the interests of Western investors. China's constitution promises to protect the "lawful rights and interests" of foreigners. It has signed a series of bilateral treaties with foreign countries (including the U.S.) providing for the mutual protection and promotion of investment. A pending amendment to the Joint Venture Law would permit expropriation only under certain circumstances and with adequate compensation. Finally, China has recently agreed to join the international intellectual property rights conventions.

As to the legal code, there are five types of law applicable to foreign companies that invest in China:

• National legislation promulgated by the National People's Congress, the State Council, and other organs of the central government. Frequently such legislation is termed "provisional" or "interim," to suggest its experimental nature.

• Legislation at the municipal and provincial level which supplements (but may or may not be consistent with) national provisions. Additional laws are often passed to guide and control foreign investment at this level.

• Legislation applied by analogy. Where no specific implementing regulations apply, Chinese officials have applied other laws by analogy.

• Regulations which are internal (*neibu*) and unavailable to foreigners, but which are nevertheless applied. Sometimes these are "trial balloons" for forthcoming laws, at other times they seem to be created and applied in an arbitrary manner to cover uncertain circumstances.

• Models, such as sample contracts for joint ventures, have also been created. These provide a common structure upon which negotiations can be based.

▲

---

firms taking advantage of this new policy were Coca-Cola, PepsiCo, Procter & Gamble, Squibb, H. J. Heinz and S. C. Johnson. The experience thus far of these and hundreds of other firms suggests that the ability to establish a manufacturing and sales presence in China—and to see steady growth in market volume—has more than made up for the frustrations experienced by many (if not most) of them during the negotiations and even for the initial period of low profitability.

The third phase of investment, now underway, was begun by government policies that had the effect of partially restricting access to the domestic market. The emphasis has also shifted from simply expanding capacity for its own sake (i.e., building new plants and facilities) to better utilization of existing capacity. The Chinese seem to be redoubling their efforts to attract large, top-ranked foreign firms that can bring suitable advanced technology.

All in all, the changes seem to augur well for a more rational approach, both in terms of the goals set and the policies and attitudes required to implement them. The virtual elimination of the balance-of-foreign-exchange problem and willingness to formally respect intellectual property rights are two clear indicators of the new attitudes.

As with the trading structure above, we now look at some of the pros and cons of the various types of investment vehicles. A more complete discussion of their structure is in chapter 3.

▼ ORGANIZATIONS THAT COORDINATE INVESTMENT

High-level organizations within the Chinese government bureaucracy that are involved in the planning, coordination, and approval of foreign investment include:

• *State Council Group on Foreign Investment.* An organ within the State Council, this body coordinates new investment policies among the ministries. A small group, it has little significance for day-to-day business.

• *Social Economic State Planning Commission.* This key body, also directly under the State Council, was formed through the merger of the State Planning Commission and the State Economic Commission in 1988 (the entities remain separate at the provincial and local level). It formulates investment policies and regulations, grants initial project approvals for large-scale projects in the provinces and municipalities, approves import substitution applications, and runs the Foreign Investment Enterprises Administration.

• *Ministry of Foreign Economic Relations and Trade.* MOFERT approves joint ventures and other investment contracts, approves export licenses and technology equipment contracts, among other responsibilities.

• *State Administration of Exchange Control.* The SAEC is another key organization in the investment structure. It approves profit repatriation and oversees the various procedures for exchanging the technically nonconvertible Renminbi for foreign currency.

• *Other Entities.* The State Administration of Industry and Commerce grants the all-important business license and sets debt/equity ratios. The Ministry of Labor and Ministry of Personnel deal with blue-collar employment issues. The State Tax Bureau collects the tax.

Equity Joint Ventures[2]

The EJV has achieved solid status within the trade and investment structure. The sheer number of such ventures means there is precedent to learn from, and that the legal framework has been well established.

● ●

SCORECARD: Advantages and disadvantages of the EJV

+	The laws and implementing regulations provide a relatively complete structure of rules and procedures
+	Many incentives are offered at both the national and local levels for this type of investment
+	There is often competition among regions for EJVs and concessions can often be negotiated
+	EJVs may provide a vehicle for selling into the local market
+	EJVs are eligible for raw material allocations (if required) & may be able to negotiate goods at subsidized state prices
−	The negotiation process may stretch out for years and can often be complex, frustrating, and expensive (although some EJVs are negotiated in a matter of months)
−	Investors are restricted from withdrawing registered capital during the life of the contract
−	Issues regarding the termination and liquidation of EJVs have not been fully addressed either by laws and regulations or in practice

Contractual Joint Ventures

All the regulations governing CJVs have been incorporated into the overall body of laws governing foreign investment (previously separate legislation and specialized regulations governed CJVs).

Although in most respects the contractual joint venture re-

---

[2] This section owes its structure and major points to the *Special Report on U.S. Investment in China*, published by the U.S.-China Business Council in 1989.

sembles the EJV in structure and operation, the legal difference is that CJVs are treated as limited liability entities with legal person status and the partners remain separate legal entities and bear liability independently.

●●●●●●●●●●●●●●●●●●●●●●●●●●●●

SCORECARD: Advantages and disadvantages of the CJV

+	Maximum flexibility in structuring assets, organization, and management
+	Registered capital is recoverable during the life of the contract
+	Can be created and dissolved with minimal legal restrictions
+	No minimum investment is required
−	CJVs do not have as much precedent in China as EJVs, and Chinese partners are more reluctant to enter into them
−	The tax rate of CJVs is somewhat higher

Wholly Foreign-Owned Ventures

As a basic rule of thumb, it can be said that the Chinese will abide a wholly foreign-owned enterprise (WFOE) when it seems clear to the local authorities that it will utilize advanced technology and equipment that will have a spill-over effect into local development plans and that it will export all or a major portion of its production.

Newly promulgated implementing regulations for China's Law on Wholly Foreign-Owned Enterprises (December 1990) tighten the investment screening process for such enterprises and require them to meet more restrictive advanced technology criteria. The law also continues to place restrictions on their operational autonomy.

Companies going it alone in China find that the road can be bumpy, but few have regrets. 3M found it difficult to clear equipment through customs and buy needed supplies locally. It was also forced to use inexperienced employees assigned by the local employment bureau until it retained a government agency as a consultant. On the other hand, the work environment can be just like home, hiring and firing can be trouble free, and there is little interference from outside bureaucracies.

Solving Key Operational Issues

Problems accompany every type of trade and investment done in China—as they do anywhere in the world. Some problems are unique to China, however. The ones cited most often are the need to balance foreign exchange, problems in sourcing products and materials locally, and issues in human resources.

●●●●●●●●●●●●●●●●●●●●●●●●●●●●●

SCORECARD: The Wholly Foreign-Owned Enterprise (WFOE)

+	Provides more protection for the investor's proprietary know-how and information utilized in the project
+	Avoids much of the complex joint venture negotiation and approval processes and does not require detailed feasibility studies
+	Does not require Chinese involvement in management or the sharing of profits
−	Greater restrictions on the types of ventures permissible
−	Fewer precedents to rely upon during negotiations and operations
−	Has the operational burden of having to negotiate all aspects of the materials, manpower and sales mechanisms with the local authorities (in a JV the Chinese partner often assumes this burden)
−	Stricter foreign exchange balancing requirements
−	Higher tax rate than for EJVs (the maximum rate is 50%, rather than the 33% for an EJV)

Balancing Foreign Exchange

All foreign-funded enterprises in China must, by law, generate the foreign exchange needed to meet foreign exchange expenses. Such expenses include imported materials and components, the salaries and other expenses associated with expatriate staff, and profit remittances. This has traditionally posed a severe challenge to many joint ventures.

Throughout the 1980s, investors had little choice but to export all or part of their production to cover this expense. Compounding the difficulty of guaranteeing a sustainable export market were the added problems associated with production in China, particularly the frequent need to import at great cost the parts and materials needed to sustain production at the level and quality required.

China's first steps towards solving the foreign exchange problem included: (1) the establishment of currency swap centers (which allow RMB profits to be exchanged for foreign exchange, albeit at a premium); (2) giving more products import substitution status (allowing them to be sold for foreign exchange on the domestic market); and (3) granting the right to let companies balance their foreign exchange needs with other ventures in which they have an interest (allowing the profits of one to cover the shortfalls of another).

By the start of the 1990s, the foreign exchange problem, while not fully solved, had been greatly ameliorated. There are at least four ways of exchanging RMB for foreign currency that can be used, either separately or in tandem.

First, there is the traditional method of exporting production. As quality has improved and localization has become more feasible (see below), this route has become increasingly successful.

Second, as shown in the case studies of Avon, PepsiCo and others, one can use RMB profits to buy local products unrelated to the venture and then export those products in foreign currency. Procter & Gamble, for example, buys flavors and fragrances, which it sells back to various P&G divisions around the world.

Third, use of the swap centers has become more viable with the gradual devaluation of the RMB to the point where it is convertible virtually at world-market rates. The elimination of all artificial tiers of the exchange rates in early 1992 will greatly facilitate this process.

Finally, sophisticated administrative methods have evolved to work around the foreign exchange issue. For example, a large Canadian food products company might develop a partnership with a Hong Kong-based firm which owns a Chinese venture making beach towels specifically for the export market. In exchange for pumping some of its RMB earnings into the towel factory, the Canadian company will receive a share of the foreign exchange profits made by the Hong Kong firm.

As a result of these changes, the Chinese government no longer withholds approval from ventures that do not guarantee to balance their foreign exchange. It is saying, in effect, that since these avenues exist, and because the foreign exchange earned by joint ventures operating in China shows a surplus overall, it is none of our concern.

Sourcing Products and Materials Locally

The reasons for developing local sources of supply and materials are clear. It reduces the cost of operation, since fewer parts will have to be imported from abroad and it avoids the instability associated with the vagaries of import duties and non-tariff barriers.

The effort to find local suppliers and educate them to meet international standards and quality requirements also pays off for political reasons. The more Chinese suppliers are involved in your business, the greater the foothold you have. To harm the foreign-funded enterprise, the reasoning goes, would harm local factories as well—factories which are now producing jobs, meeting export criteria, and paying taxes.

The solution is expensive and often complex, but it can be done (see the Xerox and Polaroid case studies). The key is training, training, and more training—and working continually and consistently with the suppliers to achieve internationally acceptable product quality standards.

THE HUMAN RESOURCE CHALLENGE

Perhaps the greatest challenge to investment ventures in China is effective management, made difficult by the wide range of abilities shown by local managers. The negotiations may have gone smoothly, and the partners may be on the best of terms, but once operations start, the relationship sometimes quickly deteriorates into an "us" versus "them" situation. Even when decisions seem to make clear business sense for both sides, the partner may not agree because of some perceived idea that it violates his or the country's best interest.

Human resource issues have been detailed in the case studies (see the PepsiCo, Ningbo Abbott Laboratories, and Shenyang Tambrands cases for different perspectives). What these cases seem to say implicitly, but which needs to be made explicit, is that the key to successful joint venture management is the ability of the foreign firm to achieve a good personal and professional relationship with the Chinese partner *without relying heavily upon the management team it inherited.* Creative methods may have to be found to honor the Chinese general manager (or deputy general manager) and his team, as well as the people they report to inside and outside the venture, while finding a way to work around them. Glaxo, for example, has kept management personnel off its board of directors. Disagreements can therefore be dealt with at that level, rather than at the factory level, where they can create severe disruption.

As one experienced trader who helped orchestrate several joint ventures put it, "Become friends and moral partners. But neutralize them sufficiently so they do not interfere with day-to-day management."

Another important tactic in human resource management is to have good recruitment practices. As a group, workers from the partner may have many ingrained habits that will hinder the rapid modernization of the venture (some individuals will stand out very positively, of course). On the other hand, the traditional lack of worker mobility in China may make it difficult to recruit workers from other factories in the region (see PepsiCo case study).

One solution pursued by some companies is to actively recruit people from universities. These people are often ambitious, open to Western-style thinking, and prefer to work in joint ventures both for prestige and for fatter pay. The government has restricted this practice (demanding that graduates first be screened by state enterprises), but, as usual, there are ways to help the schools keep some of the better people aside. Once recruited, spend the time and energy needed to convince them of your company's values, and train them to do business to international standards rather than previously existing criteria. Over time, these are the people who will replace not only the old guard now running the factory, but, as has become common in other Asian countries, the expatriates as well.

Overcoming Traditional Allegiances

Another management issue that tends to get in the way of the smooth day-to-day operation of a venture with foreign participation is the devilishly complex issue of personal allegiances.

In the U.S., people may have different functions within a company (accounting, sales, production) but their allegiance is to the company as a whole. A company, in turn, may have ties to the industry at large through professional associations or lobby groups, but it is often held accountable to the local community and always responsible for its "bottom line."

Traditionally, this is different in China. The accounting division of a factory is responsible not just to the manager, but to the accounting bureau in the city, which has ultimate control. The factory reports to the local bureau of an industrial ministry (hence names such as "The No. 6 Cosmetics Factory"), which in turn reports to a central ministry in Beijing. Steven Hendryx, former director of China operations for Otis Elevators, puts it this way: "It's just as if the treasurer of IBM reported through state channels to the Secretary of the Treasury in Washington, D.C."

When a joint venture has problems, the natural tendency of the Chinese staff is to fall back on old alliances, leaving the enterprise to fend for itself, even if it founders. This same system of vertical allegiances aggravates the inability of many managers in China to make decisions as well as the phenomenon of having people from different departments work side by side without necessarily knowing what the person at their elbow is doing.

The challenge for foreign management is to mold these traditional allegiances to the greater good of the venture, and to be just as ingenious as many local officials and factory managers are in breaking the red tape that binds this traditional system together.

✦ ✦ ✦

Planning and careful consideration of the various options in entering the market are steps familiar to any businessperson, even if the territory is not. It's when it comes time for the negotiations that you find need of a second skill. In China, every foreigner has to be a cross-cultural diplomat as well as a businessperson.

Effective Negotiations— Understanding the Chinese Business Mentality

The people of the world are bigoted and unenlightened: invariably they regard what is like them as right, and what is different from them as wrong, resulting in mutual recrimination. . . . They do not realize that the types of humanity are not uniform and that their customs are also not one, that it is not only impossible to force people to become different but also impossible to force them to become alike.

—YUNG-CHENG, EMPEROR OF CHINA, IN 1727

Doing business in China is a cultural as well as an economic transaction.

There *is* a culture gap. They *do* think differently. One of the challenges (and pleasures) of doing business in China is coming to grips with that mentality, understanding it sufficiently to try to reduce the surprises and avoid unnecessary failures.

This chapter probes the Chinese business mindset and describes some major negotiating strategies used by the Chinese. Effective counter strategy is discussed in the next chapter.

The Chinese Business Mentality

There are no ironclad guidelines to understanding the Chinese business mentality, just as there aren't for the Western business mind. People are as different from one another in China as they are anywhere, the only ironclad rule being that there will always be exceptions.

Some of the explanations given for the differences in Chinese and Western ways of thinking are almost cliches, but they have a basis in scholarly research on both sides of the Pacific. Chinese scholars, for example, explain that the followers of Confucius have always emphasized mutual needs. Western humanism has stressed concern for the individual.

The Western mind is generally trained to think in cause and effect. If something is wrong, we find the cause and fix it. The Chinese tend to think in terms of webs of thoughts and relationships. They try to unravel the pattern, wondering if it's too complex to be solved.

Americans prize directness. Chinese tend to be more comfortable with ambiguity. And what is simply an expression of duality for a Chinese may seem like a flat out contradiction to an American. To an American, for example, it may be difficult to understand how his host can display admirable character traits in a social context (subtlety, soft-spokenness, and avoidance of conflict), then turn to positioning, posturing, and calculated indecision in the context of negotiations.

The way to deal with these cultural differences is not by trying to out-Chinese the Chinese. Instead, understand the Chinese business mentality well enough to adjust your style without forsaking principle.

The Six "Classics" of Doing Business

All cultures can point to certain "classics" that seem to speak to basic attitudes and outlooks. The Bible for the West, perhaps. The Confucian classics for the Chinese. To help understand the traditional Chinese business mentality, we can imagine a mythical text known as the "Six Classics of Chinese Business."

These "Classics" may have only partially shaped the person across the table, or perhaps not at all. These traits may also be more visible in government officials or old-line managers than in young technocrats or the growing class of entrepreneurial managers. Yet old China hands will recognize the fundamentals of this text.

THE FIRST CLASSIC: CULTURAL CONTINUITY

In today's China there is also yesterday's China. The past is very much alive in the present. Centuries-old cultural traits peek through all the modern talk about making money.

The young negotiator across the table from you may seem to be thoroughly modern. He wears Western suits, listens to Voice of America, and reads *The Economist.* Yet he has a long fingernail on one pinky, which proudly signifies he is an intellectual and doesn't have to work with his hands like a common laborer. He spices his conversation with old Chinese sayings. Every Chinese New Year he passes out money in little red envelopes decorated with folk gods, symbolically wishing the recipient prosperity.

All this has an impact on how business gets done in China, or even if it gets done. For example, the urgent need to modernize requires change and adaptation, characteristics that fly in the face of centuries of cultural conservatism. This conflict can lead to hesitation and inconsistent progress in national policy as well as in individual negotiations.

For the Western businessperson, making a deal is often *the* goal. For your Chinese counterpart it may be *a* goal, but one which may conflict with underlying concerns about dependency upon foreigners and their perceived tendency to corrupt, culturally and economically.

An individual business deal may be subordinate to other, larger goals. This explains why a hotel construction project can be productively negotiated for two years, then suddenly halted because national or provincial policy has changed. The project is simply unimportant in relation to the overall goal.

The Concept of Time

Another legacy of the culture has been the elastic sense of time. Because Chinese society has been around for so long, there is no hurry. Of course they would like to see China be modern by tomorrow afternoon, but even the most optimistic people talk about the next century. The obvious implication here is the need for patience. As one veteran China trader observed: "If you're the kind of person who has trouble waiting for a red light to change, then China is not for you."

The sense of historical continuity has also taught the Chinese that things will always change, and that life holds endless possibilities that are better awaited than forced. School children all over China learn the story of the farmer who has both of life's most precious possessions, a son and a horse. One day the horse runs away. His neighbors pity him. "Never mind," the farmer says, "You never know what happens." Sure enough, two days later the horse returns, bringing a pack of wild horses with him. This time his neighbors congratulate him on his good fortune. The farmer's response is the same: "You never know what happens."

A few days later, his son breaks both his legs in a fall off a wild horse. The neighbors once again commiserate, and once again the farmer quotes his favorite saying. Finally, a group of the emperor's soldiers ride through the town, taking every able young man with them to fight in a border war. The farmer's son, disabled for now, gets to stay home.

This is seeing life as an endless stream, one thing leading to the next. There is never a definable beginning or a clear ending.

THE SECOND CLASSIC: CULTURAL SUPERIORITY

In Chinese, the characters for the word "China" literally mean "middle kingdom." For centuries, the Chinese believed themselves to be totally self-sufficient. The outer world was of no import. When British traders first arrived on Chinese shores in the late 18th century, the emperor dismissed them with an edict stating: "Our celestial empire possesses all things in prolific abundance . . . we have no need of the products of outside barbarians."

Even under today's open door policy, ethnocentrism continues to influence Chinese thinking, and it strongly affects how business is done with the outside world. Behind the hoopla of Avon's success is an underlying fear of cultural pollution. Despite the welcome mat, the Chinese are masters at creating a guest-host relationship in which the foreigner inevitably starts out in a position of inferiority and obligation, at least from the Chinese perspective.

As hosts, the Chinese are in a position to control the agenda as well as the pace of negotiations. Add to this their masterful sense of hospitality (banquets, sightseeing) and the inexperienced foreign executive may lose his or her perspective. The foreigner's tendency to be impatient with a slow-paced agenda may cause him to make concessions, or agree to deals simply to "get on with it." An insecure person wanting to prove worthy of his hosts may be tempted to share inside information, or make unplanned promises.

The "Classic of Cultural Superiority" also imbues some Chinese negotiators with the sense that China deserves special treatment. This is why the visiting executive may get signals that he should somehow see China as "deserving" and show his "friendship and understanding" by sharing technology freely or at a deep discount.

There is a flip side to cultural superiority, however, and it is a sense of technological inferiority. This can create a strong push-pull tension in the psyche of the Chinese negotiator. The fascination a Chinese factory manager displays towards the modern outside world, for example, may be counterbalanced by residual fears of being cheated and pushed around by foreigners.

THE THIRD CLASSIC: CLANNISHNESS AND CONFORMITY

The most important and basic element of Chinese society inherited through the dynasties is the sense of commitment to and conformity with the group. Sticking one's neck out is not only discouraged, it invites suspicion—particularly when it comes to dealing with foreigners.

Although this tradition is gradually being eroded, especially among educated young technocrats, the tendency towards conformity means a consensus has to be arrived at before a change of position can be agreed upon. The Western businessperson will rarely, if ever, hear a Chinese negotiator speak up in mid-meeting and say to his colleagues: "Perhaps they have a point. Let's do it their way."

And because of the need for consensus, there is indecision—and there are endless meetings. The foreigner must wait until all those who are party to the negotiations, many of them unseen, agree on how to proceed.

The tendency towards conformity also manifests itself in an "us against them" syndrome. We tend to look at joint ventures as strategic alliances—part of a vision of the globally integrated corporation. The Chinese tend to consider them tactical alliances—steps necessary until China becomes self-sufficient and reliance on the foreign company is no longer necessary. Every time a problem comes up on the shop floor and the response is, "But this is China," the focus has shifted from the issue itself to a matter of collective pride. Until extraordinary trust has been built, the foreigner is forever typecast as the "Party B" referred to in the contract.

For companies doing contract assembly work or involved in joint ventures, the "Classic of Conformity" also shows up on the factory floor—and it runs directly counter to that prized bit of Western work ethic known as initiative. A U.S. factory worker might have grown up hearing, "The early bird catches the worm." His Chinese counterpart will have learned, "The first bird in the flock is the first to be shot." The traditional system gives no rewards for taking the initiative or making right decisions, but instead punishes those who make wrong decisions. Why take the initiative? Why learn to innovate?

Further evidence of clannishness is seen in the concept of "eating from one big pot," which holds that all families in China should ideally share fortune and misfortune. In modern times this has been translated into the "iron rice bowl" syndrome common to state-owned enterprises. It means that once you have a job—and all the social welfare benefits that go with it—you won't be laid off. No wonder the Chinese partner wants to put as many as possible of its old work unit onto the foreign payroll, where the salaries and benefits are even greater.

Even as China now tries to break these shackles of tradition, it must be remembered that the chains are heavy, and linked in complex ways.

Face
Having "face" means you are viewed by your peers, superiors, and subordinates as one in harmony with the prevailing disposition of society; you've done nothing to violate conformity. As a consequence, mistakes may be minimized or ignored. To protect an organization's name, bad news may be covered with endless procrastination. Commitments are hedged with many a "maybe," "perhaps," "possibly," and other hesitations.

Face can also get in the way of successful technology transfer arrangements. Although things are changing for the better, Chinese engineers have been known to let a new piece of machinery stand idle rather than admit that they don't understand the technology. If backed too far into a corner, face may even cause someone to kill a deal.

Hierarchy and Authority
The image Westerners have of China's egalitarianism may have a grip on the popular imagination, but in reality there remains a strong sense of hierarchy. In a system where independent expression is not prized, expression through organizational rank is. Titles are valued, and rank is visibly expressed in clothes, curtained limousines, and servile aides. Superiors expect lifetime loyalty, subordinates lifetime care. (Ironically, this strong sense of hierarchy doesn't always mean that the man with the highest authority has the most power. Indeed, he may have gotten there because he has worked more effectively than anyone else in advancing the interests of his group while shielding himself from accountability.)

Seniority and rank are important in this system, and taking them into account is important in negotiations. Protocol calls for dealing with the highest-ranking person, even if the real power is sitting three overstuffed chairs away.

The point of this "Classic" of conformity and its characteristics of face and hierarchy is that in business there is a general hesitation to take responsibility as well as a slow and cumbersome system of collective decision-making. How, then, can anyone ever get anything done? By paying attention to the fourth classic: having the right connections.

THE FOURTH CLASSIC: RELATIONSHIPS AND OBLIGATIONS

Many foreign executives suspect that the phrase "It's not *what* you know but *who* you know" must have been an old Chinese saying. Relationships in China don't just add to, but may actually define, a person's life. As touched on in previous chapters, this is *guanxi*, the web of relationships and obligations that ties the system together.

The Web of Relationships

In business, how well one is connected is fundamental. The *guanxi* of the partner may literally determine just how much or how little can be accomplished. "No problem," says the factory supplying the product, but if the factory doesn't have *guanxi* with transportation, customs, and other export-related organizations, you may have to wait a long time for it.

If the potential buyer of your technology must compete for funds with others trying to buy the same piece of equipment, the one having the most *guanxi* with the bank wins the right to place the order.

One may have all the requisite permissions and approvals from a dozen bureaucracies to start a joint venture, but if there is no *guanxi* with the organization supplying the specialty steel that is on allocation, the factory won't operate until another source of supply is found.

The foreign company inevitably finds itself being drawn into the network, if only for self-preservation. You may have the needed *guanxi* with the State Supply Bureau even if your partner doesn't. *Guanxi* with higher level officials can at times also give Western and Japanese companies the aura of authority needed to pass through the bureaucratic fog.

As American Express found out, *guanxi*, no matter at what level, doesn't always guarantee success (see sidebar). Still, it's difficult to overestimate the importance of connections in China.

Guanxi has its darker side. The absence of a strong rule of law, a recognized merit system, and institutional continuity, all combine to create a vacuum in which power becomes personal. Family background and social ties may be more important than professional attainment. People with powerful connections become wealthier and build constituencies. Sons and daughters of ranking officials have been known to run companies that rake in millions. The age of the dealmaker arrives, and corruption becomes the ultimate perversion of *guanxi*.

▼ The Uses and Limitations of Connections

Seeing the *guanxi* system at work, foreign firms often draw the conclusion that the closer they get to the top, the easier life will be. Sometimes it works. Other times it doesn't.

The Tianjin-based Otsuka Pharmaceutical Company joint venture had trouble finding a market for its intravenous bottles within its home town. All attempts to resolve the problem, including meetings with the mayor and other city officials, came to no avail. Finally, the company was able to arrange for Gu Mu, a top central government official, to visit the plant. During the visit, one of the Chinese managers, at his own initiative, raised this problem with Gu. Not long afterwards the mayor of Tianjin called a conference of local hospital personnel, and convinced them to start buying the bottles.

However, the best connections possible don't by any means guarantee success. American Express and its Shearson Lehman Brothers subsidiary discovered this during their attempt to build an office/apartment complex in Beijing.

The project started in 1985 when the chairman of Shearson, Peter Cohen, traveled to China in search of investment opportunities. Within a matter of weeks, Shearson had signed letters of intent with the Beijing First Commercial Bureau for an American Express Center.

The initial site chosen for the apartment-office project was a state-run store for foreigners in the Beijing diplomatic area. To tear down the facilities and relocate the store, the Chinese demanded several million dollars. The Americans resisted. However, after New York City deputy mayor Alair Townsend brought up the issue on a visit to China, Shearson was given permission to negotiate for a new site.

The new site was a computer-parts factory and it became the joint venture partner. Negotiations dragged on for two years, despite the intervention of such well-connected figures as U.S. ambassador to China Winston Lord, Secretary of State George Shultz, former Secretary of State Cyrus Vance, and New York Mayor Ed Koch.

Finally, Richard Holbrooke, a managing director of Shearson who had taken part in the talks that led to the normalization of U.S.-China relations in 1978, met with the mayor of Beijing. The mayor said he would give instructions that the contract should be signed within one month. It was.

The Chinese factory manager didn't appreciate the meddling. He told *The Wall Street Journal*, "The U.S. side uses politics to their advantage. They never compromise; their negotiating tactics give me a big headache." The next stage—arranging the loan and getting various approvals—took nearly 17 months (to early 1988). Next came the design and construction phase but that, too has apparently stalled.

Despite extraordinary use of *guanxi*, the project has not been completed.

Sources: American Express, *Business China, The Wall Street Journal,* and other press reports.

▲

The Web of Obligations

Guanxi is not simply tapping into the network. It also implies the obligation to return the favor. It is a two-way relationship which, as Professor Lucian Pye puts it, allows each to make unlimited demands on the other. True *guanxi* means never having to say, "Sorry."

Old China hands can graphically chart the mutual deepening of obligations among those with whom they've developed *guanxi*. At first come kind words and personal conversations. Then small gifts. More substantial favors soon follow, ranging from helpful introductions and negotiation insights to financial help and trips abroad. The Japanese, whose own system of *giri* is even more rigid, understand this and play it masterfully. The American, ever ready to be the affable friend but generally unaware of the cultural implications, may more easily get mired in the quicksand of unfulfilled mutual expectations.

Once *guanxi* has been established, the term "old friend" starts to be used. Old friends have an obligation to "understand" shortcomings, bureaucratism, and all the other difficulties of doing business in China. If the responsible person of the department concerned is suddenly busy elsewhere, or the deal is abruptly postponed or canceled, you, old foreign friend, can bear the bad news because "it doesn't matter."

Western and Japanese executives also prize connections, of course. But there are two substantial differences in the *guanxi* system. The first is that the system of give and take pervades *all* business relationships at *all* levels, not just among a few chosen friends.

The second is that there is no emotional basis implied or required in China's *guanxi* network. You simply have *guanxi* or not, and if you do, obligations flow from the fact of that relationship, not necessarily from how well you know the individual personally or what your feelings are about him. Unaware of how this system works, some traders have been surprised by what they consider the impersonal nature, matter-of-factness, or even callousness of the bonds that are established. (*Guanxi* aside, close personal friendships are quite possible in China. Foreigners aware of the distinctions prize such friendships greatly.)

Yet the *guanxi* network is indispensable to the foreign businessperson. Mutual trust and obligation may in the end help get the deal done even when it seems to be crumbling apart. Things happen, visibly and often invisibly, on behalf of those who have *guanxi*. Somehow, the bid on a power project ends up being accepted, or one is introduced to someone with money in hand to buy some equipment, and so on.

Virtually every importer, exporter, agent, lawyer, banker, consultant, investor, or other businessperson who has spent time doing business in China will say that, in the end, it's often not the product or the deal, but the relationship that counts. In almost every contract completed, one can look back and say to a particular Chinese colleague, "Without you, old friend, this project would not have been accomplished."

THE FIFTH CLASSIC: RITUAL

Ritual is the glue that seems to hold Chinese society together. It is not surprising that ritual also plays an important part in business, dominating meetings, banquets, and all other forms of social and business interaction.

In an informal, first-name-basis society like the U.S., rituals can often seem quaint, and even a waste of time. But they can play a comforting role in the mind of a Chinese businessperson. Ritual provides certainty in the face of the unknown. Ritual masks, in a civilized way, a lot of indecision or uncertainty. Ritual creates an aura of sincerity in the midst of serious doubts about whether business can be done between the two of you, and also allows a way of maintaining control.

Experience dictates that ritual never be ignored, whether by a newcomer or an old China hand. An experienced trader was introduced to Mr. Wang of the cloisonné department of the Beijing Arts & Crafts Corporation by a trusted mutual friend. The trader found his young counterpart refreshingly informal, and by the second meeting the Chinese side had agreed to produce samples. On a subsequent visit to China it took only one more meeting to evaluate the samples, place a trial order, and draw up a draft contract.

With this kind of efficiency on display, the trader telefaxed Mr. Wang a week before his third visit to Beijing, telling him that he would come to Wang's office the following Tuesday unless Wang faxed back. Upon arrival, the trader did his week of other work without once calling to confirm the meeting. On the appointed day he arrived at Mr. Wang's office only to find utter confusion. Who are you? Whom do you want to see? On what business?

Finally, someone was summoned from upstairs to explain that Mr. Wang had been transferred to the furniture department, and the only person who knew something about this business was in Guangzhou.

The trader slinked out, knowing he had broken a dozen rules of ritual and protocol. He had not bothered with the getting-to-know-you conversations. He had avoided social invitations, including a banquet to meet the department heads. To top it off, his fax undoubtedly had made Mr. Wang feel as if he was an afterthought.

All this may seem petty, but it effectively demonstrates the importance of ritual even in the most basic interchanges.

THE SIXTH CLASSIC: THE BACK DOOR

Imagine the Forbidden City, in the heart of Beijing. The first five "classics" can be likened to the succession of walls, gates, moats, courtyards, and screens that guard access to the inner throne. Companies soon learn that sometimes there may be a second, more direct way of entering the palace grounds: the back door.

The tradition of the back door is deeply imbedded in China's history, and *guanxi* is the key that opens that door. What's different about the 1990s is that the fee to the doorkeeper has been raised substantially. The favors being traded are no longer simple, and the price may often be cold, hard cash (see the discussion on corruption in chapter 8).

The "Classic of the Back Door" doesn't apply to every situation, or even to most situations. But there aren't many companies doing business in China that haven't come face-to-face with the keeper of the infamous back door. An unending chain of complications awaits the incautious.

Countervailing Trends

The first five traits of the Chinese business mentality described here are no longer as pervasive as they were in the 1970s and 1980s. Fewer business people are choosing to hide behind them as a way of perpetuating inaction. The reason? Motivations have changed.

The coming of the responsibility system and its built-in incentives has made more people ready to override the old mentality in favor of the practical considerations of commerce. There is an ever increasing awareness that performance counts. Even state factories are adopting a system of contract management; if in five years the business hasn't turned around, new managers are hired. There's also the psychological pressure of knowing that it's less and less likely that the state will bail you out should you fail.

In the "old days" entrepreneurship was looked down upon. Today, Chinese society is more accepting, even admiring, of people who make lots of money in business. While the institutional memory for events such as the Cultural Revolution remains long, there's less reluctance, and less stigma, attached to sticking one's neck out.

Like everything else about China, the business mentality, too, is undergoing reform.

Chinese Negotiating Strategies:
The Art of War?

Having discussed the mental framework of the Chinese business negotiator, it's time to see how this is translated into the strategies used during the negotiation process. It's too richly textured a process to be reduced to a few Sunday-school-style lessons, but there are a number of elements that stand out when looking at the experience of other companies.

Were we to peer over the shoulder of the Chinese negotiator, we might find some or all of the following points written on his or her notepad:

1. Keep the Foreigner Off Guard

Negotiations can begin the moment the foreigner arrives in China. Instead of greeting that vice president of a multinational corporation before he goes through customs, let him wade his way through the process himself. We know he's got control over his hotel, transportation, and length of stay, but we should keep control of the schedule and agenda. If we need more time to gauge his intention, tell him our key people "have something else to do," and he'll have to repeat his presentations the day after tomorrow.

2. Get to Know the Foreign Company and Its Negotiating Team Thoroughly, and Exploit Contradictions

Launch an exhaustive quest for background information on the company, its products, and its people. Continue the personal evaluations throughout each and every encounter. Contradictions can then be exploited, whether in corporate policy (but Mr. Prechter, you sold this technology to Bangladesh, why not to us?) or among various members of the negotiating team (Mr. Weiss, your company president told us he would supply the most advanced technology, but you, Mr. Smith, are backing away from that promise).

Cultivate someone on the foreigner's team who can be counted on to be an "understanding friend" (overseas Chinese, consultants, intermediaries, newly minted China experts, and "kindhearted old gentlemen" are good candidates). This helps overcome any feeling of insecurity and establishes a sense of "friendship" which can be used to manipulate feelings of goodwill, obligation, guilt, or dependence to achieve negotiating objectives.

3. Establish Principles First, Worry About Details Later

The way we Chinese can turn our weak position into a strong one is by getting the foreigner to reveal his interests and proposals first, keeping all details of our position as guarded as possible. As necessary, use *neibu* regulations [internal, unpublished rules] and phrases such as "But this is China . . ." to keep them in the dark and off balance.

Establish a favorable agenda and get agreement on the overarching general principle first. The details can then be negotiated as endlessly or quickly as the situation requires. Foreigners will feel that they have done their part by just coming this far, literally and figuratively. To get to an agreement, their bottom line—a favored phrase—may be reflected in statements such as, "Mr. Liu, if you can assure us that the land is there, that the requisite permissions are in place, that you can offer the production capacity, and that you can accept the price of the technology we offer, then we can move forward to make this deal."

Our position should be, "We can talk about all that, but first you must agree with the principle that this will be an equity joint venture and that you will take 40% of the product and sell it overseas. Otherwise it is no use talking about these details."

4. Be Welcoming, Then Use the Pressure of Time Against Them

When the foreign boss comes to start the negotiations, allow him his "face" by showing friendliness and cooperation. Honor him with banquets and top-level meetings. Acquiesce to a memorandum of understanding if he wishes. Real negotiations can begin once he leaves town.

When the negotiations start, use the pressure of time. Westerners are always in a hurry. Ask for more time, and more meetings. Repeatedly cover the same ground at several meetings in a row, especially if separated by months. Continually probe intentions, capabilities, weaknesses, and strengths. Use good-guy bad-guy scenarios. Don't let them know which issues genuinely need time for decision and which are negotiating ploys. Gradually create an atmosphere that says: lucky foreigner, if you make everything acceptable enough to us, we can sign a contract and then you can go home.

5. Drive a Hard Bargain

Our bosses in the ministry are not interested in all the side issues. They simply want to know how big a discount was negotiated. There is no win-win, only a zero sum game in which our gain is their loss. Demand concessions. Yes, we know Americans tend to make their first offer their best offer. They're trying to show friendliness and sincerity. But bosses demand discounts, and foreigners will figure that if they turn this deal into a loss leader they'll have their foot in the door.

The Japanese understand this, and are good at letting us drive the price down, giving us our win. Never mind if the contract leaves out spare parts or other extras needed to complete the transaction, that can be negotiated later.

6. Don't Forget the End Game

When ready to conclude an agreement, move quickly. Make the impossible seem feasible. Let permissions and authorizations materialize, approve draft contracts, and arrange for the invitation to meet the head man. In this positive atmosphere, apply more pressure. Invoke the spirit of "friendship and mutual understanding" as you push for that extra concession. After all, are they going to let a few loose ends keep them from signing?

7. A Signed Contract Doesn't Mean a Settled Contract

Negotiate endlessly. When agreements and contracts are ready, consider them as drafts subject to further "friendly discussions." Once signed, continue negotiating.

▼ **POST-CONTRACT NEGOTIATIONS**

Yes is the first word of agreement, but it is definitely not the last word in negotiations. A "yes" in China may sometimes turn out to be another way of saying, "Let's now begin to talk seriously."

Post-contract negotiation blues are generally sung in two keys—obligations not spelled out in the contract and limitations dictated by bureaucracies outside the contract.

The phrase, "Based on our friendship and understanding, please . . ." often signals a request to provide things not covered in the contract. There may be requests for additional trips abroad, expectations of additional training, or a dispute regard-

ing the number of spare parts. This is why experienced negotiators never leave thorny issues to the "detail people."

This is not to say everything must be spelled out in the finest
legalese. There is no clear data supporting the notion that
highly detailed contracts assure smoother operations than ones
left purposely open and flexible (or vice versa). Successful
ventures inevitably have worked hard at creating an atmosphere
of trust and mutual respect before, during, and after the contract negotiations—something that can never be negotiated into
a contract.

If all the limitations imposed on the successful implementation of a contract were to be grouped under one heading, it
would surely be "bureaucracy." Sometimes it seems as if from
beginning to end both you and your partner are forced to
confront a bewildering maze of self-interested power centers
with whom one is forced to strike bargains without ever being
able to assert lasting control. Success of the enterprise may
depend less on whether or not the deal makes sense (even for
China) than on whether or not it fits into the particular web of
bureaucratic power one has chosen to tackle and whether or not
it suitably rewards the personal aspirations of the people who
control it.

Wrestling with entrenched officialdom is not unique to the
foreigner. Your Chinese partner has the same difficulties. Even
China's top leaders must come to grips with this morass in
trying to implement their programs. Ironically, it is the bureaucracy that has prevented implementation of the most rigid anti-
reform policies in the past few years.

▲

Building Trust

It may seem as if there's an almost unbridgeable gap between the
culture-driven negotiation tactics just described and the successful
conclusion of a contract. Sometimes, that's true, especially if neither
side has the experience, the will, or the commonality of business
interests to see it through.

Increasingly, however, elegant bridges are being built, making
the chasm seem less fearsome. The structural members of this
bridge are understanding, patience, persistence, and flexibility,
joined with common sense and mutual interests.

What allows the contractors on both sides to move forward is
trust. This trust is maintained by a willingness to show what the
Chinese would call "sincerity." It's a hard concept to define, but in
practice, sincerity means keeping the communication lines open

and well used. Trust is less blind faith than continually spelling out everything for each other.

With every bridge built, the Chinese business mentality becomes more apparent, and the opportunity for progress more concrete. There really is a usefulness in having all those meetings, and building towards consensus. There really is a chance to be enriched by an experience that is difficult to duplicate anywhere else in the world.

PART

IV

TOWARD
THE
21ST CENTURY

11

Guidelines for
Success

*There are no hard and fixed rules—only tendencies—in the
China market.*

—ROY F. GROW, "WHAT ARE THE LESSONS?" (1987)

Success in China rests on the ability to look at trade and investment
opportunities with a sense of realism while accepting the climate of
ambiguity and change in which the business must operate.

There are other ingredients, too: the willingness to do the
research and formulate a sound strategic plan; the strong backing
of senior management; an ability to take the time to find the right
partners and work with them to create an atmosphere of shared
purpose; and large doses of creativity, tenacity, flexibility, and
patience.

"It's a long haul, a very long haul," Lee Iacocca once said of
China. It *will* be a long haul. There *are* business issues that are
uniquely Chinese. But experience also shows that a great many
companies are doing very well in China and that problems there can
ultimately be dealt with as successfully as business problems
elsewhere. Failure just as often can be ascribed to a lack of research,
poor negotiating tactics, or inappropriate business strategies as to
the difficulties of the market *per se.*

Whether they are conducted by official trade groups such as
the U.S.-China Business Council, private consulting firms such as
A. T. Kearney, or experienced business school professors such as
Roy Grow and Joseph Alutto, surveys consistently show American
companies can be as inexperienced at strategic partnerships as their
Chinese counterparts. The most simple, and most easily overlooked
lesson is that to be successful, the two parties need to systematically

and thoughtfully share perspectives, assumptions and goals, from the initial negotiations through the daily give and take of decision making.

Beyond this, there is no one set of rules that will make China a good market for your company. But the case studies in this book and the lessons derived from them do suggest certain guidelines. Here we summarize them under four general headings: planning and preparation (what to know about the Chinese . . . and yourself), positioning (evaluating your potential partner), negotiating (getting to yes), and, for those who come to operate ventures in China, the lessons of day-to-day management.

Planning and Preparation

The foundation of a business plan for China begins with an understanding of China's place in the world economy and its outlook towards trade and investment. The plan can then be drawn up with certain principles in mind. Here are some of the lessons companies have learned from the successes and failures of others:

• Successful companies understand China's role in the greater Asian economy.

China is an important actor in world trade,but its foreign trade and investment goals are best viewed in the context of the rapidly growing Asian regional market. China's export capabilities (raw materials, primary products, light industrial goods, food) as well as import needs (product and process technology, manufactured goods) are complementary to the economies of its neighbors. China, as Sinologist Roy Grow points out, is looking for firms that can help the country do business with its Asian neighbors in the short run, while looking at Europe and North America in the long run. Hence the foreign-financed food processing plants that export to Southeast Asia, and the imported assembly lines to manufacture the light industrial goods needed in Hong Kong.

• At the same time, successful companies don't expect China's operating environment to be like that of other Asian countries.

The progress that factories and enterprises have made toward replacing political nonsense with commercial horse sense doesn't mean China is another Singapore or Hong Kong.

John Marshall, who has had 20 years experience in spearheading 3M's efforts in China, once said, "Even Thailand, Malaysia, and Indonesia have economic systems in place that, in varying degrees, are akin to those in the West. Their private sectors understand profit motives, balance sheets, unit costs, quality control, how to develop export markets, advertising, marketing, promotion, customer trust and all those things that are second nature to us. None of these apply universally to China; only some are now slowly developing in the more advanced regions."

The relationship between government and business is also dissimilar. In other Asian countries—Taiwan and Korea come quickly to mind—there is an unspoken pact that lets each operate more or less autonomously in its own sphere as long as social order is maintained. No such arrangement exists in China, although its outline is faintly emerging.

• Successful companies also know that "market penetration" is a relative term and that China circumscribes the foreign presence.

Self-reliance is deeply embedded in China's commercial policy. Trade and investment must first of all serve China's interests. Exports can bring in the foreign exchange for needed imports. Equity ventures are useful for jump-starting development—not as doors to foreign exploitation of the market.

Access to the market will, at least for the foreseeable future, be limited. Sums up journalist Graeme Browning, "The Chinese will never open their markets completely, because the Chinese believe they would lose much more than they would gain."

Does that mean that business can't be done in China? Of course not. Does it mean it is circumscribed and that careful research must be done before entering the market? Yes.

• Successful companies know China is not "one" market.

Experienced companies have learned to analyze and segment the market, realizing the needs of Beijing are far different from those of Shanghai. Guangzhou and Fujian are more closely linked to the economies of Hong Kong and Taiwan than with the provinces surrounding them, much less inland frontier regions such as Gansu. The point is that there are many different Chinas, operating at various levels of sophistication along a time warp stretching between the 1920s and the 1980s.

• Successful companies look for multiple points of entry.

Just as there is no one market, there is no one Buyer and no one Seller. The decentralization of the trade and investment structure, detailed in chapters 3 and 9, means that just as a company doesn't usually go to New York to find out if there is an opportunity in Phoenix, Beijing may not be helpful for learning about what buyers and sellers are up to in central and southern China. Here again homework will pay big dividends.

• Successful companies know exactly what they want . . . and are patient and flexible enough to get it.

Determine just where China fits into your company's overall strategic plan. How far must you diverge from that plan to make China happen? In any case, the goals for your China business, particularly for investors, must be clear, unambiguous, and sustainable. Without such clarity of goals, and an awareness of the limits the environment imposes, one invites frustration, mistakes, and failures.

At the same time, and because China's foreign trade and investment practices change continually, flexibility and a willingness to take a long-term approach to achieving those goals is critical.

"Long-term" is more than just a slogan. It's a tangible commitment to programs such as education, training, and shared benchmarks for the growth and evolution of the commercial relationship. The Polaroid case study offers an excellent example.

• Successful companies develop a strategy that takes into account the limitations of what can be done in China.

One rule is to begin by starting business in as simple a form as possible. There's less risk, and there's a great opportunity to get used to operating in the environment. Avon's goal, for example, was to carry out its direct sales strategy. But as an interim step it entered into a joint manufacturing agreement. 3M first bought and sold basic products before moving on to try a wholly owned subsidiary. Fluke International spent years involved in direct sales, then accepted an assembly arrangement and finally moved to licensing of technology.

• Successful companies know how to benefit from the China information network.

There is no shortage of information available about China, or experts to help evaluate it in the context of your business. Plugging into this network begins by familiarizing yourself with key publications, participating in relevant trade, government, and educational organizations, and exploring the suitability of using consultants, agents, and specialists (see chapter 8).

• Successful companies put together the right team.

The fundamental rule for picking the China team is, involve the people who are actually responsible for the business. Whether it's one person or a half dozen, the same rules apply—they should have the authority to make the deal, the expertise to understand the economic and political context in which the deal is being made, and the operational responsibility to make it work. High-level support is critical and should be continual and visible. Negotiating teams for a JV should ideally include the prospective expatriate general manager, for example, as well as the person capable of officially representing the views of the corporation.

Company representatives need not speak Chinese (and inadequate Chinese can hinder rather than help negotiations), but in cases where the project requires extensive discussions, they should certainly have access to people on their team who can. Interpreters can be hired for this purpose, and usually consultants offer this as part of their service.

A good consultant can also offer added value to the negotiating team by providing a shortcut to understanding the market, helping to develop a sound strategy, locating a partner, and assisting in the evaluation as well as the negotiations. They are not a substitute for a business plan, however, and firms committing themselves to the market should develop in-house expertise. Even if specialists continue to help in specific areas, the best information screen (as well as the best symbol of your company's commitment) is the eyes, ears and authority of someone within the company.

• Successful companies take a principled stand against corruption.

It's easy to be cynical about the pervasive corruption in China. Sometimes it seems as if there simply is no "system," and the only way something can get done is through the exercise of personal power, found through the back door, acquired and expressed through *guanxi*, and measured—directly or indirectly—in dollars.

Principled companies work hard to find ways to ensure cooperation without giving in to the temptation of "just this once," and thereby sinking into a morass of endless payoffs.

▼ A Different View

This book takes the view that China is accessible and even welcoming to foreign business, although companies approaching the market should do so conscious of the risks, aware of the realities, and understanding of the unique—but by no means insurmountable—problems presented by the market.

There are, of course, other perspectives. Stanley Lubman and his associate Gregory Wajnowski are two lawyers specializing in assisting American firms in China. They recently presented a paper in China at an "International Workshop on the Development of Shanghai." Summarized here, and in their words, are some of the problems which they believe tend to make China a hostile and inaccessible environment for investment.

1. The inconvertibility of the RMB and foreign exchange controls. Remedial measures so far have been largely insufficient . . . existing legislation should be more flexibly applied, thereby easing the anxiety of prospective investors.

2. Sourcing of inputs, high domestic costs, hidden charges and labor issues. These problems are caused, to some extent, by the underdeveloped state of the Chinese economy and the very nature of the economic system, but whatever the reasons, the consequence is that foreign investors must operate in an environment which is not necessarily hospitable.

3. The inadequacy of the legal and regulatory framework for foreign direct investment. Existing legislation often leads to a lack of clarity and inconsistent policy objectives . . . laws do not go far enough to protect foreign investment enterprises . . . broad policies are encouraging to investment, but can be undercut by specific rules and regulations.

4. The enforcement and implementation of promulgated laws. Changes in the way Chinese think about the legal system are urgently needed. Frequently cited sources of frustration are the internal, or *neibu*, rules that are only disclosed, if at all, on a selective basis.

5. The "opaque" nature of the Chinese system. All of the above problems, including an intricate bureaucracy, the inaccessibility of documents and officials, and a nascent legal system and a very different "legal culture" create a system that is difficult for foreigners to understand or deal with. This results in misunderstandings at the negotiation table . . . and a feeling among the foreign investment community that despite some encouraging words, China is still hostile to foreign investment.

Source: excerpted from *Notes*, the newsletter of the National Committee on U.S.-China Relations, Spring/Summer 1991. Copies of Mr. Lubman's full paper (which includes proposals for remedy) can be requested from the Committee, 777 UN Plaza, New York, NY 10017.

Positioning

After good planning, the next lesson to emerge from the experience of companies in China is that position is everything.

• Successful companies learn how to make the process of decentralization work for them.

Decentralization is both a curse and a blessing. A curse because all the neat organizational assumptions under the old system of centralized control over trade and investment—namely, one-stop shopping—have to be thrown out. A blessing because it is now possible to implement this basic rule: work with the partner closest to the source.

This means an importer can work directly with a factory, and an investor can complete most deals without having to get authority from Beijing.

At the same time, realize that while decentralization has been of great benefit to trader and investor alike, it also calls for delicate positioning. Apparent dependence upon central government patrimony may invoke in your partner a fear of needless meddling. Too much autonomy will make government authorities feel slighted. Hence the next point:

• Successful companies know that there is a need for allies, and don't isolate themselves.

In this era of decentralization it's all too easy to neglect the constructive aspects of having allies at all levels of the Chinese bureaucracy, including the very top. Otsuka Pharmaceuticals, Xerox, 3M, and other cases cited here testify to the need to pay careful attention to hierarchy and the use of *guanxi* (see chapter 10). The lesson is to work well with all levels of the bureaucracy so that when the time comes, multiple levers of power can be applied on your behalf.

In looking for a partner, it's wise not to neglect this need to take powerful allies into account. They can be found within municipal departments, within provincial investment corporations, within Beijing ministries, and even in Hong Kong partners. If the local Chinese partner is powerful, but their allies or yours are not, it does not always bode well for the venture.

• Successful companies realize that time and energy must not only be spent on finding *a* partner, but the *right* partner.

To help make a realistic evaluation, find answers to questions such as these:

❏ Is the proposed partner the best partner?

Ecolab, the company profiled in chapter 5, discovered the hard way that the most obvious partner isn't always the best partner. Assignment of the partner by the municipal or national authorities does not guarantee success. Procrustean beds are not comfortable—shop around for the most natural fit possible.

❏ Are the goals compatible or complementary?

The Chinese partner may be seeking to acquire technology while you are interested only in low-cost sourcing. They may seek substantial exports, while your goal is domestic sales. Even when the objectives are not the same, two partners may still be compatible, of course. The primary objective of a foreign wine company was to find a new source of grapes that was also close to a transportation center. The objective of the partner was different—to acquire technology for making better wine. Result? The successful Remy Martin-Tianjin wine-making joint venture.

❏ Does the potential partner have the authority to deal in foreign trade and does this authority specifically apply to the business being proposed?

The scope of authority of any Chinese partner is an important issue. Watch for the natural tendency to negotiate items well beyond its brief. Double check export quotas and other licensing restrictions in case someone's enthusiasm has outraced bureaucratic reality.

❏ What is the business record of the potential partner?

Now that a Chinese enterprise can no longer count on government subsidies to sustain itself, find out if the potential partner has a viable business. Asking about a credit reference in China is a sensitive issue (the first reaction may be that it's an official secret), but the question needs to be asked, and answered to your satisfaction. Ask about other customers, and general foreign trade and investment experience. Consider turning to an independent advisory group that can help evaluate the business background of the partner.

❏ How well is the partner tied into his market?

Foreign companies whose profits depend upon the product being sold in China cannot assume that a better mousetrap will automatically command an ever-growing market.

Lack of foreign exchange, bureaucratic or provincial rivalries, abrupt changes in policy, and existing or potential competitors are just some of the problems that can get in the way of selling on the domestic market. The question to ask is, Does the enterprise serve a market that is likely to remain strong?

❏ Does the partner have enough clout?

Arbitrary rules and regulations can crop up at any time, as can bureaucratic interference—witness the Olympic Hotel and Sanlian Automotive case studies. A competitor may be given the same deal, or a product can be easily knocked off. China trader Richard Engholm tells of a zipper manufacturing JV whose feasibility study showed only 11 zipper factories in China. But within two years, 105 of them were suddenly established (20 of them JVs), driving up the supply elevenfold, saturating the market and bankrupting the young venture (see also InkFont Technologies in chapter 7).

Such problems are not preventable—how can something that is a good idea and sells well be kept from being duplicated? But the partner's ability to work around such problems and to help find acceptable solutions is critical.

This is why good connections with high-level officials in a city or province are so important. In one case, a European industrial manufacturing firm selling on the domestic market has been able to keep out rivals due to its finely honed connections with provincial officials as well as its ability to make the venture profitable for both sides.

❏ **What is the prevailing management style, and the mood in the factory? Is the attitude cooperative, and entrepreneurial?**

These questions are as valuable for the importer as they are for the investor. The answers can come only through spending enough time with all who are to be involved in the enterprise—not just the agent or senior negotiator, but the factory and its manager, plant engineers and even the bureaucracies upon which the Chinese company must rely.

❏ **Is the partner a winner or a loser in the shifting sands of bureaucratic power?**

Experienced foreign companies develop a feel for the relative standing of various power centers. They know, for example, that the industrial ministries are becoming ever more powerful, even as the influence of national trading companies is diminishing. Go with the winners—but do not alienate the losers. Remain friendly with government agencies while keeping enough distance to minimize interference. Use decentralization to advantage, without losing standing with the center.

▼ WHEN IT'S THE WRONG PARTNER

National Standard International (NSI), the pseudonym for a large multinational healthcare supplier, found that changing its evaluation matrix in order to meet China's conditions instead of its own has resulted in enormous problems.

NSI evaluated the potential for sales of its product on its own, then turned to an American professor-turned-consultant for help in locating the venture. The professor advised that locating close to the source of raw materials was the key to success and NSI went ahead and found a partner in a small town in an inland province where a local factory was eager to take on a joint venture partner. In 1987, two years after the initial feasibility studies, the JV went into operation.

NSI has had none of the problems often reported by others. There has never been a lack of foreign exchange, shortage of raw materials, or absence of buyers. Instead, what has kept the JV from becoming profitable is an unproductive factory and a climate of complete mistrust between the partners.

The local partner had no experience in international business before entering this deal, nor had town officials and other officials associated with the JV. The quality of local labor was poor, and local managers totally uncooperative. All concerned seemed shortsighted and unwilling to be educated. For example, the local partner could not understand why the JV needed to spend money on marketing, on sales offices in Beijing and Shanghai, or other expenses not directly related to production. In the words of NSI, "they're all farmers."

The local partner, not seeing profits roll in, blamed NSI for the problems. For all it knew, NSI had supplied them with second-rate technology and second-rate expatriate management talent (this was partly true, since the JV's remote location could not attract better-qualified people). It got to the point where a NSI representative would say X, and the Chinese worker would do Y, simply out of spite. Even when a younger group of local Chinese managers came in to replace the old team, the atmosphere of mistrust continued.

As of this writing, the Chinese partner is demanding complete control. NSI is too close to making a profit to simply default and pull out. Only a period of solid profits are likely to restore good faith . . . but how can it be accomplished in this atmosphere?

▲

• Successful companies know that it's not just the status of the enterprise that's important, but also the qualities of the manager who runs it.

Companies negotiating technology transfer deals or joint ventures will want to pay as much attention to the qualities of the manager as they do to the qualifications of the plant he runs. Where does he fit in the local hierarchy? How tight is the bureau that is controlling him? How well does he motivate his people? Does he provide benefits to them? Does he seem to enjoy a sense of authority? Of autonomy? Of entrepreneurship? In short, is he an active participant in the reform program, or would he have preferred to see the old ways continue?

At the personal level, learn to separate the rank opportunist from the entrepreneurial deal maker, the corrupt bureaucrat from the helpful friend.

▼
SIZING UP THE CHINESE MANAGER

Roy F. Grow, an expert on technology transfer to China, makes the case that Chinese managers who successfully move through the steps of foreign technology acquisition usually demonstrate some combination of the following abilities:

• *They recognize the advantage of change.* Whether it's because their factory can no longer compete, the machinery has broken down, or heads have been turned by seeing the advanced technology of the West or Japan, they know how to seize opportunity.

• *They understand the potential disruption that a new technology can bring.* They have therefore already created a spirit of open discussion and readiness for improvement in the factory. This includes the building of a good relationship with their technical people.

• *They are sensitive to the needs of major constituencies.* The astute manager will be able to work well with the upstream levels of officialdom and the downstream users of the products that will be affected by the technology.

• *They are relatively autonomous, and not wedded to any one government agency or ministry.* A strong patron can help provide access to the technology and support for its acquisition, but he also has a tendency to interfere. The manager should be free to bargain and maneuver as necessary with various bureaucracies in order to get the job done, both during the negotiation process and after the technology is in place.

• *They are entrepreneurial.* Nothing could be more mistaken than to consider the phrase "Chinese entrepreneurs" a contradiction in terms. There are managers all over China who excel at maneuvering through the various bureaucracies to accomplish their goals—both within and outside of the factory. Chinese managers who are most effective in acquiring foreign technology are entrepreneurial types who play multiple points of access and control off against each other and take a certain joy in the process.

Adapted from "Acquiring Foreign Technology: What Makes The Transfer Process Work?" by Roy F. Grow. In *Science and Technology in Post-Mao China*, Cambridge, Mass.: Harvard University Press, 1989.

▲

Negotiating

Companies that underestimate the importance of a close, straight-forward relationship with the Chinese are likely to encounter serious difficulties. That relationship is built from the first day of negotiations and should inform all subsequent interaction.

> ### • Successful companies know that the effectiveness of the negotiations depends upon the effectiveness of the negotiator.

Ideally, the person chosen to spearhead the China negotiations is senior enough to have authority, seasoned enough to be experienced internationally, and patient and consistent enough not to be daunted by what can be a lengthy process.

The person(s) having the best chance of accomplishing the task at hand is someone who (1) has enough self-assurance to weather the continual drain of psychic energy and "hardship" circumstances imposed by the Chinese negotiating process; (2) has had prior experience in Asia, and (3) does not fear that his or her career is riding on the outcome. This type of negotiator will not be tempted to feel that any deal is better than no deal.

If a team approach is required, as is often the case in technology transfer agreements or equity ventures, then the first rule is continuity. The same person should clearly be in charge throughout the negotiating process (which can take months or even years) and, ideally, the people involved in the implementation of the deal (e.g., the general manager of a JV) should also take part. High turnover in negotiation teams breeds uncertainty in the minds of the Chinese and inconsistency in a company's posture.

> ### • Successful companies formulate a positive strategy to cope with Chinese negotiation tactics.

Your Chinese counterparts come to the table with a clear negotiating strategy in mind. The experienced foreign company does likewise.

An effective negotiation posture begins with the formulation of sound goals, which are stated clearly to both your own negotiating team as well as the Chinese. Ambiguous or shifting goals will always put one at a disadvantage. The person or persons presenting the proposal should know it, and all company policies and products related to it, cold. Improvisation usually leads to disaster.

The second element of an effective negotiating strategy is to let the prospective partner know that the deal will be made only if it meets the realistic strategic and economic goals your company has set for it. Flexibility and "mutual understanding" are, of course, required, but the Chinese will respect a company only if they know that it sticks to its principles and can't be moved by the pressure simply to make the deal.

The third element is to figure out who the key players are on the Chinese side and make them part of the negotiations to the extent possible. The people in the overstuffed chairs around the room taking notes are not necessarily those authorized to make the deal or those having the responsibility for carrying it out. Try to ensure that the Chinese team includes the relevant technical experts, project managers, and government officials responsible for facilitating and/or authorizing the deal. If they're not included, figure out a way to establish a relationship with them informally without making your partner lose face.

Fourth, realize that just as consistency and open communications are the keys to effectiveness, so anger and impatience are the doorways to failure. With a clear understanding of the partner's interests and point of view, be patient but persistent in the effort to communicate yours. Don't issue timetables, either for your own ability to stay or for the deal to have to be concluded. Negotiating deadlocks are rarely broken through displays of anger and impatience. These are seen as a character weaknesses, and are easily exploitable.

• Successful companies understand that creativity and flexibility are necessary, too.

Honor the principles behind the prospective partner's major negotiating points. If a deadlock occurs, search for ways around it that allow both sides to save face. Something not possible one way may be perfectly acceptable another way, even if the only difference is what you end up calling it.

Similarly, forceful bending does not make an accord. Flexibility does. An agreement that leaves either side with the feeling of being force-fed like a Peking duck will face a lot of indigestion.

• Successful companies don't underestimate the power of traditional political and cultural values that may lie under the surface.

As discussed in chapter 10, underlying cultural values influence the negotiation process as well as the implementation of the contract. For example, when conflicts or misinterpretations arise, it may lead either or both sides to feel used—the Chinese for their cheap labor and access to the market, the foreigners for their technology and the money they seem to be willing to spend in buckets.

• Successful companies know assumptions are dangerous companions.

Treat all those you meet with equal respect. Don't assume that a political heavy doesn't want to do the project while the understanding and aggressive young turk does. Don't assume that because she doesn't speak up at meetings or sits at the third table at a banquet she isn't important now, or won't be in the future.

Assume nothing, from the apparent power (or lack thereof) of your counterparts to the assurances of working this or that aspect out after the contract has been signed.

Loose ends do not straighten themselves out. Vagueness enables further pressure for concessions. Spell out all problems. Disputes based upon understandings and intentions not spelled out in the final contract inevitably surface. The signal phrase is, "Based on our friendship and understanding, please . . ." There may be requests for additional trips abroad, expectations of additional training, or a dispute regarding the number of spare parts.

The temptation is to leave an issue that seems particularly thorny, but not of overriding importance, to the "detail" people, or to worry about that understood-but-not-specified extra week of technical training later. The Chinese certainly prefer it this way, but commitments of any kind, and even clear understandings of what is not committed, are best put in writing.

This is not to say everything must be spelled out in the finest legalese. There is no clear data supporting the notion that highly detailed contracts assure smoother operations than those left purposefully open and flexible. A company that places a heavy emphasis on writing contractual terms in the best legalese money can buy may be at a double disadvantage. A spirit of mistrust is likely to arise, and everything may take much longer to accomplish.

▼ Things That Make the Negotiations Move Faster

A survey carried out by the Manchester School of Business (U.K.) showed negotiations were likely to progress well if:

1. The project is compatible with central government development priorities.

2. The project is compatible with municipal and/or district priorities.

3. There are few Chinese organizations involved.

4. A trading relationship already exists between the Chinese and the foreign firm.

5. The complexity of the technology is low.

6. The Chinese negotiators have previous experience of negotiations with foreign companies and understand Western business concepts.

7. The composition of the Chinese negotiating team remains stable.

8. The foreign company remains flexible and creative during the negotiations, rather than legalistic.

Source: Nigel Campbell and Peter Adlington, *China Business Strategies: A Survey of Foreign Business Activity in the PRC.* Oxford: Pergamon Press, 1988.

▼ THINGS THAT MAY MAKE THE NEGOTIATIONS STUMBLE

A survey done jointly by the consulting firm of A. T. Kearney and China's International Trade Institute in 1987 found that each of the following issues, common to most joint venture negotiations, could become a serious stumbling block:

- amount of investment and equity shares
- valuation of "in-kind" contributions
- apportionment of board of directors and selection of chair
- autonomy and decision-making
- finance and borrowing
- pricing of product, both domestically and internationally
- salary and benefits of expatriates
- training and associated payments
- marketing ratios for domestic and export sales
- local content
- contract form and arbitration

Source: Manufacturing Equity Joint Ventures in China, a report by A. T. Kearney Management Consultants, 1987; updated 1989.

Managing and Operating

The essential element to carry from the negotiations into the implementation of the contract is a sense of shared purpose. Nurturing this goal will help ease the strains all ventures are likely to encounter at one time or another.

• Successful companies realize that a contract neither defines nor governs the venture.

A contract establishes the venture, but is obviously no substitute for competent efforts to implement it. Success is shaped through human relationships and the conduct of the business rather than through rigid rules and contracts.

Successful ventures inevitably have worked hard to create an atmosphere of trust and mutual respect before, during, and after the negotiations—something that can never be secured by a contract.

Trust is built through consistency and mutual respect. As one veteran Chinese negotiator said, "Show respect in the first place, and ask their opinions, and they will not want to say 'no.' On the other hand, if you don't show respect, they have this ugly feeling about you. Then even the smallest matter becomes a big deal and questions are always answered with a 'no.' And if it's 'no,' the foreign company can't do anything about it."

• Successful companies know there is a difference between ownership and control.

Management control is among the most difficult issues faced by equity ventures. Autonomy from outside interference must be guaranteed to the extent possible, and is partly controlled by the makeup of the board of directors. Companies are also learning to leave day-to-day managers off the board so that disputes are confined to the principals rather than spilled down to the managerial level where they can have a negative effect on morale and operations.

The foreign presence is usually needed for management supervision in the early stages of operation, even when there has been a chance to recruit and train workers especially for the venture (see Tambrands and United Biscuits).

As to questions of day-to-day management, the balance many foreign companies strive for is to be in control without seeming to dictate. Decision-making tends to work best when foreign managers are put into key positions initially and an active training program is then instituted to phase in local managers as they become qualified.

• Successful companies actively recruit and train Chinese workers.

Recruitment of personnel can be a serious problem, due to the lack of trained personnel, limited mobility of labor, and regulations designed to stem the flow of skilled workers from state-owned enterprises. Solutions are discussed throughout the case studies as well as in chapters 8 and 9, but one key seems to lie in maintaining control over the process of recruitment and training (see the Avon, PepsiCo, and Abbott examples).

Training is perhaps one of the most underestimated challenges faced by a new investor. The experience of almost every JV, and especially those involved in areas of high-technology, dictates that an aggressive policy of indoctrination and training must be implemented to ensure the smooth transfer of knowledge and expertise.

Training is also of paramount importance in changing the attitude of those workers who have little concept of the link between success and competent performance.

• Successful companies learn how to operate in a climate of ambivalence, ambiguity, and uncertainty.

Doing business with China has never been an either/or proposition. Business is rarely either trouble free or all that terrible. Ventures are never either closely defined or totally open ended. The trick is to have this uncertainty work for you instead of against you.

✦ ✦ ✦

These are some of the lessons garnered from the experience of hundreds of companies that have done business in China. It's now time for the ultimate question: Is China a place for you?

Reading the Fortune Cookies: Predictions for the Decade to Come

Reforms and greater openness are China's only way out.

—DENG XIAOPING, JANUARY 1992

We are waiting. . . . Change is happening in the world and China cannot resist it.

—FORMER CHINESE OFFICIAL TURNED ENTREPRENEUR

Is China a Good Investment?

Much of this book has dealt with issues that make China a unique business challenge.

The country is just emerging from a centuries-long commercial slumber during which the prevailing feeling was that the less contact with foreigners, the better. Even today what happens in trade and investment often seems more like experiment than policy.

Looking at China's status in the world and its significant economic clout, we tend to expect of it a mature body of commercial law and well-established norms of commercial behavior. It has neither. Accustomed to open markets and free societies, we find in China only a rudimentary start towards a market economy, and an authoritarian regime. Doing business with China is most assuredly not a neat, clean, and easy proposition.

The evidence that the effort is worthwhile is shown by the experience of hundreds of companies doing very successful business in China, companies that have shaped their strategy to a vision of China as a country in process rather than a country frozen in any particular moment of time.

What makes the effort worthwhile for many companies is that China is an inseparable part of the global market. South China and the East Asian nations beyond Japan boast the world's fastest-growing consumer economy—an economy that will swell by 80 million consumers in the next eight years and whose collective gross domestic product will approach $5 trillion by the end of the century (roughly equal to that of Europe).

Within China, a more profound revolution is under way than anything Chairman Mao ever contemplated. A staggering number of Chinese are in the process of gaining not only the desire but the means to be significant consumers. Thousands of enterprises are transforming themselves from inefficient, isolated entities into businesses operated on modified market principles and run by management contracts. Stock markets, commodity markets, property transactions, and other mainstays of the market economy are being established.

This is not to say progress has been, or will be, continuous. Chinese politics is unstable; the economy is still subject to stuttering periods of stop and go.

Which brings us back to the fundamental question. Is China a good investment?

For a growing number of forward-looking companies, the answer is "Yes." China is accessible and even welcoming to foreign business—and daily growing more so. China is an excellent source for raw materials. China is also a wonderful market for many importers and exporters, and an important place for investors looking for the right combination of labor, resources, and market position.

There are problems and risks associated with China, but these exist everywhere. Those unique to China loom large, but are by no means insurmountable. They *can* be understood and dealt with, just as they can in Thailand and Taiwan. But not if we allow ourselves to be overwhelmed by the wide pendulum swings of perception that saw the last decade start with a naive rush to invest and end with an exaggerated sense of peril. Neither boundless expectations nor narrow cynicism contribute to success in China. A solid sense of who benefits from what, does.

Whether China is a part of *your* future will depend upon your business strategy and how well you understand the nature of the market and the requirements for success.

It also depends upon an understanding of what is most likely to happen in China and the region in the next decade and the ability to assess the likely impact of these economic and political changes on your company's future.

A Look into the Future

Making predictions in any era is risky business. Making predictions about China in this period of transition is a doubly dubious affair. But answering the question of whether or not China is a good investment demands a look at the major trends shaping the Asian marketplace in the decade ahead. Cast as predictions to help challenge thinking, they are offered less as predetermined fact than as a way to inform the context of a period of extraordinary change.

It is China, not Central Europe or the former Soviet republics, that will be the economic success story of the 1990s. The road to economic progress will be long and arduous in Eastern Europe and, especially, for the newly-formed Commonwealth of Independent States. Despite the immense progress of political reform, these nations are just now taking the steps toward economic reform that China took in the late 1970s and early 1980s. They'll have to struggle for a decade or more to see the beginnings of the kinds of fundamental changes from which China is ready now to reap the benefits.

The economy of southern China will continue to outpace the rest of the nation, encouraging regionalism and leading to open speculation on whether a "Southern Dynasty" will emerge to take *de facto* control of the country. **By the end of the decade, South China will be catching up to France** in economic terms. At the same time, the economic integration of Guangdong and Fujian with Hong Kong and Taiwan will create a "Greater China" regional powerhouse. Already Hong Kong and Taiwan account for nearly a third of all foreign investment in China. A third or more of Hong Kong's industries have moved into the Pearl River delta; roughly $20 billion worth of process trade has flowed from China back into Hong Kong annually since the early 1990s. The combined strength of these three economies is so compelling that **talks will be held between officials from Guangdong, Hong Kong, and Taiwan on how to form a "Greater Chinese Economic Zone."** This gradual economic merger bodes well for the resolution of the remaining political conflicts in the region as well.

There will be no "big shock" in 1997. By then, Hong Kong will already be fully integrated into the Pearl River Delta economy. From Victoria Peak to Shamian Island, Hong Kong,

Guangzhou, and the towns and cities along the Pearl River estuary in between will merge into one huge metropolis. Hong Kong manufacturers already employ more than 4 million workers in southern China. and trade between Hong Kong and China is already roughly equivalent to Hong Kong's entire GDP (about $63.2 billion). Hong Kong will become ever more important as a capital-raising center for China and Southeast Asia; Guangdong, which currently emphasizes light industrial and processing and assembly operations, will become a major industrial supplier and trading center. **Fears of China will ebb and gradually prove irrelevant** as these mutually beneficial roles are realized. By 1997, Hong Kong will have a quasi-independent ruling body as a political face-saving device to placate the small but prestigious group of self-determinationists. But all that will be left to keep it from being fully integrated as a semi-autonomous part of China are the formalities.

The success of the process of regionalization will also mean that China and Taiwan will announce an accommodation during Chinese New Year celebrations in the next "Year of the Dragon"— A.D. 2000. Three trends will pave the way for a political merger as significant as that of East and West Germany. First, the Taiwan economy will continue to be further integrated with China's. Trade and investment have mushroomed: In 1993 trade, even though indirect, amounted to over $10 billion. Investment totaled $15 billion. As Taiwan faces rising labor costs, lower productivity, and shrinking exports, further investment on the mainland will be openly encouraged—even as the island's growing economic dependency on China becomes a major political issue. Second, the island's leaders are keeping a weather-eye out on China's treatment of Hong Kong. As fears there subside, sentiment for some form of a Taiwan-China merger will increase. At the same time, the passing of the old communist guard in Beijing will mean China can rethink its notions about sovereignty in its Taiwan policy and accept a semi-autonomous arrangement similar to the one to be negotiated with Hong Kong.

By the year 2001 China, Hong Kong, and Taiwan will also have joined the six ASEAN countries and Australia to form a regional economic alliance. In a variation of a scenario created by analyst Daniel Burstein, the first half of the 1990s will see ASEAN take the initiative in developing a lower Pacific Rim alliance in response to the global trend toward economic regionalism. **Singapore will become the "Brussels" of this alliance**, serving as its secretariat. Japan will quietly help weld the region together through economic muscle while staying out of the political limelight. In the end, for reasons both economic and cultural, **Japan will not play a leading role**. It will be given observer status, as will the U.S. The resulting alliance, which will include Vietnam, Laos and Cambodia, will stimulate still further growth. **By 2010, the region— including the Hong Kong/Guangzhou city state—will constitute itself economically as the Greater Asia Free Trade Zone (GAZE).**

By the early 21st century, Japan and China could become intense geopolitical rivals. The traditional cultural and political rivalries that are being overcome in the Europe of 1992 (e.g., between France and Germany) will take a great deal longer to heal in Asia. History is never far below the surface here, and the strategic turmoil that led to 19th and 20th century wars involving Russia, China, Japan, and Korea may yet resurface. The coming withdrawal of American troops from Korea and Japan will leave a power vacuum, resulting in a stronger and independent-minded Korea, and growing pressure within Japan for remilitarization. This will increase wariness in China, where military spending has increased significantly in the past few years and which is the region's only large nuclear power. On the surface, economic suspicions will dominate, and as Japanese direct investment in China increases in each of the years 1992 through 1994, the themes that dominated U.S.-Japan relations in the 1980s and early 1990s will reincarnate themselves in the China-Japan relationship, which will be characterized by mutual need but often publicly expressed as mutual hostility. In mid-decade, as Beijing gets distracted by the end of the communist dynasty, **Japan will try to pressure China** to grant it special favors for operating in the Shenyang/Dalian corridor to help speed the growing economic ties between that region and Japan. China, invoking fear of another Manchukuo, will balk. **As tension grows, the U.S. will begin to wonder if eventually it might have to make a choice whether to play its Japan card or its China card**, providing an odd coda to the long-forgotten Cold War maneuvering of the 1970s.

Domestically, the tempo of China's economic and trade reforms will continue in 1995–96, despite succession uncertainties. Reforms will continue to be introduced at a rate leaders consider consistent with maintaining stability. Many of these reforms—such as the elimination of the dual pricing system, subsidies, and so on—will benefit foreign traders and investors, as will China's increasing acceptance of international trade and regulatory standards such as the intellectual property rights conventions. Such reforms, **plus promises of greater transparency, will mean China will join GATT in 1995**.

China will develop a surprisingly robust capital market by 1997. While not yet a rival to the world's other financial capitals, Shanghai will be the focus of major changes in the country's financial life. China's leaders will move cautiously, but more stock and commodity markets will open in the next few years. **Hundreds of companies are now being groomed for listing at home and abroad**. Holding companies will be created for state-owned enterprises, and shares in these holding companies will be sold or distributed as workers' bonuses. Money will move freely through banks and markets. The amount of savings being held outside the system will astound foreign economists as people all over China rush to buy into their future through bonds, securities, and real estate.

Although Western analysts scoff at the notion that China can make consistent economic progress while stuck halfway between the command economy and the market, **"market socialism" will remain the ideology driving economic policy for at least the next five years**. This is not simply political indecision: China is consciously attempting to steer a road to development that incorporates Western-style reliance on markets but avoids the social turmoil they associate with Western-style democratic practices. **By 1996 China will at last begin to reverse its underwriting of state enterprises**, which by now contribute less than 50% of industrial output. Bankruptcy laws will finally be invoked. As a consequence, **many state-run firms will be allowed to go out of business in 1996**. The rest will be absorbed over time by private and/or foreign-funded ventures, **although the government will continue to keep foreign investors from taking majority control of enterprises** deemed essential to China's independence. As the "iron rice bowl" cracks, the government will begin experimenting with national welfare reform, rationalizing that one large welfare state is less expensive to maintain than the thousands of mini-ones now associated with state-run enterprises. The new welfare system will be implemented during the Ninth Five Year Plan (1997–2001).

Ministries will coninue to evolve into regulatory bodies, gradually shedding their role as planning agencies. **The foreign trade and investment system will continue the process of decentralization**, with more and more cities and provinces having significant control of the process. **China will develop large commercial entities, tied together in mutually reinforcing ways on the Japanese *keiretsu* model. These will, by 1997, effectively control more than half of China's foreign trade and investment.** Despite its bow to Japan as model, China will not become another Japan in the near term. There may be reorganization and growing prosperity, and the GDP will continue its dramatic rise, but it will take years to build the infrastructure—physical and intellectual—capable of propelling the country as a whole beyond an intermediate stage of development.

Favorable foreign sentiment towards China— stretched to yet another round of excessive optimism in the early 1990s—will ebb considerably in 1995– 1996. As overblown expectations once again meet the realities of China's growing pains, company executives can be expected to vent publicly their anger at perceived corruption, double-dealing, excessive bureaucratism, lack of legal protection, and a general unwillingness to play by the "rules." Chinese actions (or lack thereof) will certainly add easy ammunition to such negativism. Knowing that China can be a painful experience in the short run but essential to corporate growth in the long run, experienced foreign companies will expand, learn to be ever more "local," and reap consistent benefits from their presence.

The greatest *social* danger facing Chinese society is not a hard-line Stalinist coup or an army putsch but the re-emergence of 1930s-style chaos. There's a remarkable degree of venality abroad in the land, fueled by the absence of a strong moral center and fanned by the chaos just underneath the surface of a society in flux. The cast-off work force and the migratory unemployed are envious of the "haves." Stability is always a question mark. **Sporadic unrest will break out in major cities in 1995–96, and pockets of resentment against foreigners will become evident**. But continued economic progress, a generally stable and available supply of food and, most of all, a strong natural desire for stability will help ensure the social order.

The greatest *economic* danger will come in the form of economic warlordism. Decentralization will continue to be the buzzword of the 1990s. Provincial and local authorities will continue jockeying with the authorities in Beijing for economic control. **Along with decentralization will come economic factionalization.** The gap between inland and coast will grow wider, just as will the gap between foreign-involved businesses and the state enterprises. Steps toward inter-provincial cooperation have recently picked up steam, but China, mimicking the pattern already established in other parts of Asia, will have **several disproportionately wealthy city-states or "islands" serving as hubs for trade and investment.** Perhaps the best analogy is to see these areas as a group of Taiwans—a number of strong economic islands that will put their own development first but will be tied in various ways to their neighbors. Guangzhou, Shanghai, Tianjin, and Shenyang-Dalian will be among these wealthy areas. Despite its continued administrative importance (at least until 2010) **Beijing will be excluded**

from this scenario. Together with Beijing in the second tier will be Hunan, Zhejiang, Jiangsu, and Hebei provinces. Further removed yet from prosperity will be the inland provinces.

Political **power, like economic power, will continue to devolve to the provinces.** Preoccupied with their own goals, the leadership will trade off their authority for continued recognition, all the while becoming more irrelevant to provincial authorities. Local politicians will fashion their own, regional, solutions to economic problems. **But China will not break up into independent states as was the case with the Soviet Union**. While there may be much testing, and perhaps even some breaking away at the periphery (Tibet, Xinjiang, Inner Mongolia), the weight of China's history and culture speaks to the struggle for unity, even though in many ways that unity may end up being largely symbolic in the transitional period ahead.

The death of Deng Xiaoping in 1995 will not result in the turmoil generally forecast. Nevertheless, a struggle will be underway behind the scenes to see who among the present front-runners—Zhang Zemin, Zhu Rongji, Li Peng—can wrest clear leadership. The army will monitor events and attempt to influence their outcome but will not move to directly intervene—either for or against any faction—unless there is severe instability. If the leadership can maintain a façade of shared decision-making (and indications are that it can), the old communist guard will merely collapse—under the weight of time, mortality, and its failure to adequately cope with a series of natural disasters. As none of the present contenders for leadership have the stature and authority of Deng, **China will have to wait until 1996–97 to see strong central leadership   re-emerge**. In the meantime, China's authoritarian bent, disdained by the West but generally accepted in China in the name of stability, will continue.

The post-Deng leadership structure will go through three distinct phases in the near term. **As Western consensus has it, the immediate leadership mantle will be passed to Jiang Zemin**, who along with Li Peng and Zhu Rongji, will gain the chance to govern during the initial transition period. **A surprise choice (at least to outsiders) will be made for the post of premier: Wu Bangguo**, a protege of Jiang's from Shanghai. By 1996, however, another faction within the government will gain control, having been able to point to a number of key failures during the Jiang-Li-Zhu interregnum. This more pragmatic faction will be led by the carpenter from Tianjin: **Li Ruihua**. Standing with him will be Zhao Shi and Tian Jijun. Wu Bangguo will also be a member. In the third and final phase of the immediate post-Deng era, the national

People's Congress will reform itself by the end of the decade and spawn a "New Democratic" Party from which a new Chinese leader will emerge by consensus.

The Party is over. **The Chinese Communist Party will lose control of the government in 1999. Various interest groups will emerge in the wake of Deng Xiaoping's death, and power will be brokered instead of dictatorially seized, but true democracy will not come to China in this century**. Democracy has no history in China. The last free election was in 1912 and was nullified within six months. Instead, we are, by late century, likely to see a variation of the "Asian model" of democracy where a popularly elected legislature remains under the "tutelage" of a strong central figure put in place through a consensus-building process. Parties will exist, and democratic ideas will be discussed and even adopted, but the search for what type of "democratic" system is best for China will be long and arduous. Not until the next century will there be a more institutionalized and consensus-based management of affairs.

Foreign traders and investors will face an environment in which the economy will continue to improve even as large economic and political issues remain unsettled. Corruption will become increasingly blatant. Another challenge will come from an increasingly complex regulatory environment. Provinces will place greater restrictions on inter-regional trade as an outgrowth of regionalism. **The business issues that will preoccupy the China trade publications of the mid-1990s will be decentralization and localization**, both in an economic and political sense.

The key indicator of China's long-term success will be Shanghai, not Guangzhou. The transformation of Guangdong Province was easy compared to the challenges facing Shanghai: a woefully inadequate infrastructure, huge population, and a long-suppressed spirit of entrepreneurship. In recent years, however, Shanghai has been adept at taking advantage of the central government's willingness to let it have its head. Hence the rush to build highways, bridges, office buildings, industrial zones. Ultimately the confidence of foreign investors will ride upon whether Shanghai can transform its flash of growth into a sustainable boom. **After a bust in the late 1990s—which will help hasten the end of communist rule—Shangai will eclipse Hong Kong, Tokyo, and Singapore to be the focal point of Asian growth in the 21st century.**

At present, that's the future. Some of these predictions may be overtaken by the rush of events, others may strike the reader as fanciful. In some cases the disagreement may come only in the timing. Of course, alternate scenarios can be constructed as well (see sidebar).

In these scenarios some companies may find complications and uncertainties that deter them from investing. Others will see an opportunity to source materials, sell product, and make strategic alliances that will position them to enjoy the unprecedented growth this region will experience.

For the anxious, impatient and inflexible, China is an invitation to frustration. For the company capable of doing the homework, able to work with the market instead of against it, and understanding of the risks and complications, the results can be most worthwhile.

Yes, China can be a good investment.

APPENDICES

Appendix 1

Further Reading

This appendix contains full bibliographic reference to the works of people quoted or otherwise cited in the text. The section of the chapter in which their work was cited is indicated by the heading. There are also suggestions for additional reading to facilitate further research into particular topics.

CHAPTER 1

James McGregor, "Success Stories in China Stay Untold as U.S. Firms Strive for Low Profiles," *The Wall Street Journal*, November 7, 1991.

Barber B. Conable, Jr., in remarks before the National Committee on U.S.-China Relations, January 29, 1992.

James Stepanek, "It's Business as Usual, China-style," *The Asian Wall Street Journal*, September 4, 1989. Stepanek's writing is particularly lucid and well worth searching out.

Roy F. Grow, "Brighter Outside the Beijing Beltway," *Current Issues*, February 1991.

Robert Delfs, "Saying No to Peking," *Far Eastern Economic Review*, April 4, 1991.

Elizabeth Cheng and Michael Taylor, "Delta Force," *Far Eastern Economic Review*, May 16, 1991.

"As China's Economy Withers, Reform May Bloom Again," *Business Week*, November 4, 1991.

"Beijing Issues Renewed Warning About Finances," *The Financial Times of London*, October 22, 1991.

"They Couldn't Keep It Down," an overview of the economy in *The Economist*, June 1, 1991.

James McGregor, "China's Trade Status? Most Annoying," *The Wall Street Journal*, May 3, 1991.

Jonathan Spence's quote came from a speech delivered at the 1991 Annual Meeting of the National Committee on U.S.-China Relations.

CHAPTER 2

David Hale, "Future Conditional: U.S. Trade Relations with
    China," *The Financial Times of London*, July 24, 1991.

"They Couldn't Keep It Down," an overview of the economy in *The
    Economist*, June 1, 1991.

The Economic Foundations

"One Billion and Counting," a survey of the 1990 census by
    Judith Bannister in *The China Business Review*, May–June,
1991 *CBR*, as the bi-monthly magazine is known, is an indispensable resource.

"It All Depends on How You Count Them," *Far Eastern Economic
    Review*, March 2, 1989.

Barry Naughton, "The Economy Emerges from a Rough Patch," in a
    special China issue of *Current History*, 1991.

Kyoichi Ishihara, "The Post-NPC Chinese Economy—Present State
    and Outlook," in *JETRO China Newsletter* 93, July–August,
    1991.

James Stepanek, "China's Enduring State Factories: Why Ten Years
    of Reform Have Left China's Big State Factories Unchanged,"
    in U.S. Congress, *Joint Economic Committee, Hearings on
    China's Economic Dilemma in the 1990s*, Vol. 2, April 1991.
    Hereafter cited as U.S. Congressional Hearings, April 1991.

"If It Works, It's Private," *The Economist*, November 30, 1991.

Infrastructure

J. P. Huang, "Fueling the Economy," *The China Business Review*,
    March–April 1991.

David G. Fridley and James P. Dorian, "China's Resource Crisis,"
    Far Eastern Economic Review, September 27, 1990. See also
    other work by Fridley, e.g., "China's Energy Outlook," in U.S.
    Congressional Hearings, April 1991.

James Stepanek, U.S. Congressional Hearings, April 1991.

Ralph W. Huenemann, "Modernizing China's Transport System," in
    U.S. Congressional Hearings, April 1991.

Ken Zita, "China's Telecommunications and American Strategic Interests," in U.S. Congressional Hearings, April 1991.

The Political Framework

Kenneth Lieberthal and Michel Oksenberg, *Policy Making in China: Leaders, Structures, Processes*. Princeton: Princeton University Press, 1991.

Tai Ming Cheung, "Policy in Paralysis," *Far Eastern Economic Review*, January 10, 1991.

Steven W. Mosher, "Year of the Phoenix," *New Republic*, April 29, 1991.

David M. Lampton, "China's Biggest Problem: Gridlock, Not Revolution," U.S. Congressional Hearings, April 1991.

Professor Oksenberg's quote appeared in James McGregor's article, "Old Guard in Beijing Finds Itself Trapped by Its Own Ideology," *The Wall Street Journal*, September 24, 1991.

CHAPTER 3

Theodore H. White, *In Search of History*. New York: Harper & Row, 1978, p. 119.

Daniel Burstein, "Their Man in Hong Kong," *Mainliner*, August 1985.

Trade and Investment

Arlene Wilson, "Overview," U.S. Congressional Hearings, April 1991.

Martin Weil, "The Business Climate in China: Half Empty or Half Full?" U.S. Congressional Hearings, April 1991. Weil's writing is also well worth searching out.

U.S.-China Business Council, *China's Trade and Investment Organizations*, June 1989.

Aspy Palia and Oded Shenkar, "Counting on Countertrade?" *The China Business Review*, March–April 1990.

U.S.-China Business Council, *U.S. Investment in China*, 1990.

China International Consultants. *China Investment Guide*, 4th ed. Hong Kong: Longman Group, 1989.

"China's New Rules on Wholly Foreign-Owned Enterprises." Two essays by Mao Tong and Ji Zhao, in *East Asian Executive Reports*, February 1991.

Manufacturing Equity Joint Ventures in China, a report by A. T. Kearney Management Consultants and the International Trade Research Institute of the P.R.C., 1987. Updates of this survey are available from A. T. Kearney.

Foreign Borrowing

Satoshi Imai, "China's Foreign Debt—Where It Stands Today," JETRO *China Newsletter* 93, July–August 1991.

Vanessa Lide, "The World Bank in China," *The China Business Review*, January–February 1991.

"World Bank Loans to China," *Business China*, July 15, 1991.

Elizabeth Cheng, "Guarantor's Market," *Far Eastern Economic Review*, June 20, 1991.

William R. Feeney, "China's Relations with Multilateral Economic Institutions," U.S. Congressional Hearings, April 1991.

Special Zones

All major China business publications (*The China Business Review, Business China, China Trade Report* and *China Trade*) run regular profiles of the SEZs, ETDZs, and open cities.

Lawrence C. Reardon, "The SEZs Come of Age," *The China Business Review*, November–December 1991.

Investment Opportunities in Shanghai. Cambridge: Asia Pacific Resource Group, Inc., 1991.

Manufacturing in Guangdong: An Executive Guide to Operating in Southern China. Hong Kong: Business International, 1990.

Norman P. Givant, "Putting Pudong in Perspective," *The China Business Review*, November–December 1991.

Thomas B. Gold, "Can Pudong Deliver?" *The China Business Review*, November–December, 1991.

———. "A Great Leap Forward," *The Economist*, October 5, 1991.

CHAPTER 4

Carl Crow, *400 Million Customers.* New York: Halcyon House, 1937.

CHAPTER 5

David Bonavia, *The Chinese.* New York: Lippincott & Crowell, 1980.

"Ecolab: A Different Partnership Approach," *China Trade,* June, 1991.

Roy F. Grow, "Acquiring Foreign Technology: What Makes the Transfer Process Work?" *In Science and Technology in Post-Mao China.* Merle Goldman and Denis Simon, eds. Cambridge: Harvard University Press, 1989.

CHAPTER 6

Carl Crow, *400 Million Customers.* New York: Halcyon House, 1937.

Steven R. Hendryx, "The China Trade: Making the Deal Work," *Harvard Business Review,* July–August, 1986.

Andrew Tanzer, "Ding-dong, Capitalism Calling," *Forbes,* October 14, 1991.

————. "U.S. Cosmetics Firm Breaks New Ground with Its P.R.C. JV," *Business China,* July 16, 1990.

Adi Ignatius, "U.S. Companies Going It Alone in China Find Road Bumpy but Have Few Regrets," *The Wall Street Journal,* October 10, 1990.

CHAPTER 7

Carl Crow, *400 Million Customers.* New York: Halcyon House, 1937.

"Coping with Corruption," a two-part series in *Business China,* May 27, 1991 and June 24, 1991.

CHAPTER 8

Roderick Macleod, *China, Inc.* New York: Bantam Books, 1988, pp. 172–74.

Robert Thomson, "China Juggles with Commercial Reality and Socialist Realism," *The Financial Times of London,* September 25, 1991. This article discusses the machine tool exhibition.

"Fair Enough," *China Trade Report*, June 1991, covered the electronics exhibition cited.

"Coping with Corruption," a two-part series in *Business China*, May 17, 1991 and June 24, 1991.

Chapter 9

Roderick Macleod, *China, Inc.* New York: Bantam Books, 1988.

Manufacturing Equity Joint Ventures in China, a report by A. T. Kearney Management Consultants and the International Trade Research Institute of the P.R.C., 1987.

U.S.-China Business Council, *U.S. Investment in China*, 1990.

Nigel Campbell, *A Strategic Guide to Equity Joint Ventures in China.* New York, London: Pergamon, 1989.

Steven R. Hendryx, "The China Trade: Making the Deal Work," *Harvard Business Review*, July–August 1986.

Chapter 10

Chapter head quote is from Nigel Cameron, *Barbarians and Mandarins: Thirteen Centuries of Western Travelers in China.* New York: Walker/Weatherhill, 1970.

Lucian Pye, *Chinese Commercial Negotiating Style.* Cambridge: Oelgeschlager, Gunn & Hain, 1982.

———. "The China Trade: Making the Deal," *Harvard Business Review*, July–August, 1986.

Chapter 11

Roy F. Grow, "What Are the Lessons?" In *The Midwest USA/China Resource Guide*, P. Richard Bohr, ed. Minneapolis: Midwest China Center and The Minnesota World Trade Center, 1987.

Roy F. Grow, "Reconsidering the China Market: Guidelines for Success," *Euro-Asia Business Review*, October 1987.

Jim Mann, *Beijing Jeep: The Short, Unhappy Romance of American Business in China.* New York: Simon and Schuster, 1989, p. 296.

Special Report on U.S. Investment in China. Washington, D.C: U.S.-China Business Council, 1989.

Manufacturing Equity Joint Ventures in China, a report by A. T. Kearney Management Consultants and the International Trade Research Institute of the P.R.C., 1987.

Joseph A. Alutto, "Sino-U.S. Joint Ventures: Seeking Corporate Success in Transitional Economies." Manuscript provided to the author. Dean Alutto of the Ohio State University College of Business was on the faculty of the National Center for Science and Technology Management Development in Dalian, P.R.C.

Interview with John Marshall by Siew Wong of the Midwest China Center, 1987. Transcript provided to the author by P. Richard Bohr.

Graeme Browning, *If Everybody Bought One Shoe: American Capitalism in Communist China.* New York: Hill and Wang, 1989, p. 39.

Christopher Engholm, *The China Venture: America's Corporate Encounter with the People's Republic of China.* New York: Scott, Foresman, 1989, p. 114.

Other reading

Randall E. Stross, *Bulls in the China Shop.* New York: Pantheon, 1990, p. 278.

Steven R. Hendryx, "The China Trade: Making the Deal Work," *Harvard Business Review,* July–August 1986.

Lucian Pye, "The China Trade: Making the Deal," *Harvard Business Review,* July–August 1986.

CHAPTER 12

Daniel Burstein, *Euroquake.* New York: Simon & Schuster, 1991, p. 339. Burstein, who knows Asia well, has also written the influential book *Yen! Japan's New Financial Empire and Its Threat to America.* New York: Simon & Schuster, 1988.

Appendix 2

The China Business Bookshelf

The following is an indication of the wealth of materials now available on China. Those publications marked with an "•" were particularly helpful to the author.

SUBSCRIPTION PUBLICATIONS

•*The Asian Wall Street Journal.* 200 Burnett Road, Chicopee, MA 01020.

Asia Week. 30/F Vicwood Plaza, 199 Des Voeux Road, Central, Hong Kong.

•*Business China.* Twice-monthly. Business International/Pacific Ltd., 10/F Luk Kwok Centre, 72 Gloucester Road, Hong Kong.

China-Britain Trade Review. Abford House, 15 Wilton Road, London SW1V 1LT.

•*China Business Review.* Bi-monthly. The U.S.-China Business Council, 1818 N Street NW, Suite 500, Washington, DC 20036.

China Daily Business Weekly. China Daily Distribution Corporation, 15 Mercer Street, New York, NY 10013.

China Economic Information Newsletter. CA Technology, 55 East 9th Street, New York, NY 10003.

China Economic News. Published weekly by Economic Daily (MOFERT/Beijing), distributed by Economic Information & Agency, Ltd. 10-16/Fl 342 Hennessy Road, Wanchai, Hong Kong.

China Hand: Investing, Licensing and Trading Conditions in the People's Republic of China. Two-volume binder with regular updates. Hong Kong: Business International Asia/Pacific, Ltd., 1990.

China Market. Economic Information & Agency Holdings, Ltd. 10-16/Fl 342 Hennessy Road, Wanchai, Hong Kong.

China Monthly Statistics. China Statistical Information and Consultancy Service, Beijing. U.S. partner: China Statistics Archives, University of Illinois, 1033 West Van Buren Street, Chicago, IL 60607.

China Phone Book and Business Directory. Bi-annual. China Phone Book and Address Directory Company, Ltd., 181 Gloucester Road, Hong Kong.

China Quarterly. London: Contemporary China Institute of the School of Oriental and African Studies, London University.

•*China Trade.* Monthly. China Trade Corporation, 334 Broadway, Cambridge, MA 02139.

•*China Trade Report.* Monthly. Review Publishing Company, GPO Box 160, Hong Kong.

China's Customs Statistics. Annual. Economic Information & Agency Holdings, Ltd. 10-16/Fl 342 Hennessy Road, Wanchai, Hong Kong.

China's Foreign Trade. Monthly. China Council for the Promotion of International Trade. Subscription agent: Guoji Shudian, PO Box 399, Beijing.

East Asian Executive Reports. Monthly. East Asian Executive Reports, 717 D Street NW, Suite 300, Washington, DC 20004.

•*Far Eastern Economic Review.* Weekly. Review Publishing Company, GPO Box 160, Hong Kong.

Tax and Investment in the People's Republic of China. International Bureau of Fiscal Documentation. PO Box 20237, 1000 HE Amsterdam, The Netherlands.

Intertrade. International Business Monthly, Ministry of Foreign Economic Relations and Trade. U.S. agent: CMA International, 7515 Topton Street, New Carrollton, MD 20784.

•*JETRO China Newsletter.* Monthly. JETRO Publications Department, 2-2-5 Toranomon, Minato-ku, Tokyo 105, Japan.

Articles, Speeches, Hearings, Seminar Papers

Cheng Chu-yuan. "China's Economy in Retrenchment," *Current History,* September 1990.

Hendryx, Steve R. "The China Trade: Making the Deal Work," *Harvard Business Review,* July–August, 1986.

Naughton, Barry. "The Economy Emerges from a Rough Patch," *Current History,* September 1990.

Oksenberg, Michel. "The China Problem," *Foreign Affairs,* Summer 1991.

Pye, Lucian. "China: Erratic State, Frustrated Society," *Foreign Affairs,* Fall 1990.

Stepanek, James. "It's Business as Usual, China-Style," *The Asian Wall Street Journal Weekly,* September 4, 1989.

•U.S. Congress, Joint Economic Committee. April 1991. *Hearings on China's Economic Dilemmas in the 1990s.* U.S. Government Printing Office, 1991.

U.S. Congress. House. Committee on Foreign Affairs. Subcommittee on Asia and Pacific Affairs. *Hearings on U.S. Political and Economic Policy Toward China.* 1990.

U.S. Congress. House. Committee on Banking and Finance. Subcommittee on International Development, Finance, Trade and Monetary Policy. *Hearing on World Bank Lending to the People's Republic Of China,* 1989.

Worthy, Ford S. "What's Next for Business in China," *Fortune*, July 17, 1989.

DATABASES FOR RESEARCHING ARTICLES, TRADE LEADS, AND OTHER INFORMATION

DIALOG. (800) 334-2564

F&S INTERNATIONAL. (617) 969-2332

MEAD DATA CENTRAL. (800) 543-6862

NEWSNET. (800) 345-1301

ON! USCBC. (202) 429-0340

WILSONLINE. (800) 367-6770

BOOKS AND OTHER RESOURCES

Bohr, P. Richard, ed. *Midwest USA/China Resource Guide*. Minneapolis: Midwest China Center and The Minnesota World Trade Center, 1987.

Browning, Graeme. *If Everybody Bought One Shoe*. New York: Farrar, Straus & Giroux, 1989.

Business International. *Manufacturing in Guangdong: An Executive Guide to Operating in Southern China*. Hong Kong: Business International, 1990.

Bonavia, David. *The Chinese*. New York: Lippincott & Crowell, 1980.

Byrd, William A. *The Market Mechanism and Economic Reforms in Chinese Industry*. Sharpe, 1990.

•Campbell, Nigel. *A Strategic Guide to Equity Joint Ventures in China*. New York, London: Pergamon, 1989

China Directory 1992. Tokyo: Radio Press, 1991.

China Media Book: China's Advertising Rates and Media 1988/89. Bath, U.K.: Anglo-Chinese Publications, 1988.

China International Consultants. *China Investment Guide*. 4th ed. Hong Kong: Longman Group, 4th Edition, 1989.

Chiu, C. W. China Trade Documents. Philadelphia: Taylor & Francis, 1989.

Colling, John. A *Guide to the Government and Leadership of the People's Republic of China*. Hong Kong: Longman Group, 1989.

Engholm, Christopher. *The China Venture: America's Corporate Encounter with the People's Republic of China*. New York: Scott, Foresman, 1989.

Gelatt, Timothy A., and Ta-kuang Chang. *Corporate and Individual Taxation in the People's Republic of China*. 3rd ed. Hong Kong: Longman Group, 1989.

•Grow, Roy F. "Comparing Japanese and American Technology Transfer in China." In *Technology Transfer in International Business.* Tami Agmon and Mary Ann Von Glinow, eds. New York, Oxford: Oxford University Press, 1991.

•Grow, Roy F. "Acquiring Foreign Technology: What Makes the Transfer Process Work?" In *Science and Technology in Post-Mao China.* Merle Goldman and Denis Simon, eds. Cambridge: Harvard University Press, 1989.

Grummit, Ann, ed. *China Economic Handbook.* London: Euromoney Publications, 1986.

Harding, Harry. *China's Second Revolution: Reform After Mao.* Washington, D.C.: Brookings Institution, 1987.

Hartland-Thunberg, Penelope. *China, Hong Kong, Taiwan and the World Trading System.* London: Macmillan, 1990.

•Ho, Alfred Kuo-liang. *Joint Ventures in the People's Republic of China: Can Capitalism and Communism Coexist?* New York: Praeger, 1990.

Hope, Ann, and Marcus Jacobson. *China's Motor Industry: Risk and Opportunities to 2000.* London: Economist Intelligence Unit, 1989.

Hsu, John. *China's Foreign Trade Reforms: Impact on Growth and Stability.* New York: Cambridge University Press, 1989.

International Trade Administration. *Doing Business with China.* Department of Commerce. U.S. Government Printing Office, 1988.

Jacobson, Harold Karan, and Michel Oksenberg. *China's Participation in the IMF, the World Bank, and GATT: Toward a Global Economic Order.* Ann Arbor: University of Michigan Press, 1990.

Kenworthy, James L. *Guide to the Laws, Regulations and Policies of the PRC on Foreign Trade and Investment.* W. S. Hein, 1989.

Kleinberg, Robert. *China's Opening to the Outside World: The Experiment with Foreign Capitalism.* Boulder: Westview Press, 1990.

Landsberger, Stefan. *China's Provincial Foreign Trade Statistics, 1978–1988.* London: Royal Institute of International Affairs, 1989.

Lawson, Eugene K., ed. *U.S.-China Trade: Problems and Prospects.* New York: Praeger, 1988.

Lieberthal, Kenneth, and Michael Oksenberg. *Policy Making in China: Leaders, Structures and Processes.* Princeton, N.J.: Princeton University Press, 1991.

Mann, Jim. *Beijing Jeep.* New York: Simon & Schuster, 1989.

Macleod, Roderick. *China, Inc.* New York: Bantam, 1988.

Morrison, Charles E., and Robert F. Dernberger. *Asia Pacific Report: Focus, China in the Reform Era.* Honolulu, East-West Center, 1989.

Nathan, Andrew. *China's Crisis.* New York: Columbia University Press, 1990.

•Pearson, Margaret. *Joint Ventures in the People's Republic of China: The Control of Foreign Direct Investment under Socialism.* Princeton, N.J.: Princeton University Press, 1991.

•Pye, Lucian. *Chinese Commercial Negotiating Style.* Cambridge: Oelgeschlager, Gunn & Hain, 1982.

Pomfret, Richard. *Investing in China.* Ames, Iowa: Iowa State University Press, 1991.

Ross, Lester. *Environmental Policy in China.* Bloomington, Indiana: Indiana University Press, 1988.

Riskin, Carl. *China's Political Economy.* Oxford: Oxford University Press, 1987.

Selden, Mark. *The Political Economy of Chinese Socialism.* Armonk, N.Y.: M.E. Sharpe, 1989.

Seligman, Scott. *Dealing with the Chinese.* New York: Warner Books, 1989.

•Stross, Randall E. *Bulls in the China Shop.* New York: Pantheon, 1990.

Thoburn, John T., et al. *Foreign Investment in China under the Open Door Policy and the Experience of Hong Kong.* Aldershot, U.K.: Avebury, 1990.

Tsao, James T. H. *China's Development Strategies and Foreign Trade.* Lexington, Mass., Lexington Books, 1987.

•*Trade Contacts in China: A Directory of Import and Export Corporations.* Hong Kong: China Prospect Publishing House, 1987.

•U.S.-China Business Council. *China's Trade and Investment Organizations.* Washington, D.C.: 1989.

•U.S.-China Business Council. *Special Report on U.S. Investment in China.* Washington, D.C.:1990.

Vogel, Ezra. *One Step Ahead in China: Guangdong under Reform.* Cambridge: Harvard University Press, 1989.

Wang, N.T., "Entrepreneurship in China." In *Micro and Macro-Level Entrepreneurship: The Experience of China's Economic Policies at Home and Abroad.* A. Hernadi, ed. Budapest: Hungarian Scientific Council for World Economy, 1990.

Wang, N. T. *China: Legal Framework for Foreign Investment and Its Implications.* New York: East Asian Institute, Columbia University, 1986.

Appendix 3

Useful Organizations and Contacts

A. J. de Keijzer & Associates
30 Salem Road
Weston, CT 06883
Tel: (203) 226-7840
Fax: (203) 226-7820

A. T. Kearney, Inc.
225 Reinekers Lane
Alexandria, VA 22313
Tel: (703) 836-6210
Fax: (703) 739-4741

American Chamber of Commerce in China
International Club
Jianguomenwai
Beijing
Tel: 86-1-5322491
Fax: 86-1-5127345

American Chamber of Commerce in Hong Kong
1030 Swire Road
Hong Kong
Tel: (852) 526-0165

American Consulate General
26 Garden Road
Hong Kong
Tel: (852) 523-9011

American Embassy Commercial Section
Xiu Shui Bei Jie 3
10060 Beijing
Tel: 86-1-532-3831

Asia Pacific Resource Group, Inc.
334 Broadway
Cambridge, MA 02139
Tel: (617) 868-0981
Fax: (617) 491-0476

Baker & McKenzie
815 Connecticut Avenue, N.W.
Washington, DC. 20006
Tel: (202) 452-7000
Fax: (202) 452-7074

Business International Asia/Pacific, Ltd.
10/F, Luk Kwok Centre
72 Gloucester Road
Hong Kong
Tel: (852) 529-0833
Fax: (852) 865-1554

China United Resources Corporation, Ltd.
China United Trading Corporation
One World Trade Center, Suite 3333
New York, NY 10048
Tel: (212) 775-7079
Fax: (212) 775-7273

Japan External Trade Organization
1221 Avenue of the Americas
New York, NY 10020
Tel: (212) 997-0400
Fax: (212) 977-0464

National Committee on U.S.-China Relations, Inc.
777 United Nations Plaza, 9B
New York, NY 10017
Tel: (212) 922-1385
Fax: (212) 557-8258

Office of People's Republic of China and Hong Kong Affairs
International Trade Administration
U.S. Department of Commerce
Washington, DC 20230
Tel: (202) 377-3583

Pacific Rim Resources
201 Spear Street, Suite 1600
San Francisco, CA 94105
Tel: (415) 896-6715
Fax: (415) 495-1821

U.S.-China Business Council
1818 N Street N.W., Suite 500
Washington, DC 20036
Tel: (202) 429-0340
Fax: (202) 775-2476

Appendix 4

Investing in China

The emergence of a capital market in China has generated great
enthusiasm among both Chinese and foreign investors. While on the
surface there's not yet much to see (three exchanges, two dozen
stocks, and few regulations as of early 1992), these markets represent
a critical shift away from state socialism and toward the open market
system of the not-too-distant future.

The Securities Market

The main force behind the development of securities markets in China
is the serious financial condition of the central government. Since
China launched a taxation system in the mid-1980s, the government's
financial position has gone into steady decline. The deficit has soared,
largely because 65% or more of revenues go toward supporting the
inefficient state factories. Infrastructure projects and other severe
bottlenecks to growth were not being adequately addressed. The
government simply had to think up a new way to raise money.

Accordingly, the government began issuing large amounts of
treasury bonds. The intent was to absorb excess liquidity in the
system, thereby curbing demand and inflation, and at the same time
creating a direct path from the pockets, bank accounts and mattresses
of individuals (an amount estimated at $300 billion) to central govern-
ment coffers.

The bonds were not so much sold as coerced—workers and officials
were "persuaded" to accept up to one-third of their salary in bonds. In
many cases, the "lucky" recipients would sell these bonds on the street
to raise cash. The price was never near the face value, but what it
meant, of course, was that the yield rose dramatically, to the point
where it became a real hedge against inflation. A similar process took
place with some of the non-government issues. As a result, a lively
secondary market emerged.

The story in equities is a mirror image. Companies began in 1984 to
convert themselves to limited companies, and offered shares paying
dividend and interest rates far higher than the bank was offering
(shares are still hybrid; i.e., part of the payout is in interest, part as
dividend—they are not actually ownership shares).

An informal market—literally over the counters of bank branches—
began to evolve. The government began to tidy up these markets by
commissioning the Stock Exchange Executive Council (SEEC) to
produce a trading system designed to be usable at exchanges throughout the country. The result was a system patterned after the NASDAQ
system in the U.S. and implemented in December 1990. Over 90% of
the trade is in bonds.

There were a number of significant developments during 1991. A Chinese Securities Association, formed in Beijing by the People's Bank of China, has enormous influence in deciding which cities can have stock exchanges and which companies can list stocks (and the association seems to be doing its best to slow down the process). Nevertheless, Guangzhou announced it would open a bond market, with a stock exchange to follow. Tianjin, Xiamen, and Wenzhou also announced active interest in developing exchanges.

In mid-year, the two exchanges dealing in stocks (Shenzhen and Shanghai) began to issue special "B" shares expressly for foreign investors, denominated in domestic currency (but paid for in foreign exchange). The first issue, on behalf of the Shanghai Vacuum Electronic Device Corporation (SVEDC), had foreign underwriters placing about a million B shares valued at about $74 million.

The Shenzhen exchange is by far the most active. When it was about to distribute application forms for subscription to 11 company flotations planned for 1992, more than 100,000 Chinese investors came to Shenzhen and literally camped outside the doors.

Foreign mutual funds and unit trusts targeted at China have allocated at least $150 million to buy shares in quoted companies on the Shenzhen exchange and Shanghai stock markets—a figure equal to the total equity in Chinese stocks so far issued.

China's bid to sell stocks to foreigners has its critics. The foundations are simply not yet in place, they note. One of the underwriters of the SVEDC withdrew because of the way the B stock was quickly shoved onto the market without a full audit of the company. Lack of liquidity is another major obstacle to confidence, as is the lack of any type of regulatory system underlying the trading system. Even Wang Poming, a vice-president of the SEEC admits equities are rare and not very liquid and that the market is still primitive in terms of trading behavior.

The first public scandal has also hit China's stock exchange in Shenzhen. The government claims it intervened in the trading of Champaign Industrial Company (a JV between China and a group of American, Australian, and Malaysian investors) because of financial irregularities. The company suggests it got into trouble because it refused to sell shares to the government at a cut-rate price. Observers believe both sides could be right.

Despite growing pains, the central bank has announced its commitment to expand the number of markets, albeit cautiously and slowly. For example, the government wouldn't permit new listings on the Shanghai exchange for the first year of operation and now lets them come on only slowly. That's the view from Beijing. In South China there is a different perspective, as usual.

There, many Chinese factories are not waiting for the opening of official exchanges. In August 1991, for example, five factories in Xiamen prepared to issue nearly RMB 1 billion in stock. These will be sold to eager Chinese clients by "internal liaison enterprises," which already outnumber foreign firms in the city, notes James Stepanek.

Security firms are eager to sell stock and help privatize Chinese industry . . . which of course is the opposite of what Beijing wants.

Stepanek quotes one official of Xiamen Securities Co, Ltd. as saying, "Our goal is to do everything a Hong Kong securities company does. We want to help factories make themselves into companies owned by shareholders."

Factories all over China are quietly planning to do just that, making the appearance of stock markets in China one of the biggest stories of the 1990s.

Venture Capital Funds

Foreign investors, meanwhile, have not been waiting for the exchanges to be established before trying to get in on the action.

In the early 1980s, foreign venture capitalists invested in China indirectly by buying stock in Hong Kong-listed companies that were already actively producing goods for export as part of joint ventures or assembly and processing operations. Two of the early funds using this approach were China and Eastern (managed by Baring Brothers) and ChinaVest I (Nassau Capital).

By the mid-1980s, these and other investors began to take steps towards direct involvement, putting capital into joint ventures that were at the "mezzanine" stage (i.e., companies in China already operating and now looking to expand).

Examples of venture capital funds currently doing this type of investing are ChinaVest II, JF China Investments (Jardine Fleming), FP Special Assets (First Pacific), and a fund set up by AdVest (USA).

One fund of note brings together three powerful partners: Standard Chartered Bank, the brokerage James Capel, and China Venturetech Investment Corporation, China's only venture capital firm. Operating under the name of China Assets (Holdings) Ltd., this fund concentrates on companies suitable for listing on either the Hong Kong or new Chinese exchanges.

China Assets has a powerful board, ranging from Liu Hongru, a vice chairman of the State Commission for Restructuring the Economy, to Donald Kendall, former CEO of PepsiCo. Even the Asian Development Bank has a 10% stake in the venture. The three major partners raised $39 million in Europe, Japan, and Asia (not a single investor was found in the U.S.).

According to E. M. Rule, director of the fund, deal flows have been excellent. Funds will be at least a third invested by the end of 1991. Typical investments are made for a two-to-three-year payback period and are placed in light industry with strong cash flow in the Pearl River Delta and the coastal areas. There are also some state-owned industrial enterprises with good access to export markets under examination.

China Assets (Holdings) Ltd. is not a classic venture capital fund but an investment company, and its shares will be listed on the Hong

Kong stock exchange within nine months of the complete placement of these loans.

"It seems only a matter of time," says Wang Poming, "before China truly becomes a major consideration for foreign portfolio managers. . . . What we need in the meantime is a bit of patience and a lot of prayer."

Reading for Profit

Recent articles on China's stock markets and Hong Kong venture capital funds include:

"China's Evolving Capital Markets," by James Stepanek, in *China Trade*, September 1991.

"China's Open-Door Stock Policy," by Sheryl Wu Dunn, in *The New York Times*, December 24, 1991.

"Foreigners Join the Queue for Shenzhen Flotations," by Simon Holberton, in *The Financial Times of London*, April 3, 1992.

"Funds Open New Investment Channels," *China Banking and Finance*, September 30, 1991.

"New Business on the Bund," by Fred Burke, *The China Business Review*, May–June 1991.

"Rebuilding China's Securities Markets," by Paul Schroeder, *The China Business Review*, May–June 1991.

"Securities in China: Peking Uses STAQS to Structure Market," *Business China*, March 11, 1991.

"Small Leap Forward," by Elizabeth Cheng, *Far Eastern Economic Review*, July 18, 1991.

"A Socialist Paradox," by Sylvia Yau, *China Trade Report*, June 1990.

"Stock in Trades," by Elizabeth Cheng, *Far Eastern Economic Review*, March 21, 1991.

"Venture Capitalists Eye Opportunities in China," *Business China*, September 24, 1990.

FOR MORE INFORMATION

If you would like to receive further information or have
special research requirements,
write on your letterhead to:

Business Research China
30 Salem Road
Weston, CT 06883 U.S.A.

Services include business intelligence on
✦ prospective partners,
✦ independent project analysis and evaluation,
✦ information on China's evolving capital markets,
✦ and survey research.

Also available from Pacific View Press

CHINA ON THE EDGE:
Crisis of Ecology and Development
He Bochuan

One of China's leading futurists paints a grim picture of the environmental situation and the problems of development in his country. His thesis is that years of overpopulation and the demands of a growing economy have put China on the brink of a major environmental disaster. Originally published in Chinese in 1988, this is the first English language edition with thoroughly updated statistics.

Cloth $29.95   **Paper $16.95**

STRANGERS ALWAYS:
A Jewish Family in Wartime Shanghai
Rena Krasno

A community of outsiders within a larger community of outsiders—this was the Jewish community of Shanghai before 1945. Rena Krasno provides a fascinating account of this world and its history, and of the life of her family and friends during the Japanese occupation, and a poignant view of exile life for the young people of this little-known community.

Cloth $24.95

VIETNAM:
Business Opportunities and Risks

A timely new resource for the business professional that provides a quick, comprehensive snapshot of the country and identifies the key variables that must be considered in evaluating the potential for business success.

Paper $19.95

LÓNG IS A DRAGON:
Chinese Writing for Children
Peggy Goldstein

An award winning introduction to Chinese writing with explanations about how the language developed and clear instructions on how to draw the characters. Written for children ages 9-12, this beautifully illustrated book provides instruction for 75 simple characters and the numbering system.

Cloth $15.95

For a complete catalog, write:

Pacific View Press
P.O. Box 2657
Berkeley, CA 94702